Zeitgeschichte im Kontext

Band 23

Herausgegeben von Oliver Rathkolb

Die Bände dieser Reihe sind peer-reviewed.

Oliver Rathkolb / Agnes Meisinger (eds.)

Controlled Freedom

Allied Cultural Policy in Vienna, 1945–1955

With 40 figures

This volume is published in cooperation with the Vienna Institute for Cultural and Contemporary History and Arts (VICCA).

V&R unipress

Vienna University Press

Bibliografische Information der Deutschen Nationalbibliothek
Die Deutsche Nationalbibliothek verzeichnet diese Publikation in der Deutschen
Nationalbibliografie; detaillierte bibliografische Daten sind im Internet über
https://dnb.de abrufbar.

**Veröffentlichungen der Vienna University Press
erscheinen bei V&R unipress.**

Gedruckt mit freundlicher Unterstützung des Wiener Instituts für Kultur- und Zeitgeschichte
(VICCA), des Instituts für Historische Sozialforschung (IHSF), der Arbeiterkammer Wien, des
Dekanats der Historisch-Kulturwissenschaftlichen Fakultät und des Rektorats der Universität Wien.

© 2025 Brill | V&R unipress, Robert-Bosch-Breite 10, D-37079 Göttingen, info@v-r.de,
ein Imprint der Brill-Gruppe
(Koninklijke Brill BV, Leiden, Niederlande; Brill USA Inc., Boston MA, USA; Brill Asia Pte Ltd,
Singapore; Brill Deutschland GmbH, Paderborn, Deutschland; Brill Österreich GmbH, Wien,
Österreich)
Koninklijke Brill BV umfasst die Imprints Brill, Brill Nijhoff, Brill Schöningh, Brill Fink, Brill mentis,
Brill Wageningen Academic, Vandenhoeck & Ruprecht, Böhlau und V&R unipress.
Alle Rechte vorbehalten. Das Werk und seine Teile sind urheberrechtlich geschützt.
Jede Verwertung in anderen als den gesetzlich zugelassenen Fällen bedarf der vorherigen
schriftlichen Einwilligung des Verlages.

Umschlagabbildung: Anton Marek, The International Patrol for your protection (Vienna City
Library, P-7026).
Englische Übersetzung: © John Heath 2025
Druck und Bindung: CPI books GmbH, Birkstraße 10, D-25917 Leck
Printed in the EU.

Vandenhoeck & Ruprecht Verlage | www.vandenhoeck-ruprecht-verlage.com

ISSN 2198-5413
ISBN 978-3-8471-1852-7

Contents

Oliver Rathkolb
Introduction. Allied Cultural Policy in Vienna: Contemporary History
Meets Archaeology   9

Thomas Angerer
A Dazzling New Beginning. French Cultural Policy in Occupied Vienna,
1945–1955 15

Wolfgang Mueller
Soviet Propaganda, Media, and Cultural Policy in Vienna, 1945–1955 . . . 27

Manfred Mugrauer
KPÖ Cultural Policy under Soviet Occupation 39

Oliver Rathkolb
US Occupying Cultural Policy between Denazification, Cold War, and
Democratic Reorientation 49

Richard Hufschmied
British Cultural Policy in Vienna, 1945–1955. Intentions, Actions, and
a Jewish Underground Struggle 59

Johanna Lerchner
The Allied Topography of Vienna 67

Wolfgang Duchkowitsch
The Allies and the Press, 1945/46 75

Marion Krammer / Margarethe Szeless
Press Photography in the Cold War. Photo Policy in Austria,
1945–1955 87

Wolfgang Pensold
Radio between the Zones 97

Karin Moser
Allied Film Policy between Cooperation, Control, Enlightenment, and
Self-interest 109

Agnes Meisinger
Ready, Set, Go! Allied Sport and the Revival of Sporting Events in Vienna,
1945–1955 119

Veronika Floch
"Our souls approach, understand, and agree with one another through
admiration of the work of art." Allied Cultural Policy and Visual Art in
Vienna, 1945–1955 131

Monika Knofler
Art as a Weapon – on the Allies' Exhibitions Policy 143

Monika Platzer
Architecture in Four Acts, 1945–1955 153

Markus Stumpf
"Books are undoubtedly not furniture." The Library as a Battleground:
Reorientation through Denazification and Book Donations 163

Günther Stocker
The Allies and Austrian Literature 177

Peter Roessler
Dramatic Outlooks. The Allies' Dramas on Vienna Stages 187

Michael Kraus
Vienna State Opera in Occupied Post-War Austria, 1945–1955 197

Christian Glanz
Out of Nowhere? Observations on the Characteristics and Locations of
Jazz in Vienna in the Early Post-War Era 207

Hans Petschar
Porgy and Bess: A Case Study of the Impact of US Cultural Policy in
Vienna, 1945–1955 215

Selected Bibliography 227

Authors 231

Oliver Rathkolb

Introduction. Allied Cultural Policy in Vienna: Contemporary History Meets Archaeology

By presenting a case study of Austria as a small country amongst large international players, the present edited collection seeks to contribute to the international historiography of the New Cold War, which in recent years has begun to focus on transnational cultural exchange.[1] In the research on Austria, recent studies, particularly on literary history after 1945[2] but also on press photography[3] and sport,[4] have investigated the new groups that emerged in the immediate postwar era. This approach, focusing on the societal impact of the Cold War and Allied policy and using cultural networks, exchange, and ties as tools of analysis, generally remains heavily underrepresented in Austria.

The diverse positions in the arena of cultural policy and concrete initiatives taken by the four Allies between 1945 and 1955 had a strong influence on the art scene – an influence that has been suppressed, however. Now, eighty years later, it is returned to the memory via an archaeological approach to contemporary history. Never before had so many Viennese been confronted so intensively with international cultural influences as they were after liberation in April 1945.

Evidently, the strong emphasis on Austrian cultural tradition and strengths during the era of rebuilding was so dominant that there was no room for the international influences in cultural history. Even the National Socialists under Reichsstatthalter and Gauleiter Baldur von Schirach had stressed "Viennese culture", sometimes placing it above Berlin's.

---

1 Simo Mikkonen, Giles Scott-Smith, Jari Parkikinnen (eds.): Entangled East and West. Cultural Diplomacy and Artistic Interaction during the Cold War, Berlin 2018.
2 Stefan Maurer, Wolfgang Kraus und der österreichische Literaturbetrieb nach 1945, Vienna 2020 and https://kk-diskurse.univie.ac.at/das-team/index.htm (1 June 2024).
3 Marlies Dornig, Hans Petschar (eds.): Bild – Macht – Politik. Yoichi Okamoto. Ikone der Nachkriegsfotografie, Vienna 2023. Marion Krammer, Rasender Stillstand oder Stunde Null? Österreichische PressefotografInnen 1945–1955, Vienna 2021.
4 Maximilian Graf, Agnes Meisinger (eds.): Österreich im Kalten Krieg. Neue Forschungen im internationalen Kontext, Göttingen 2016.

Whereas before 1938 many Austrians had considered themselves German but culturally superior to the "Prussians", after 1945 this superiority complex contributed to the development of an identity as a small country and helped suppress collaboration in the National Socialist war of aggression, the Shoah, and the other crimes of the National Socialist regime.

It remains important to show and analyse Austrian artists, writers, journalists, and their work, along with their own interests and strategies. The specific form of Allied cultural policy is certainly much stronger than the traditional cultural diplomacy during the Cold War, although in the era of Allied administration of Austria it represents merely soft power.

However, international historiography too lacks a critical media history of the early Cold War, with the exception of studies on international radio in Europe[5] and on journalists in the Cold War.[6]

Hence this volume will open up innovative fields of research and is based on a group of outstanding experts' long-term research on the cultural and media history of the early post-war era and of the Cold War in Austria.

The book seeks to shift the historiography of the Cold War away from political and economic analysis towards the impact on the cultural and political behaviour of people after seven years of racist and antisemitic totalitarianism and collaboration with the National Socialists in Austria, following five years of right-wing clerical and authoritarian politics under the Dollfuss–Schnuschnigg dictatorship.

All four Allies of the anti-Hitler coalition declared both (classically defined) culture and the media a key element of planning before 1945. The USA in particular (initially in collaboration with Britain) sought to develop concrete plans to use culture and the media as an important tool for the re-education of the Germans and Austrians after the war, concentrating on denazification and the replacement of the Nazi elites by placing democratic personalities as key players in the cultural and media spheres. By replacing the elites and providing new cultural offerings, including contemporary music, international theatre productions, and international literature, films, and exhibitions, they aimed to deepen the process of democratic transformation.

After the early months of 1946 and especially after 1947, the primary political aim shifted to geopolitical reorientation and integrating the Germans and Austrians into the Western, US-dominated anti-communist camp, including former members of the NSDAP, irrespective of how closely they had been involved in its propaganda institutions as artists, writers, or journalists.

---

5 Alexander Badenoch, Andreas Fickers, Christian Henrich-Franke (eds.): Airy Curtains in European Ether. Broadcasting and the Cold War, Baden-Baden 2013.
6 Dina Fainberg: Cold War Correspondents. Soviet and American Reporters on the Ideological Frontlines, Baltimore 2021.

In Austria, the Soviets pursued a policy completely different to that of the USA and Britain, since their main aim, especially in Austria, was to weaken Germany and destroy the traditional enthusiasm for annexation and the Austrians' strong German cultural consciousness. To this end, they ordered cultural institutions such as the State Opera, the Vienna Philharmonic, and all theatres to reopen just weeks after the liberation of Vienna on 13 April 1945. The music of Johann Strauss in particular was celebrated, and thousands of photos were taken of Soviet soldiers and officers in front of his grave and monuments to him.

Immediately after liberation in 1945, by insisting on cultural separation from Germany, the Soviets in particular also promoted the doctrine of Austrian victimhood, but with it the construction of an independent, non-German identity, taking up earlier narratives based on claims of cultural superiority over militaristic Prussia à la Frederick the Great that had existed since the days of Maria Theresa. Here, the views of the Communist cultural ideologue Ernst Fischer (*Der österreichische Volkscharakter* [The Austrian National Character]) and the Christian Social Dollfuss–Schuschnigg dictatorship, which had defined itself as a second German state, collide.

In contrast, in the Western zones of occupation, all media and theatres remained closed and under strict military control, only US-licensed newspapers and cultural activities being permitted.

The authors of this volume concentrate on the short- and long-term impact of these political aims in the fields of music, theatre, and the media (newspapers, publishing houses, and radio) in Vienna, where the Western Allies were not active before September 1945: how did the cultural elites and the public respond to these political aims, and how did this affect the aim of eradicating National Socialism and German-ness in Austria?

The main purpose of the various chapters in this volume, however, is not only to describe to analyse the political aims and describe activities, as earlier publications have done, but to reconstruct the short- and long-term impacts of Austrian's cultural and media consumption and their influence on cultural and political attitudes. Further, the volume discusses the educational effects on artists and journalists who worked for the Allied media both in the print arena and for the four radio stations (the RAVAG's *Die Russische Stunde*, US-controlled Rot-Weiss-Rot, the British sector's Radio Alpenland, and the French authorities' Sendergruppe West).

These aspects, which had an impact on both the cultural attitudes and the professionalization of Austrian artists, writers, and journalists, remain under-researched to this day; usually, they are simply overlooked.

An important element analysed in these pages is connected to the fact that this internationally intensive cultural period from 1945 to 1955 has not become part of Austria's cultural history. Quite on the contrary: many authors, such as the prominent writer Ingeborg Bachmann, who spent more than two years working for the US broadcaster Rot-Weiss-Rot, suppressed this fact in their autobiographical testimonies. It would seem that this could have been interpreted by the Austrians as "cultural collaboration". This tendency to ostracize artists, writers, and journalists active in Allied cultural institutions is particularly striking with respect to communists.

An important role was played by another aspect of everyday emotional culture: sport – both in Allied policy and in the Austrian political setting. Here too, the significance of the Allies' attempts to cultivate a tradition has often been suppressed and has been neglected by official sporting history.

A third, general question pertaining to all cultural spheres and media concerns how cultural policy contributed to the development of Austrian identity as a small country and as decidedly non-German: both the Soviets and the Communists pursued a very conservative cultural doctrine, reinventing the age of Maria Theresa, Grillparzer, and Nestroy as a counterpoint to the Prussian king and German authors – thereby reproducing political frameworks from the Dollfuss–Schuschnigg dictatorship and earlier. It was not until 1947 that Socialist Realism was introduced to Austrian audiences, with little success.

The French, the British, and the Americans, on the other hand, promoted modern art in order to counter Stalinist communism, which attacked modern international painting as "daubing" ("Kleckserei" – which is not far from the National Socialist term "degenerate art"). This influence of international art, literature, and music on young Austrian artists and writers is of particular interest to many authors of this volume. French literature and philosophy formed an important foundation for contemporary literature.

US films and comics were a very popular element of youth culture, and in response, the Soviets and Communists, supported by Austrian conservatives, attempted to counter this development via censorship in order to protect Austrian youth from "filth and trash".

In general, the secondary literature to date has concentrated only on the political aspect of the funding of culture in Austria and Germany by the CIA and others, primarily as a means of strengthening the anti-communist camp and preventing communist authors such as Bert Brecht from being performed at Austrian theatres into the 1960s.

A more thorough analysis will show that these "operations" had important side effects, such as funding the journal *FORVM*, founded by the writer Friedrich Torberg after he had returned from exile; *FORVM* went some way to overcoming Austrian culture's deep-rooted patriarchal, nationalistic, and German framework, including the racist and antisemitic political impact of the National Socialist regime, which had been able to build on Austrian traditions.

In other chapters, the authors will critically discuss the long-term institutional impact of a century of intensive cultural interventions and intertwining – such as the foundation of the independent press agencies APA (Austria Presse Agentur) by the USA and Britain or the newspapers established by the US press officers: *Tiroler Tageszeitung, Salzburger Nachrichten, Oberösterreichische Nachrichten,* and *Wiener Kurier*. The Lycée Français de Vienne, an international school for boys and girls also open to Austrians, was opened by the French in 1946 and offers progressive all-day teaching seldom found in the traditional, backward-looking Austrian education system.

In the everyday topography of the city, the Allies are actually present only in 1945, during the liberation of Vienna, and in 1955, when the State Treaty was concluded – the fact that in 1948 over 8,000 buildings, shops, hotels, and villas were still confiscated by the four Allies is also reconstructed by a chapter drawing on an extensive database.

The authors have succeeded in reconstructing the suppression of the intensive surge in internationalization from liberation to the State Treaty and the withdrawal of the Big Four in 1955, providing many illustrative, specific examples and analysis of the four Allies' internal political planning and aims, and placing them in their context with respect to cultural policy. In doing so, however, they demonstrate with the same clarity how these awakenings merged or clashed with conservative trends and continuities (from local Modernism to the Dollfuss–Schuschnigg era and the National Socialist cultural terror).

This publication fills a lacuna in cultural history, since young artists came into contact with the critical Modernism banned under National Socialism and revolted against the dominant cultural restoration.

The present volume is based on the scholarly publication accompanying the exhibition *Controlled Freedom: The Allied Forces in Vienna* at the Wien Museum (10 April – 7 September 2025). We extend our thanks to John Heath for his English translations of the contributions and to Hans Petschar and Peter Prokop (Austrian National Library) and Maximilian Zauner (Vienna City Library) for providing historical photographic material. Thanks are also due to Liane Popa for her support with archival research, and to our colleagues at the Wien Museum, Sonja Maria Gruber and Andrea Ruscher.

Thomas Angerer

A Dazzling New Beginning. French Cultural Policy in Occupied Vienna, 1945–1955

Newspaper articles and press services; magazines; radio broadcasts; film screenings, festivals, and distribution; a bookshop with an exhibition room and a reading room with newspapers, magazines, books, and reference works, both venues soon in the city centre like the Cultural Institute with its language courses, lectures, film and record evenings, talks, exhibitions, library, and its contacts; concerts; exhibitions; visiting theatre, opera, ballet, and folklore performances; a French school; a language offensive in the education sector; visiting professors at universities; visiting lecturers; documentation centres, free subscriptions, donations of books, and language assistants for diverse education establishments; prizes, scholarships to go to France, and summer and ski camps for pupils and students; grants for artists; and much more: culture was a main concern of the French occupation authorities and diplomacy in Vienna. It met with great expectations, provided important impetus, and left strong memories and sustained institutions.

Why did the French occupation authorities rely so heavily on culture? It was for at least four reasons. Firstly, it was where its strengths lay. Materially, the country had been weakened so much by occupation and war that food rationing in Paris was at times worse than in Vienna. For supplying their sector (Mariahilf, Penzing, Rudolfsheim-Fünfhaus, and Ottakring), the French occupation authorities were thus as reliant on US help as they were in their own country.[1] Culturally, France was incomparably better off: Paris was a Mecca for art; the country continued to set benchmarks in theatre and philosophy, in architecture, and also in film; and French remained a global language. Culture was France's last ace, and cultural foreign policy was more important than ever for its great power politics.[2] Although

---

1 Stefan Vogel: Frankreich und die Alliierte Besetzung Wiens von 1945 bis 1955. Motive und Grenzen der französischen Vermittlungspolitik, in: Jahrbuch des Vereins für die Geschichte der Stadt Wien 55 (1999), 173–210; idem: Der französische Sektor in Wien 1945–1955, in: ibid., 61 (2005), 293–331.
2 Guillaume Frantzwa: L'image de la puissance. Un siècle de diplomatie culturelle, Paris 2023, 97–101.

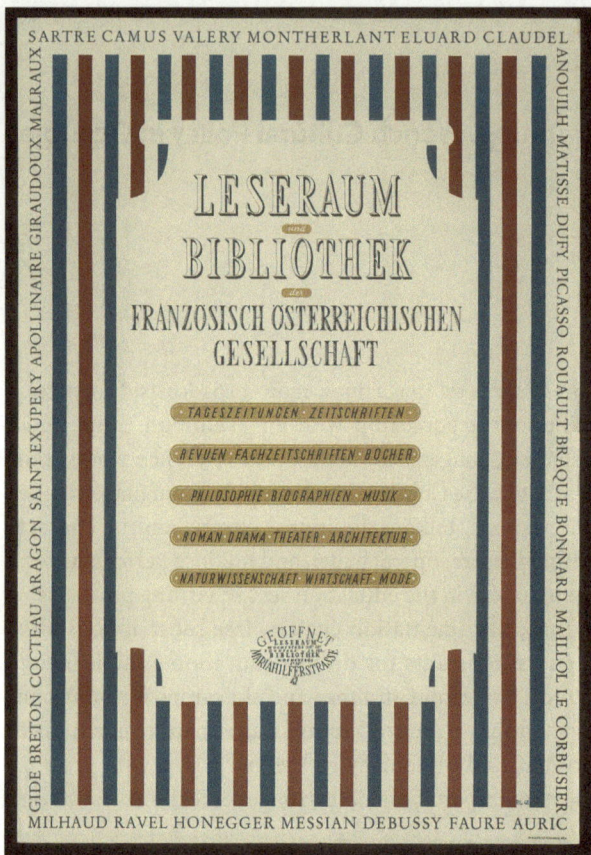

Fig. 1: The reading room and library of the Französisch-Österreichische Gesellschaft (Franco-Austrian Society) in the documentation centre of the French Information Service, Mariahilfer Strasse 47 (Wienbibliothek im Rathaus, P-246997)

defeat, occupation, and collaboration had damaged its reputation and self-confidence, France's sense of mission remained unbroken, with deep historical roots, and bolstered even by victory over the Greater German Reich. Hence it sent to restored Austria the last head of its Cultural Institute that had been established in Vienna in 1931, Eugène Susini (1900–1982), in order to reopen it and renew the cultural agreement signed with the country in 1936. It also saw in Vienna a bridgehead to Central Europe, where it sought to regain a foothold.[3]

---

3 Michel Cullin: Eugène Susini, in: Thomas Angerer, Jacques Le Rider (eds.): "Ein Frühling, dem kein Sommer folgte"? Französisch-österreichische Kulturtransfers seit 1945, Vienna/Cologne/Weimar 1999; 41–50; Barbara Porpaczy: Frankreich – Österreich 1945–1960. Kulturpolitik und Identität (Innsbrucker Forschungen zur Zeitgeschichte, Vol. 18), Innsbruck 2002, 80–84 and 12 respectively (with older literature).

Another reason for banking on culture in Vienna was the city's then extraordinarily high receptiveness to French culture. The war had barely ended, and it would be months before the Soviets let the French in, but there was already an Association Artistique Franco-Autrichienne holding its first high-profile events, and when the French occupation authorities took over its sectors, in the Fédération France–Autriche it already had on site a partner organization with interim manager of the Burgtheater Raoul Aslan as president, over 1,500 applicants for membership, and a host of initiatives.[4] Not only in Paris, whence old friends of Austria and exiles soon put out feelers, but also in Vienna there was a desire to restore cultural ties. "Finally [...], finally [...]"[5]: many newspaper articles on the first French concerts, exhibitions, and theatre performances spoke of gratitude at regaining what people had been missing after spending seven years barred from international cultural life.

Culture from France, a melting pot of international cultural figures, had the advantage of being more than just French culture. Pablo Picasso, Juan Gris, Amedeo Modigliani, Jules Pascin, Chaim Soutine, Marc Chagall, Giorgio de Chirico, ...: the artists of the École de Paris who had been on display in Vienna in 1926 and 1938 and returned in 1947 as "classics of modern French painting"[6] came from all over Europe. The Cinémathèque française, with which the Gesellschaft der Filmfreunde Österreichs (Austrian Society for Friends of Film) reached an exchange agreement brokered by the French Information Service in 1946, documented filmmaking from around the world and thus offered, as the *Wiener Zeitung* wrote, a "glimpse of freedom".[7] For a country seeking to catch up and reorient itself in the early post-war years, French cultural policy in Vienna often opened the first windows on Europe and the world – or, as the painter Georg Eisler put it, "a window, not so much on Paris, but on modern art". In postwar Vienna, it was not necessary to be a Francophile to see in French cultural mediators "cultural rescuers", to cite Eisler once more.[8]

---

4 Unpublished research by the author, on which the rest of this chapter is based too (!) unless indicated otherwise. On the dissolution of the Fédération at the instigation of the French, cf. Lydia Lettner: Die französische Österreichpolitik von 1943 bis 1946, doctoral thesis, University of Salzburg 1980, 320f.
5 [Leopold W.] Rochowanski: Begegnung mit französischer Graphik. Zur Ausstellung in der Akademie der bildenden Künste, in: Wiener Kurier, 13 December 1945, 4.
6 Porpaczy, Frankreich, 48 and 243; Christian Huemer: Paris—Vienna: Modern Art Markets and the Transmission of Culture, 1873–1937, PhD thesis, City University of New York 2013, 106–203.
7 Französisch-österreichisches Filmabkommen, in: Wiener Zeitung, 5 April 1946, 3.
8 Georg Eisler: [Erinnerung] in: Institut français de Vienne (ed.): Österreichisch-französisches Jahrbuch/Annales franco-autrichiennes, Vienna/Cologne/Graz 1984, 70; idem, Lokalaugenschein, in: Liesbeth Waechter-Böhm (ed.): Wien 1945, davor – danach, Vienna 1985, 139.

This brings us to the third reason why cultural policy was so important to the French occupation authorities: it was essential for overcoming National Socialist values and spreading democratic ones. French cultural policy, with its broad programme of publications, courses, talks, and exhibitions, represented humaneness, openness, and a critical outlook, humanist, Enlightenment traditions, and new approaches both Christian and secular (above all *Renouveau catholique* and existentialism).[9] A large graphic art exhibition from the Salon d'Automne at Vienna's Museum of Arts and Crafts at the turn of 1945 and 1946 also showed works by artists who had been taboo under National Socialism (such as Raoul Dufy, André Lhote, Jean Lurçat, Henri Matisse, Pablo Picasso, or Georges Rouault) and seventeen drawings by Léon Delabre from his time in a concentration camp.[10] With a sense for controversial topics, Susini, a Germanist, gave lectures at the University of Vienna open to all faculties on Richard Wagner, Friedrich Nietzsche, and Stefan George.

To open minds, the French occupation authorities relied from the outset on personal encounter and exchange. To this end, in the Tyrol, part of the French Zone, it did a lot to support the Tyrolian-Viennese initiative for International University Weeks hosted by the Austrian College in Alpbach, Louis Aragon and Elsa Triolet featuring among the first French guests.[11] Great emphasis was placed on youth work: as early as December 1945, a delegation of Austrian youth organizations (including Hugo Potyka, later to become a renowned architect) was sent to Paris to prepare an exchange with French organizations, and from 1946 onwards hundreds of Viennese pupils and students were sent to the French Zone for international summer and skiing camps or university weeks, with André Gide as the highest-profile guest in Pertisau. The French also initiated a school exchange for the holidays, opened the Lycée français de Vienne to Austrian pupils, awarded scholarships for the Lycée in Fulpmes (near Innsbruck), including to pupils from Vienna, rewarded the best pupils in French with language weeks in France, and gave students scholarships at French universities. (Early exchange pupils and scholarship holders included the later diplomat Heinrich Blechner and the later historian Gerald Stourzh.)[12] Grants for art were particularly coveted:

---

9 Juliane Werner: Existentialismus in Österreich. Kultureller Transfer und literarische Resonanz, Berlin/Boston 2021. A comparable study on Reform Catholicism is lacking. For the entire cultural program, see the passages concerning Vienna in Porpaczy: Frankreich, chapters IV and V.

10 Exposition d'œuvres de la gravure française contemporaine. Académie des Beaux-Arts, Vienne, du 11 décembre 1945 au 13 janvier 1946. Vienne 1945, 10, 13f., 18 (no. 75–91).

11 Dinah Lepuschitz: Ein österreichisches Pontigny?, in: Angerer, Le Rider, "Frühling", 281–302; Maria Wirth: Ein Fenster zur Welt. Das Europäische Forum Alpbach 1945–2015, Innsbruck/Bozen/Vienna 2015, 25–39.

12 Porpaczy, Frankreich, 103; Michaela Feurstein-Prasser: Die französische Jugendpolitik in Tirol, in: Christian Fornwagner, Richard Schober (eds.): Freiheit und Wiederaufbau, Inns-

Fig. 2: The exhibition "Salon d'Automne" at the Kunstgewerbemuseum (Museum of Arts and Crafts) was opened in 1946. *Wiener Kurier*, 11 July 1946 (ANNO, Austrian National Library, ANL/Vienna)

in Vienna at the turn of the 1940s and 1950s, they went to artists such as the weavers Johanna Schidlo, Louise Autzinger, and Fritz Riedl, the set designer Elisabeth Urbancic, and the graphic artists and painters Florian Jakowitsch, Josef Pillhofer, Maria Lassnig (with Arnulf Rainer riding on her coat tails), Oswald

bruck 2007, 9–20; eadem: Von der Besatzungspolitik zur Kulturmission. Französische Schul- und Bildungspolitik in Österreich 1945–1955, doctoral thesis, University of Vienna 2002, 199–201; Monika Platzer: Kalter Krieg und Architektur. Beiträge zur Demokratisierung Österreichs nach 1945, Zurich/Vienna 2019, 97; the contributions by Carolyn Oliva and Jean-Michel Casset in: Angerer, Le Rider, "Frühling", 262–264 and 110–116 respectively; Béthouart, Note pour Monsieur Susini, 12 March 1946, Ministère des Affaires Étrangères, Archives diplomatiques (henceforth: MAE) 5AUT/194/1a; Kurzmeldungen, Das kleine Volksblatt, 6 July 1946, 6.

Oberhuber, and Kurt Moldovan, or to art scholars such as Werner Hofmann, who would later found the Museum of the Twentieth Century.[13]

Fourthly, and no less importantly, French cultural policy sought to help emancipate Austrians' cultural self-awareness from that of Germany and strengthen their desire for independence. Keeping Austria apart from Germany, politically, militarily, and above all as a state, had been an axiom of France's Germany and European policy since the nineteenth century; it was now combined with a targeted policy of nation building.[14] The French-led media promoted features on Austrian identity,[15] the French reading room contained Austrian literature banned by the Nazis, access to which had to be restored in Vienna's libraries, and Susini gave lectures on Rainer Maria Rilke, Hugo von Hofmannsthal, and Franz Kafka at the University of Vienna. Along with the (re)discovery of Austrian traditions, not least over two centuries of vibrant cultural ties with France, which had been suppressed by German nationalism, the French authorities also promoted new approaches. For instance, the French bookshop Kosmos in the Wollzeile held an exhibition of works by the twenty-year-old Ernst Fuchs, who was already spending most of his time in Paris, and the first solo exhibitions in Vienna of works by Florian Jakowitsch and Maria Lassnig, before their fellowships in Paris even.[16]

France also attempted to raise Austrian self-awareness by helping the country present itself culturally in France. For instance, French cultural diplomacy enabled the Philharmonic and the State Opera to undertake their first tour abroad after the war (Paul Paray and Josef Krips alternating as conductors from both countries as a further symbol of bilateral cooperation). Incidentally, the French authorities continued to organize and fund appearances by Austrian ensembles in France, both directly and indirectly, for many years even though the Austrians did not do the same for French artists,[17] and even though France was particularly keen to show to Vienna as the city of music that it possessed world-class musicians and ensembles. The Philharmonic Concerts with the violinist Ginette Neveu

---

13 Only few made it to Paris on their own, such as Ernst Fuchs, Erich [later: Arik] Brauer, Friedensreich Hundertwasser, or Marc Adrian. There is not sufficient space here for full references; my thanks to Natalie Lettner for her bibliographical assistance.
14 Thomas Angerer: Kontinuitäten und Kontraste der französischen Österreichpolitik 1919–1955, in: Klaus Koch, Walter Rauscher, Arnold Suppan, Elisabeth Vyslonzil (eds.): Von Saint-Germain zum Belvedere. Österreich und Europa 1919–1955, Vienna 2007, 129–157; idem: Französische Freundschaftspolitik in Österreich nach 1945, in: Manfried Rauchensteiner, Robert Kriechbaumer (eds.): Die Gunst des Augenblicks. Neuere Forschungen zu Staatsvertrag und Neutralität, Vienna/Cologne/Weimar 2005, 113–138, here 115–122.
15 Georges Dumaine: Österreichertum, in: Welt am Montag, 18 February 1946, 3.
16 nic, Ausstellung Florian Jakowitsch, in: Weltpresse, 2 June 1949, 6. Natalie Lettner: Maria Lassnig. Die Biografie, Vienna, third edition 2022, 107.
17 Éric Dussault: La dénazification de l'Autriche par la France. La politique culturelle de la France dans la zone d'occupation, 1945–1955, Sainte-Foy, QC 2005, 41–43.

between 1946 and 1948 became legendary.[18] In the visual arts, the French authorities liaised with venues in Paris such as the Petit Palais, the National Library, and the Musée National d'Art Moderne to host travelling exhibitions of the Kunsthistorisches Museum in 1947, the Albertina in 1950, or a solo exhibition of works by Fritz Wotruba in 1948.[19] A member of the French Information Service in Vienna, the Germanist Armand Jacob, moved in Viennese avant-garde circles, wrote about new Austrian art in French newspapers, and before Jean Cocteau's appearance in Oedipus Rex at Vienna's Konzerthaus in 1952 he took him to the avant-garde rendezvous Strohkoffer before the rolling cameras of the *Österreichische Wochenschau* newsreel, to the lasting pride of the Art Club.[20]

Most significantly, in 1947 France concluded a new, much more extensive cultural agreement with Austria, enabling cultural institutes in each other's countries, with firmer guarantees than in the agreement of 1936, and set up a Mixed Commission with stronger powers in order to set in motion exchange and collaboration in all areas of culture. It was Austria's first international agreement after the war and allowed the country, although then only partly sovereign, to restore cultural ties with France on an equal footing – an expression of a French policy of friendship that was cause for much satisfaction in political and cultural circles and was intended to show the Austrians once again that it was well worth being independent from Germany. The agreement contained a clause providing a kind of most-favoured status to French lessons at Austrian schools: the language (only an optional subject during the National Socialist era) was not to receive worse treatment than other living foreign languages – that is, English. While this article was unable to arrest the triumph of English, an additional agreement in 1952 helped greatly increase the popularity of the Lycée: as a modern all-day school with neither confessional nor political ties, over the decades it guided thousands of Viennese from pre-school to a dual Franco-Austrian school-leaving certificate, among them renowned creative artists (Timna Brauer, Claudia Messner, Elisabeth Schweeger et al.), journalists (Roland Barazon, Ben Segenreich et al.), and academics (Otto Pfersmann, Walter Schachermayer et al.).[21]

In late 1947, a French Cultural Institute much larger and more representative than had existed before the war opened in Palais Lobkowitz, which had housed

---

18 Online-Konzertarchiv der Wiener Philharmoniker. Alexander Golovlev: French and Soviet Musical Diplomacies in Post-War Austria, 1945–1955, London/New York 2023.
19 Paul Rachler, Matthias Boeckl: Das Medium als Botschaft. Ausstellungen als Verbreitungsmotor von Ideen der Moderne, in: Agnes Husslein-Arco (eds.), Wien – Paris. Van Gogh, Cézanne und Österreichs Moderne 1880–1960, Vienna 2007, 19 f.
20 Eisler, [Erinnerung], 69 f; Maria Fialik: "Strohkoffer"-Gespräche, Vienna 1998, 87; Werner, Existenzialismus, 109 f.
21 Porpaczy, Frankreich, 89–100; the texts by Michaela Feurstein and Jean-Michel Casset in: Angerer, Le Rider, "Frühling", 83–98 and 99–118 respectively.

the French Embassy at the turn of the century. Eugène Susini enjoyed the baroque-ified setting and hosting large receptions, gaining the nickname "Prince Eugène". He integrated the Culture Department of the High Commission into the building. Since the Culture Department was responsible for Austria as a whole and under his own direction, Susini could ask the head of the Cultural Institute in Innsbruck, Maurice Besset (1921-2008), a young, outstanding connoisseur of art, for help with programming exhibitions in Vienna too.[22] Just as importantly, there was also the Information Department of the High Commission in Mariahilferstrasse (the Delkahaus) headed by an old connoisseur and friend of Austria, the Germanist, translator, journalist, and diplomat Marcel Ray (1878-1951).[23]

The remits of the Culture and the Information Departments were not as clearly demarcated as their British counterparts, which led to friction but also to synergy. With the Apollokino, the Culture Department had in its sector the "most beautiful and largest Viennese cinema", organized film festivals, and provided a high-quality selection of French filmmaking, also making it available to other cinemas in Vienna, although the use of subtitles did not quite overcome the language barrier; it was not until 1948 that it reluctantly accepted the need for dubbing, a reticence born out of an aversion to dependence on the German market and to German accents.[24] The Information Department's main business, however, was media work, ranging from reporting on culture in its own publications (principally *Welt am Montag [mit Sport]* and *Welt am Abend*, 1945/ 1946-1948) to press conferences and press material for other local media.[25] Along with the culture magazines *Wort und Tat* (1946-1948) and *Europäische Rundschau* (1946-1949), both of which quickly became important in Germany too but

---

22 Porpaczy, Frankreich, S. 85-87.
23 Cécile Poulot, Marcel Ray: "traducteur et passeur" d'Adolf Loos en France, ou la construction d'un classique international en histoire de l'architecture, in: Revue germanique internationale 32 (2020), 77-92.
24 Hermann Schreiber: Eine Chance für Frankreich, in: Literatur und Kritik 40 (2005) 30 (quotation); Barbara Porpaczy: Kultur- und Propagandapolitik der französischen Besatzungsmacht, in: Karin Moser (ed.): Besetzte Bilder. Film, Kultur und Propaganda in Österreich 1945-1955, Vienna 2005, 133-154; Myriam Gourlet: Die französische Medienpolitik in Österreich während der Besatzungszeit 1945-1949, Mémoire pour la maîtrise. Université Catholique de l'Ouest, Angers, 2002, 98.
25 French-controlled radio from the French Zone was difficult to receive in Vienna; after the Second Control Agreement, the French left it to the federal provinces. The weekly newsreels for the cinemas and the wall newspaper *Hallo Hallo ... hier spricht Paris!* contained hardly any reporting on culture. Karin Moser: Les actualités françaises. Die Exotik der französischen Besatzungswochenschau, in: eadem (ed.): Besetzte Bilder, 547-561; eadem: Propaganda und Gegenpropaganda. Das "kalte" Wechselspiel während der alliierten Besatzung in Österreich, in: medien & zeit 17 (2002/1), 27-42; Barbara Semper: "Hallo Hallo ... hier spricht Paris!" 1945-1947, Diplomarbeit, University of Vienna 2013.

proved unsustainable,²⁶ a cultural press service also played a significant role: *Kulturelles*, later *Geistiges Frankreich*. From 1947 to 1953, it provided radio, newspapers, and magazines with short news items, articles, and sometimes short literary translations free of charge. With a circulation of up to 200 copies, it was delivered to editors, journalists, and many cultural figures. It had a significant impact, not least due to the professional leadership of the young Austrian writer and Francophile Hermann Schreiber (under the overall direction of the abovementioned Armand Jacob).²⁷ The press service drew on a documentation centre with a public reading room and lending library; the writer H. C. Artmann observed, "It was fantastic."²⁸ In 1948, the reading room moved from Capistrangasse 5 to the Delkahaus, and in 1950 to the house on the corner of Kärtnerstrasse/Walfischgasse (the Fensterguckerhaus). When occupation ended, it was receiving between 100 and 250 visitors a day.²⁹

It remains to take a closer look at cooperation by all French authorities and levels involved in making cultural policy in Vienna during the early post-war years and at some of its numerous protagonists. (For instance, there were at least seven *normaliens* from 1945 to 1947 alone,³⁰ and the wife and colleague of the first head of information in Vienna was a respected artist and the younger sister of Simone de Beauvoir, Hélène de Beauvoir, who painted frescoes in the first French bookshop.)³¹ Initially, for staff and financing, French cultural policy received greater support from the High Commission (from 1945 to 1950 under the direction of General Marie-Emile Béthouart) than from the Foreign Ministry, including even the diverting of Austrian payments for the costs of French occupation (just as improperly as in Germany, but apparently not as systematically, and not least for the repair of war-damaged buildings).³² By the early 1950s, however, due to a shortage of funds France had already reduced its occupation of

---

26 Holger Englerth: "... das war etwas besonderes ..." Wort und Tat (1945–1948); idem: Europa oder Lipizzaner? Europäische Rundschau (1946–1949), both in: Österreichische Nationalbibliothek, Österreichische Literaturzeitschriften 1945–1990 [2010], https://www.onb.ac.at/oe-literaturzeitschriften/; Roger Vorderegger: Die Zeitschrift *Wort und Tat* im Kontext des geistig-kulturellen Klimas der Nachkriegszeit, in: Sandra Unterweger, idem, Verena Zankl (eds.): Bonjour Autriche. Literatur und Kunst in Tirol und Vorarlberg 1945–1955, Innsbruck/Vienna/Bozen 2010, 315–69; Ina Ulrike Paul: Die "Europäische Rundschau" (1946–1949), in: Michael Grunewald (ed.): Le discours européen dans les revues allemandes (1945–1950), Bern 2001, 363–387.
27 Porpaczy, Frankreich, 262–267; Werner, Existenzialismus, 76–80, 93–100.
28 H. C. Artmann: [Erinnerung], in: Österreichisch-Französisches Jahrbuch, 41.
29 Porpaczy, Frankreich, 184.
30 Roger Bauer, Jean Clément, Jean Derré, Pierre Moisy, Marcel Ray, Eugène Susini, later Armand Jacob et al. For a first account, cf. Emmanuelle Picard: Des usages de l'Allemagne. Politique culturelle française en Allemagne, 1945–1963, Villeneuve d'Ascq 2001, 265.
31 Werner, Existenzialismus, 109/note 224.
32 Porpaczy, Frankreich, 193–196.

Austria to the extent that nothing remained of the High Commission's Cultural Service, and hardly anything of its Information Service. Nevertheless, the Cultural Institute was able to take over the important reading room in Walfischgasse, along with its financing, cultural policy now coming entirely under its auspices.

The reach of French cultural policy's impact in Vienna should not be underestimated. Certainly, up to the late 1950s, French Cultural Institutes were academic institutions formally run by the University of Paris, despite being funded and controlled by the Foreign Ministry. Attendances at Palais Lobkowitz continued to rise beyond the 1950s, however, reaching around 1,000 per semester during the final year of occupation.[33] Numbers were bolstered by audiences at the University of Vienna and the Catholic Academy. From the perspective of cultural diplomacy, audiences at all three institutions were not closed elites but multipliers: future teachers, civil servants, media and cultural figures, etc. Cultural Institute professors and members of the Information Service regularly spoke at adult education centres (Volkshochschulen) and on the radio and wrote for Viennese newspapers and magazines. When the Information Service provided reports on culture in its *Welt am Montag mit Sport*, they appeared in the Austrian weekly with the largest reach: it "informed us about the most modern literary life abroad – about the Sartre–Breton debate or the new Goncourt – as if we were French", wrote the poet Andreas Okopenko looking back on his youth.[34]

For talks, the Eroica-Saal in Palais Lobkowitz often proved too small – three examples: for Raymond Aron, the Brahms-Saal was required, for Robert d'Harcourt the Auditorium maximum, and for Le Corbusier the Mozart-Saal. Aron and d'Harcourt spoke in German; Le Corbusier was translated. The press reported on these events, Aron's talk appearing in *Europäische Rundschau* and Le Corbusier's in *Der Aufbau*, the magazine published by Vienna's Municipal Planning Office (Wiener Stadtbauamt).[35] Guest concerts filled the Großer Musikvereinssaal up to three times in succession and were occasionally broadcast on the radio. For the exhibition "Meister der modernen französischen Malerei" (Masters of Modern French Painting) in 1947, there was a radio broadcast and a short film by the Österreichische Werbegesellschaft (Austrian Advertising Company), screened before the main feature at cinemas, and some 2,000 placards; within three weeks, it drew no fewer than 20,000 visitors to the Kunstgewerbemuseum (Museum of Arts and Crafts), whose opening times had to be extended to 7 p.m. The catalogue, with thirty-three full-page plates, had a print

---

33 Porpaczy, Frankreich, 183.
34 Andreas Okopenko, cit. Werner, Existenzialismus, 75f.
35 Platzer, Kalter Krieg, 80, cf. too 77.

run of 15,000.[36] The previous year at the same venue, the exhibition of works by the Salon d'automne, planned for three weeks, had to be extended to five, attracting some 35,000 visitors.[37] Incidentally, French cultural policy, despite banking on high culture, also had great success in Vienna with French folk music and folk dance groups.[38] If it neglected chansons, this was also because they were often played on the radio anyway.

From the above it is already clear that the programme of events promoted by French cultural policy was not as conservative as one might associate with Susini as an individual. Besides the fact that he is said to be the first to have lectured on Bert Brecht at the University of Vienna,[39] the Cultural Institute's range of courses extended to the most contemporary developments and a large variety of styles. The Salon d'automne, to which the two abovementioned large shows of 1945/46 were dedicated, was the most important exhibition of new art in Paris. Already in early 1946, Francis Poulenc and Olivier Messiaen came to premiere their own works in Vienna, including some of their most recent.[40]

Above all, however, "classics" of French Modernism – such as the abovementioned art exhibition at the Kunstgewerbemuseum in 1947 or the exhibition on architecture and municipal planning at the same venue the next year – were still revolutionary in Vienna and entirely new to younger generations, particularly "Die Klassiker des Kubismus in Frankreich" (The Classics of Cubism in France) at the Albertina in 1950: a large-format tabloid devoted a full page to an appeal to the Ministry for Education, protesting against such "outlandishness".[41] Reporting on the performance of Debussy's *Pelléas et Mélisande* by the touring Opéra Comique at the Theater an der Wien (the State Opera's alternative venue due to bomb damage) and at the Volksoper, the first time the work had been performed in Vienna for thirty-five years, and the first time in its original language, the *Wiener Kurier* ran with the headline: "All of modern music derives from this". The performances by the touring Paris Opera Ballet in 1950–1952 triggered a debate in the press on new conceptions of classical ballet, and while

---

36 Porpaczy, Frankreich, 234. Haut Commissariat de la République française en Autriche, Division des Affaires Culturelles, Compte rendu Exposition "Les Classiques […]", 21 February 1947, MAE, 5AUT/191.
37 Porpaczy, Frankreich, 234. Verlängerung des "Salon d'Automne", in: Die Kleine Volkszeitung, 31 August 1946, 7.
38 Golovlev, Music Diplomacy, 151f., 173–175.
39 Jean-Marie Valentin: Avant-propos, in: Revue d'Allemagne et des pays de langue allemande 13 (1981), 196.
40 Konzert der Wiener Philharmoniker, 16/17 February 1946, https://www.wienerphilharmoniker.at/de/konzerte/konzert/6794/; Helmut A. Fiechtner: Olivier Messiaen, in: Die Furche, 27 April 1946, 9.
41 Abwegiges um unser Geld. Ein Nekrolog zu einer Ausstellung und ein Appell ans Unterrichtsministerium, in: Wiener Wochenausgabe, 25 March 1950, 9; Porpaczy, Frankreich, 265.

touring theatre companies mainly performed classics, they reinterpreted them for the new times; in the case of the Théâtre National Populaire in 1953, the company also presented a new model for making classics more accessible for broader sections of the population.[42]

Michel Cullin, a student of Susini's at the Sorbonne and one of the most important successors to him in Vienna in the early 1980s, wrote of a "golden age of Franco-Austrian cultural relations", and the renowned journalist and high official Kurt Skalnik, a student himself at the time, described it as a "spring that was unfortunately not followed by a summer".[43] Despite the hardship in France, thanks to excellent personnel and huge assistance by the High Commission, French cultural policy in Allied-occupied Vienna was able not only to swiftly regain a footing but also to enjoy a brilliant revival, as well as stabilizing at a high level before the occupiers withdrew. Its outstanding significance in the visual arts and its inferiority in popular culture and media policy are beyond dispute. Its legacy in terms of impetus and infrastructure – temporarily, a reading room, permanently, the Cultural Institute and the Lycée, and for decades, large scholarships, grants, and cooperation programmes – can still be felt to this day.

---

42 Golovlev, Music Diplomacy, 167/35 (citation), 150, and 152f.; idem: Dancing the Nation? French Dance Diplomacy in Allied-Occupied Austria, 1945–55, in: Austrian History Yearbook 50 (2019), 166–183; Porpaczy, Frankreich, 216.
43 Michel Cullin: L'action culturelle française en Autriche après 1945, in: Felix Kreissler (ed.): Relations franco-autrichiennes 1870–1970, Mont-Saint-Aignan 1986, 328; Kurt Skalnik: [Erinnerung], in: Österreichisch-französisches Jahrbuch, 67.

Wolfgang Mueller

Soviet Propaganda, Media, and Cultural Policy in Vienna, 1945–1955

For the Soviet Union, the first modern "propaganda state", state dissemination of ideological content via culture and the media, the press, images, radio, and film, but also theatre and the visual arts, was of central importance.[1]

During the Second World War, the USSR had transmitted radio broadcasts for the population of Austria, having declared its commitment to the country's restoration in the Moscow Declaration of 1 November 1943, together with the USA and Britain. Whereas the focus had then been on distancing Austria from National Socialism and reinforcing an Austrian identity, after the war and Austria's liberation from the National Socialist dictatorship, the emphasis was placed on re-establishing the media and culture. As early as 1945, however, priority was given to stressing the aims and achievements of the Soviet Union and Stalinism along with Russian, but also non-Russian culture in the USSR. Shortly thereafter, negative portrayals of the West and also, later, non-communist actors took on increasing significance in Soviet media and cultural events. Media and culture thus became stages for the early Cold War.

The organization and control over the content of Soviet propaganda, media, and cultural policy both in the USSR itself and abroad were the responsibility of central state and party organs such as the Soviet Information Bureau, the telegraph agency TASS, and the Committee on the Arts, all three under the Council of Ministers of the USSR, as well as the Department for Agitation and Propaganda of the CPSU, the All-Union Society for Cultural Relations Abroad (VOKS), etc. In Austria too, several Soviet institutions operated, initially under the control of the Political Administration of the 3rd Ukrainian Front (Army Group) of the Red Army. In October 1945, all officers involved were placed under the newly created Propaganda Department of the Soviet section of the Allied Commission for

---

1 Cf. Peter Kenez: The Birth of the Propaganda State. Soviet Methods of Mass Mobilization, Cambridge 1985; Vladimir O. Pechatnov: Strel'ba kholostymi: sovetskaia propaganda na Zapad v nachale kholodnoi voiny, in: A. O. Chubar'ian et al. (eds.): Stalinskoe desiatiletie kholodnoi voiny, Moscow 1999,108–133; Jeffrey Brooks: Thank You, Comrade Stalin! Soviet Public Culture from Revolution to Cold War, Princeton 2000.

Austria. Its remit included censorship of the press, radio, film, theatre, and literature, as well as presenting Soviet propaganda and culture. Performances by touring Soviet artists and the import of Soviet dramas, records, etc., were initiated by the VOKS's Vienna office, and imports of books and films via the Vienna branch of the Soviet companies Mezhdunarodnaia kniga (International Book, MK) and Sovexportfilm. In the late 1940s, the Propaganda Department (excluding its subordinate institutions) employed 115 Soviet functionaries, in addition to some 4,171 Austrians, mostly from the Communist Party of Austria (Kommunistische Partei Österreichs, KPÖ) and circles close to it, which may have contributed to Soviet propaganda in Austria's increasing focus on domestic policy.[2]

Moreover, with Ernst Fischer as state secretary for education and art (1945) and Viktor Matejka as city councillor for culture (1945–1949), Communists also took over key nerve centres of Austrian cultural policy,[3] which was clearly the Soviet intention; in terms of personnel but also, increasingly, content, Soviet cultural policy was characterized by the complex patron–client relationship between the USSR and the KPÖ, which it had levered into many positions of power (including the Ministry of the Interior, and with it the police) and which it supported both politically and financially. In 1945, the print works of the formerly "Aryanized" Steyrermühl-Verlag publishing house were leased to the KPÖ "for reasons pertaining to state policy". The facilities were henceforth used for the party's own press, Globus-Verlag.[4] A further role in transmission was taken on by the Österreichisch–Sowjetische Gesellschaft (Austro-Soviet Society, ÖSG), newly formed in 1945 on Soviet initiative. Initially, the ÖSG sought to position itself as an above-party organization, despite its financial dependence on the USSR and the fact that Communists held strategic positions in it. It also published the journal *Die Brücke Österreich–Sowjetunion* (The Bridge Austria–Soviet Union) and organized exhibitions, talks, and concerts.

---

2 Cf. Wolfgang Mueller: "Die Kanonen schießen nicht … Aber der Kampf geht weiter." Die Propaganda der sowjetischen Besatzungsmacht in Österreich im Kalten Krieg, in: Stefan Karner, Barbara Stelzl-Marx (eds.): Die Rote Armee in Österreich. Sowjetische Besatzung 1945–1955, Vol. 1: Beiträge (Veröffentlichungen des Ludwig-Boltzmann-Instituts für Kriegsfolgenforschung, special edition 4), Graz/Vienna/Munich 2005, 339–362.
3 Cf. Manfred Mugrauer: Die Politik der KPÖ in der Provisorischen Regierung Renner, Vienna 2006.
4 Murray G. Hall: Verlag der "Tagblatt-Bibliothek" (Steyrermühl-Verlag), in: idem (ed.): Österreichische Verlagsgeschichte, http://verlagsgeschichte.murrayhall.com/?page_id=611 (21 July 2024).

Rebuilding

Some of the first tasks of Soviet occupation authorities was to inform the population of instructions given by the Red Army in Austria via pamphlets, placards, and announcements via loudspeaker, to promote denazification and the creation of an Austrian identity, and to "create correct ideas about the Soviet Union", as a Soviet directive put it.[5] From 15 April 1945 onwards, such information was also printed in the *Österreichische Zeitung* (*ÖZ*), the newspaper published by the Red Army for the local population. Its circulation soon rose to 50,000 and later to 150,000 copies. The country's first post-war newspaper, it reported on the state of affairs at the fronts and progress made in rebuilding political, economic, and cultural life in Austria. From 1946, it was supplemented by the *Welt-Illustrierte* and the wall newspaper *Sowjetunion im Bild*.

But efforts were also made to cultivate a positive image of the Soviet Union and to entertain. Before the war was over, the song and dance ensemble of the 3rd Ukrainian Front had already made its first appearance in Vienna's Stadttheater and later at the Konzerthaus. Folk dance groups from Russia, Ukraine, and Georgia and soldiers' choirs would remain one of the most enduring attractions of Soviet cultural policy into the late occupation era. From 24 April, the Apollo-Kino screened Stalin's favourite film, Sergei Eisenstein's *Iwan der Schreckliche*, (German; Russian: *Ivan Groznyi*, English: *Ivan the Terrible*), and from 27 April some nine cinemas were showing Soviet war newsreels,[6] comedies, and monumental films – most of them without subtitles and of poor quality. A visitor noted that they had "zero" success with the public.[7] In the early May, some seventeen cinemas in Vienna were supplied with Soviet films. The same month, a delegation of the Kyiv Academy Theatre arrived, and between 14 July and 11 August 1945, a tour including the violist David Oistrakh and the ballerina Galina Ulanova was very well received by audiences.

Of course, reviving culture was possible only with Austrian involvement. In the April, Order No. 2 of the Soviet local commander had allowed theatres, cinemas, "and other entertainment venues" to open in the same month.[8] By Soviet order, the State Opera began rehearsals, and the Vienna Philharmonic received the Soviet request to start performances as soon as possible under the management of the conductor Clemens Krauss, whose role in National Socialist cultural life

---

5 Cit. Wolfgang Mueller: Die sowjetische Besatzung in Österreich 1945–1955 und ihre politische Mission, Vienna 2005, 96.
6 Cf. Felix Czeike: April und Mai 1945 in Wien, in: Wiener Geschichtsblätter 30 (1975), 33–48.
7 Josef Schöner, Wiener Tagebuch 1944/45, ed. by Eva-Marie Csáky, Franz Matscher, Gerald Stourzh, Vienna 1992, 197–199.
8 Wilfried Aichinger: Sowjetische Österreichpolitik 1943–1945, doctoral thesis, University of Vienna 1977, 241 f.; for the text, cf. ibid., 421.

was evidently of no concern to the Soviet side. A little later, the new impresario of the Burgtheater, Raoul Aslan, was instructed to open his stage. After two public rehearsals, the first Philharmonic concert after the war took place on 27 April, and three days later the Burgtheater ensemble launched its new season with Grillparzer's *Sappho* at the Varieté Ronacher. On 1 May, there followed a general opening of Vienna's theatres, including the State Opera at its alternative venue, the Volksoper, since the opera house on the Ring had been severely damaged during an air raid on 12 March 1945. Although Gerhart Hauptmann's *Elga* had to be replaced at the Akademietheater by Ibsen's *Hedda Gabler* following Soviet objections,[9] initially, there were hardly any cases of denazification, problems due to Soviet censorship, or interventions in artistic matters. The swift revival of the cultural scene represented a peculiarity of Soviet occupation policy which could also be observed in Berlin and stood in contrast to the Western powers' ban on locals' activities.

The Soviet forces also supported the Vienna State Opera's reconstruction on the Ring – by supplying building materials, trucks, and a donation of two million schillings granted shortly before the parliamentary elections in the autumn. In the August, the Soviet Union had inscribed itself into Vienna's cityscape with the Red Army Monument, realized in Stalinist architectural language.

Concerts were broadcast by Radio Wien, which with Soviet approval had become operational again on 29 April. In the late May, the Soviet occupation authorities introduced prior censorship of the station's daily offerings, and from 7 June the *Russische Stunde* (Russian Hour, *RS*) was broadcast, a programme put together by Austrian staff using Soviet materials.[10]

The Russian Contribution

Building on the reputation of "Russian" art, under which Ukrainian, Belarusian, Georgian, Armenian, etc. works were often subsumed too, it was possible to regain a firm footing in cultural life by non-binding, but also by obligatory measures (for instance in the field of film distribution). In the *Russische Stunde*, Russian music could be listened to practically daily; Tchaikovsky, Prokof'ev, and

---

9 Cf. Oliver Rathkolb: Politische Propaganda der amerikanischen Besatzungsmacht in Österreich 1945–1950. Ein Beitrag zur Geschichte des Kalten Kriegs in der Presse-, Kultur- und Rundfunkpolitik, doctoral thesis, University of Vienna 1981, 295–298.
10 Cf. Wolfgang Mueller: Eine "scharfe Waffe" im Kalten Krieg? Die sowjetische Rundfunkpolitik in Österreich 1945–1955. Wiederaufbau, Zensur, Radio Moskau und Russische Stunde, in: Anita Mayer-Hirzberger, Cornelia Szabó-Knotik (eds.): Zur Russischen Stunde der RAVAG (1945–55). Ein Kapitel österreichischer Radiogeschichte (Anklaenge. Wiener Jahrbuch für Musikwissenschaft 2022/23), Vienna 2023, 11–46.

Shostakovich were some of the most-played non-Austrian composers. Following the big tour in 1945, the concert halls hosted visits by classical and folk musicians such as the Sveshnikov Choir and the Moiseev Dance Ensemble in 1946; Evgenii Mravinskii, Lev Oborin, and David Oistrakh in 1946, Jakob Flier in 1946, a Georgian dance group in 1949, the Berioska Folk Dance Ensemble in 1949 and 1953, the Piatnitskii Choir in 1950, the cellist Mstislav Rostropovich in 1951, the ballerina Maiia Plisetskaia in 1954, and the pianist Emil Gilel's in 1955. The programme comprised works by Tchaikovsky, Musorgskii, Rakhmaninov, Shostakovich, and Khachaturian, or folk music. While the 186 performances of Tchaikovsky during the occupation era placed him well behind Beethoven (626), Mozart (483), and Bach (415), he was one of the most-played non-German-speaking composers, roughly matching the frequency with which his works were performed between the wars, although this was not sustained in the following decade.[11] From 1949, several guest performances were given as part of Austro-Soviet "Friendship Weeks".

Vienna's theatres regularly staged Russian and Soviet plays: the Burgtheater and the Akademie put on Griboedov, Tolstoi, Gor'kii, and Chekhov; the Volkstheater, headed by Günther Haenel, a figure with close ties to the KPÖ, offered Ostrovskii, Turgenev, and a play by the Soviet writer and politician Anatolii Lunacharskii; and the equally left-wing theatre Die Insel staged one to two Russian pieces a year, by writers such as Chekhov, Ostrovskii, Afinogenov, and Gor'kii.[12]

In the cinemas, developments were less satisfactory for the Soviet Union, since despite the Soviet film festivals held from 1946 onwards, the avant-garde of a Pudovkin or Eisenstein, which now seemed somewhat antiquated, and the trivial comedies and emotional propaganda films such as *Der Schwur* (German; Russian: *Kliatva*, English: *The Vow*) proved far less appealing than the sometimes high-quality and less ideologized children's films such as *Die steinerne Blume* (German; Russian: *Kamennyi tsvetok*, English: *The Stone Flower*). Faced with a shrinking market share, the Soviet authorities went on the offensive, introducing compulsory subscriptions for cinemas and founding the Austrian Universalfilm-Verleihgesellschaft (Universal Film Distribution Company) for the distribution of Soviet films.[13]

---

11 Cf. Alexander Golovlev: French and Soviet Musical Diplomacies in Post-War Austria, 1945–1955, London 2023, 46–49, 179f.
12 Cf. Michael Kraus: "Kultura". Der Einfluss der sowjetischen Besatzung auf die österreichische Kultur 1945–1955, Diplomarbeit, University of Vienna 2008, 138, 220–222.
13 Cf. Wolfgang Mueller et al. (eds.): Sowjetische Politik in Österreich 1945–1955. Dokumente aus russischen Archiven (Fontes Rerum Austriacarum. Österreichische Geschichtsquellen, second section: Diplomataria et Acta, Vol. 93), Vienna 2005, 501.

The distribution programme was supplemented with productions by the Wien-Film studios on Vienna's Rosenhügel hill, which had been confiscated by the Soviet Union in 1946 and remained under Soviet control. Some of these films were of artistic value, some lacked depth, but they all toed the party line.[14] Following the production of Austrian newsreels in 1946, in 1948 the KPÖ suggested local feature film production. In 1950, the Nova-Film-Gesellschaft, a front company for the Soviet Military Bank, released its first colour production, the dance film *Das Kind der Donau* (Child of the Danube), starring Marika Rökk.[15]

Another medium that, like theatre and film, oscillated between 'hard' and 'soft' propaganda was exhibitions. The Austrian public had its first opportunity to become acquainted with Soviet painting in 1947, at a large exhibition of Socialist Realism at the Vienna Museum of Applied Art (Wiener Museum für angewandte Kunst, MAK). The ÖZ had already praised the "healthiness of this art, its inexhaustible vitality" and observed that Soviet art was free from any of "that mystic degeneration and [...] formalist affectation" that characterized the visual arts in other countries.[16] The large-scale works by the Soviet state artists Gerasimov, Deineka, and Plastov on display in Vienna comprised genre and historical paintings and portraits of Stalin. According to Soviet figures, the exhibition was attended by 30,000 during its four-week run; the media cited positive reactions in line with Stalinist (and also National Socialist) aesthetics.[17] The show at MAK was the largest the Soviet Union staged in Austria. The many other exhibitions, from 1950 onwards mostly at the Soviet Information Centre, were dedicated to topics such as Romanian stamps, Soviet children's books, the achievements of socialism in the USSR and Eastern Europe, and the alleged "use of bacteriological weapons in Korea by the American warmongers".[18]

---

14 Cf. Oliver Rathkolb: Die "Wien-Film"-Produktion am Rosenhügel. Österreichische Filmproduktion und Kalter Krieg, in: Hans Heinz Fabris, Kurt Luger (eds.): Medienkultur in Österreich. Film, Fotografie, Fernsehen und Video in der Zweiten Republik (Kulturstudien, Vol. 11), Vienna/Cologne/Graz 1988, 117–132; Martin Prucha: Agfacolor und Kalter Krieg. Die Geschichte der Wien-Film am Rosenhügel 1946–1955, in: Ruth Beckermann, Christa Blümlinger (ed.): Ohne Untertitel. Fragmente einer Geschichte des österreichischen Kinos, Vienna 1996, 53–79.
15 Cf. Kraus, "Kultura", 134.
16 M. Sokolow: Große Kunstausstellung in Moskau, in: ÖZ, 20 February 1946, 3.
17 Cf. Peter Acht: "Keine Dekadenz! Gesund, schön!", in: ÖZ, 25 March 1947, 5.
18 Cit. Wolfgang Mueller: "Leuchtturm des Sozialismus" oder "Zentrum der Freundschaft"? Das Sowjetische Informationszentrum im Wiener Porr-Haus: ein Instrument der Besatzungspolitik zwischen Volksbildung und Propaganda, in: Wiener Geschichtsblätter 55 (2000) 4, 261–285, here: 279f.

Fig. 1: Placard for the exhibition "Kinder- und Jugendbücher aus der Sowjetunion" (Children's and Adolescents' Books from the Soviet Union) at the Soviet Information Centre, 1954 (Vienna City Library, P-6884)

The Cold War

At this point, the beginnings of a new phase of Stalinist terror and the Cold War it fostered had already had a profound influence on Soviet cultural policy in Vienna. The end of the war saw the end of so-called wartime liberalism in the USSR; returning soldiers were banished to the Gulag, artists were subjected to repressions, Jews were marginalized, and leading Jewish figures, such as the head of the Jewish Theatre and the Jewish Antifascist Committee, Solomon Mikhoels, were murdered. The campaign against "formalism" in art launched by Stalin's political disciple Andrei Zhdanov and a wave of new political show trials and repressions in the Soviet Union and Soviet-occupied Eastern Europe instigated by Stalin himself not only put an end to the opera *Velikaia druzhba* (The Great Friendship) by the Georgian Vano Muradeli, but also drove Shostakovich to a nervous breakdown and took the lives of thousands. The Soviet machinery and the KPÖ were gripped by waves of Stalinist "purges". While the ÖSG, led by the doctor Hugo Glaser and the Catholic Communist Nikolaus Howorka, was a heavily left-wing institution, it was not considered entirely trustworthy in the late Stalinist period, and was "purged" and transformed into a "combat organization".[19] From 1947, the Soviet media in Austria also presented themselves using the metaphor of culture and media as "weapons" – despite Stalinist peace propaganda.

The Soviet ÖZ was characterized by glorification of the Soviet Union and Stalinism; from 1946 onwards, it also displayed growing – and later extreme – anti-Americanism, increasing polemic against Austrian non-communists, and KPÖ propaganda. In a series of articles published by *Pravda* and the ÖZ in early October 1946, the Vienna TASS correspondent accused the Austrian People's Party (Österreichische Volkspartei, ÖVP) and the Social Democratic Party of Austria (Sozialistische Partei Österreichs), which it termed "enemies of the people", and the Western powers of sabotaging the reconstruction of Austria, persecuting communists, starving the workers, supporting fascist groups, and wanting to sell Austria to England and the USA. It was claimed that "progressive forces" had begun to form, and it remained unclear who would triumph in the heavy "struggle" that had broken out: the forces of "reaction [...] or the new, progressive forces".[20] In 1950, the newspaper even dreamed of the "total annihilation of capitalist rule" and cited Stalin's dictum that social democracy had to be eradicated.

The *Russische Stunde* radio program, increased to around seventeen hours a week by mid-1949, transformed into a "propaganda weapon" taking aim at the West and the non-communist parties, and there was also an increase in Soviet pressure to read out one-sided or untruthful announcements and help increase the influence of Communist editors. This development peaked in the lead-up to and during the KPÖ riots in October 1950.

Soviet newsreels and films were also used as a propaganda "weapon". The Soviet Rosenhügel newsreel *Wir sind dabei* juxtaposed pictures intended to show misery, corruption, and oppression in the West with alleged progress and joy under Stalinism; non-Communist Austrian politicians were denigrated as "capitalism's lackeys".[21]

---

19 Golovlev, French and Soviet Musical Diplomacies, 72 f; Kraus, "Kultura", 101.
20 Die Ursachen der Stagnation, in: ÖZ, 5 October 1946, 1. Further pieces appeared on 9, 11, and 12 October 1946. On the following, cf.: P. Grigorjew: Strategie und Taktik der Bolschewistischen Partei, in: ÖZ, 28 April 1950, 4.
21 Karin Moser: Die sowjetischen Wochenschauproduktionen für Österreich, in: eadem (ed.): Besetzte Bilder. Film, Kultur und Propaganda in Österreich 1945–1955, Vienna 2005, 527–546.

In 1947/48, the Soviet propaganda offensive also spilled over into theatre. An important step in this respect was the theatre production of the anti-American play *Die russische Frage* (German; Russian: *Russkii vopros*, English: *The Russian Question*) by Konstantin Simonov, which had already caused political scandals elsewhere. After American representatives had intervened to prevent its premiering in Vienna in 1947, it was staged there in the following March after a performance in Urfahr.

Lavishly staged for the propaganda drive, the production not only represented a quantum leap in theatre's involvement in the Cold War,[22] but also gave rise to a communist theatre group funded by the Soviet occupying forces, the Neues Theater in der Scala. Several proposals for its foundation had already been put before the Soviet authorities by the Communist actor Karl Paryla in 1946.[23] After his troupe of actors had proven their political usefulness with their performance of *Die Russsische Frage*, they received a permanent home in Vienna's former Johann-Strauss-Theater (then the Scala Cinema) with over 1,200 seats. The house staged works such as Beaumarchais's *Figaro*, Brecht's *Mutter Courage*, and *Der große Verrat* (The Great Betrayal) – a Stalinist propaganda piece taking aim at Tito by the KPÖ's figurehead intellectual Ernst Fischer.

In 1950, a second significant theatre project was launched with the Theater im Sowjetischen Informationszentrum. Its programme comprised anti-Western political pieces; between 1951 and 1953, the only moderate works it staged were for children. The theatre put on the tendentious works by the Tur brothers and Lev Sheinin, such as *Geheimarchiv des strategischen Dienstes* (The Secret Archive of the Strategic Service) or *Begegnung an der Elbe* (Encounter by the Elbe), the aims of which was to show "the intrigues of the American imperialists". The Soviet Information Centre (SIZ) also staged political cabaret; headed by Kurt Sobotka, its programme polemicized against the "Austrian cultural deputies and their transatlantic string-pullers". Overall, both the Scala and the SIZ demonstrated the Soviet use of theatre as a propaganda "weapon". The six Information Centres established at the Porr-Haus in Karlsplatz, in Stadlau, Sankt Pölten, Wiener Neustadt, and Eisenstadt in 1950–1953, based on the "Amerika-Häuser" model, provided not only theatres but also libraries and rooms for lectures and exhibitions.[24]

---

22 Cf. Oliver Rathkolb: Planspiele im Kalten Krieg. Sondierungen zur Kultur- und Theaterpolitik der Alliierten in: Hilde Haider-Pregler, Peter Roessler (eds.): Zeit der Befreiung. Wiener Theater nach 1945, Vienna 1997, 40–64, here: 46.
23 Cf. Wilhelm Pellert: Roter Vorhang, rotes Tuch. Das Neue Theater in der Scala 1948–1956, Vienna 1979, 22, 34, 36; Carmen-Renate Köper: Ein unheiliges Experiment. Das Neue Theater in der Scala 1948–1956, Vienna 1995.
24 Cf. Mueller, Leuchtturm des Sozialismus, 272–277, 284f.

Fig. 2: Anti-American slogan "Ami Go Home" in lights in front of the Porr-Haus (the Soviet Information Centre) (ANL/Vienna, US 24.081)

Assessing Impact

With Stalin's death in 1953, Soviet propaganda was toned down a little, and the State Treaty of 1955 brought an end to the era of Soviet 'cultural policy' in Vienna. The Scala and the SIZ were closed due to a lack of financing, and several artists who had worked for it or for Soviet propaganda, such as Karl Paryla and Otto Tausig, emigrated to the GDR, some of them having been 'blacklisted' by their political opponents. Writing in the Social Democratic *Arbeiter-Zeitung* in 1955, Franz Kreuzer criticized those who had "put on a show for the agents of the foreign power: the dubious individuals from the Russische Stunde, the petrol station stars from USIA-Rosenhügel, the communo-comedians from the Scala, and many others who only made the music for the communist dance".[25] Those who later voiced a critical assessment of the Soviet Union, such as Viktor Matjeka, left the KPÖ or were expelled from it, like Ernst Fischer.

Soviet policy had enabled a rapid restart to cultural life in 1945 and, moreover, had provided a good deal of impetus for cultural exchange and the creation of cultural institutions. Leading Soviet musicians as well as dance groups, children's film festivals, and much more besides enriched cultural life and were often accepted by the public. While years of National Socialist propaganda did not represent an easy starting point, there is no indication that this constituted a significant barrier to the Austrian reception of Chekhov, Khachaturian, or Ulanova in 1945.

A more critical assessment must be made of the political substance and characteristics of Soviet cultural exports such as the dissemination of Stalinist propaganda, the ridiculing of the Western avant-garde, but also the ruthless treatment of many artists and other people who were subjected to constant "tests" and "purges". The more open the genre or medium in question was to transporting political messages, the more strongly it was instrumentalized for political ends. While classical concerts could be staged relatively unideologically, this was not the case with baseless propaganda and columns laden with bogeymen. Increasingly, cultural figures were forced to take sides: with the Western liberal system or with the Soviet totalitarian dictatorship. Faced with this choice, but also given the Austrian traditions and Western support, the overwhelming majority of Austrians opted for the West. When Soviet authorities internally criticized the growing piles of unsold Soviet books, the dwindling sales of the *Österreichische Zeitung* and Soviet films, or the sect-like atmosphere in affiliated cultural organizations, the underlying reason for these phenomena remained unspoken: the nature of Stalinism, its view of the world and of human existence.

---

25 Arbeiter-Zeitung, 21 May 1955, cit. Kraus, "Kultura", 182.

Manfred Mugrauer

KPÖ Cultural Policy under Soviet Occupation

The Communist Party of Austria (Kommunistische Partei Österreichs, KPÖ) had the largest influence on domestic political development during the period from 1945 to 1955.[1] It was one of the three founding parties of the Second Republic, and until November 1947 it formed part of the all-party government together with the Austrian People's Party (Österreichische Volkspartei, ÖVP) and the Socialist Party of Austria (Sozialistische Partei Österreichs, SPÖ). The KPÖ shaped trade unions, companies, and the communes, had an impact on intellectual life, and was also able to exercise a certain influence on culture and sport.

An important factor for the KPÖ's political weight and societal standing was its close ties with the Soviet Union. The Soviet occupation authorities in Austria developed extensive activities in the field of cultural policy, for instance with its newspaper *Österreichische Zeitung*, the RAVAG *Russische Stunde* (Russian Hour) broadcast by Radio Wien, the Soviet Information Centres it founded, or the Wien-Film studios on the Rosenhügel hill in Vienna. These institutions were an important element of Communist cultural and information policy and also offered Austrian Communists opportunities to work and to play a role in culture and society.

The Party of Cultural Reconstruction

After the liberation of Austria in April 1945, the KPÖ was a considerable factor in cultural reconstruction, which initially took place under the leadership of KPÖ Secretary of State Ernst Fischer and Vienna's Communist city councillor for culture, Viktor Matejka. In reviving the cultural scene, especially with the reopening of theatres, Fischer could count on support from the Soviet authorities,

---

1 Manfred Mugrauer: Die Politik der KPÖ 1945–1955. Von der Regierungsbank in die innenpolitische Isolation (Zeitgeschichte im Kontext, Vol. 14), Göttingen 2020.

the "theatre-mad Russians".² More than a few cultural figures sought a radical break with the largely discredited past, which even drove artists who had hitherto kept their distance from the workers' movement, such as the composer Friedrich Wildgans, to the KPÖ.

The KPÖ had already made a significant contribution to anti-fascist cultural work in the countries in which its members had been exiled. In exile, the focus had been on communicating Austrian cultural traditions in order to emphasize the independence of the Austrian nation. Cultural work reinforcing Austrian identity was also undertaken in the Soviet prisoner of war camps, where Communist Antifa activists created theatre and music groups. In its immediate action programme of 6 August 1945, the KPÖ demanded the "radical purge" of cultural life "of all remnants of fascism" and the "cultivation of Austrian cultural traditions",³ with an eye on the folk traditions of Austrian culture and democratic sources of a national identity.

"High Culture" and Working-Class Culture

The KPÖ's cultural policy initiatives after 1945 aimed to have an impact both "from above" and "from below": on the one hand, the party sought to infuse "high culture" with democratic and socialist ideas. For instance, when the Dmitrii Shostakovich's 7th ("Leningrad") Symphony premiered in Austria at a concert by the Wiener Symphoniker at the Musikverein, headed by Josef Krips, on 28 October 1945, the event was organized by the KPÖ.⁴ In the following years, the party was able to exert influence on concert life in Vienna via the Gesellschaft zur Pflege der kulturellen und wirtschaftlichen Beziehungen zur Sowjetunion (Society for the Cultivation of Cultural and Economic Relations with the Soviet Union) – what would later become known as the Österreichisch-Sowjetische Gesellschaft (Austro-Soviet Society, ÖSG). The concerts organized by the ÖSG were an opportunity to give Austrian audiences their first taste of composers such as Dmitrii Shostakovich, Sergei Prokof'ev, and Aram Khachaturian. RAVAG's *Russische Stunde* revived the worker symphony concerts of the First Republic.

The main focus, however, was placed on "mass cultural work". On the initiative of the KPÖ and its closely related Free Austrian Youth (Freie Österreichische

---

2 Ernst Fischer: Das Ende einer Illusion. Erinnerungen 1945–1955, Vienna/Munich/Zurich 1973, 120.
3 Kommunistische Partei Österreichs (ed.): Sofortprogramm zur Wiederaufrichtung Österreichs, no place [Vienna], n.d. [1945], 1, 7.
4 Manfred Mugrauer: Schostakowitsch in Wien, in: Barbara Boisits, Cornelia Szabó-Knotik (eds.): Musicologica Austriaca 27 (2008). Freie Beiträge. Jahresschrift der Österreichischen Gesellschaft für Musikwissenschaft, Vienna 2009, 211–275, here: 238.

Fig. 1: The Austrian premiere of Dmitrii Shostakovich's 7th ("Leningrad") Symphony took place at Vienna's Musikverein on 28 October 1945, during a concert by the Vienna Symphonic, conducted by Josef Krips. The concert was organized by the KPÖ city management. (Vienna City Library, P-5379)

Jugend, FÖJ), dozens of amateur dramatic groups, choirs, and dance and instrumental ensembles emerged after 1945,[5] holding annual national gatherings from 1947 onwards. In 1951, they came together in the Verband der Volkskunstgruppen (Association of Folk Art Groups). In 1954, the association comprised around 120 singing groups and choirs, dance, theatre, and cabaret groups, and orchestras playing especially in Vienna and Lower Austria in the Soviet-administered factories. Some 2,300 amateur artists participated in these groups.[6] In a sense, the KPÖ thus took up the legacy of the workers' movement of the First Republic, which the Social Democrats abandoned after 1945.

---

5 Evelyn Deutsch-Schreiner: Theater im "Wiederaufbau". Zur Kulturpolitik im österreichischen Parteien- und Verbändestaat, Vienna 2001, 127–140.
6 Zentrales Parteiarchiv (ZPA) der KPÖ, Material zum XVI. Parteitag Mai 1954, vorgelegt vom Zentralkomitee der KPÖ, 75.

The Neues Theater in der Scala

Fig. 2: The Neues Theater in der Scala, founded by members of the KPÖ, at Favoritenstrasse 8 in Vienna's 4th District (Wieden), 1948–1956 (KPÖ Picture Archive)

Overall, the KPÖ sought to reinforce the beginnings of what Lenin had termed a "second culture" offering an emancipatory counterweight to the dominant capitalist culture. The most striking expression of such a "second culture" was the Neues Theater in der Scala, founded by Communist remigrants in 1948. The Soviet occupation authorities made the building available to the KPÖ "for the organization of an Austrian people's theatre".[7] With the Scala, the Communist leadership collective possessed its own venue of undisputed historical theatrical

---
7 Wiener Stadt- und Landesarchiv, 1.3.2.350.A12.5, High Commissioner Vladimir Kurasov to Günther Haenel, Karl Paryla, Wolfgang Heinz, Emil Stöhr, Franz Neubauer, Gustav Manker, 1 April 1948.

significance.[8] Since the theatre, with a staff of around eighty,[9] was beyond the KPÖ's budget, closure was often on the cards – as early as 1949, and finally in 1951. The programme could be maintained only with the financial support of the Soviet Union.[10]

Besides actors with permanent contracts like Wolfgang Heinz, Karl Paryla, Hortense Raky, and Otto Tausig, international greats of theatre such as Bertolt Brecht, Ernst Busch, Therese Giehse, and Helene Weigel also worked at the Scala. The house staged works of world literature, modern Americana and Soviet drama, and contemporary pieces by Austrian authors – a total of 89 works in eight years. The Scala was the only Austrian theatre to break the Brecht boycott during the Cold War. The Theaterfreunde (Friends of the Theatre) was formed as an audience body with the aim of making visiting the theatre affordable for broad sections of the population via cheap subscription rates.

Party Press and Publishing House Policy

A relevant factor behind public opinion during the decade of occupation was the KPÖ's party press.[11] The cultural journal *(Österreichisches) Tagebuch*, founded by the KPÖ in 1946, was a discussion forum for progressive intellectuals beyond the party itself and became the "main organ of cultural-political understanding" in the immediate post-war era.[12] In later years too, *Tagebuch* remained an important voice in a cultural life that was increasingly shaped by forces of conservatism and restoration. Besides the central publication *Österreichische Volksstimme* (Austrian Voice of the People), the federal provinces each had their own Communist Party newspapers. In the years up to 1955 (and beyond), several other newspapers

---

8 Wilhelm Pellert: Roter Vorhang. Rotes Tuch. Das Neue Theater in der Scala (1948–1956) (In Sachen 8), Vienna 1979; Carmen-Renate Köper: Ein unheiliges Experiment. Das Neue Theater in der Scala (1948–1956), Vienna 1995.
9 ZPA der KPÖ, Bericht der Betriebsorganisation "Neues Theater in der Scala" an den 15. Parteitag der KPÖ, 23 August 1951.
10 Cf. Peter Ruggenthaler: Warum Österreich nicht sowjetisiert wurde. Sowjetische Österreich-Politik 1945–1953/55, in: Stefan Karner, Barbara Stelzl-Marx (eds.): Die Rote Armee in Österreich. Sowjetische Besatzung 1945–1955. Beiträge (Veröffentlichungen des Ludwig Boltzmann-Instituts für Kriegsfolgen-Forschung, Special Edition 4), Graz/Vienna/Munich 2005, 650–726, here: 713.
11 For an overview, cf. Georg Friesenbichler: Sprachrohr der Partei – oder wessen? Betrachtungen zur linken Medienlandschaft nach 1945, in: idem., Hubert Friesenbichler: Die drei Leben des Hubert F. Vom jungen Nazi-Gegner zum linken Journalisten. Mit einem Anhang zur Parteipublizistik nach 1945, Vienna 2014, 111–154.
12 Sebastian Meissl: Der "Fall Nadler" 1945–1950, in: idem., Klaus-Dieter Mulley, Oliver Rathkolb (eds.): Verdrängte Schuld, verfehlte Sühne. Entnazifizierung in Österreich 1945–1955, Vienna 1986, 281–301, here: 290.

and journals were published for various target audiences (women, adolescents, smallholders, etc.), such as the tabloid *Der Abend* (The Evening) edited by Bruno Frei, the illustrated children's paper *Unsere Zeitung* (Our Newspaper), the *Stimme der Frau* (Woman's Voice), *Jugend voran* (Youth to the Fore), or *Landpost* (Country Post) and *Der kleine Landwirt* (The Smallholder).

The press founded by the KPÖ, Globus-Verlag, was the only publishing house to extensively offer works by authors banned and forced into exile by the Nazis.[13] In 1945, Globus-Verlag published the exile works of Egon Erwin Kisch; it was the first time they had appeared in German. In 1946, the poet Theodor Kramer, who had fled to England, found in Globus an Austrian publisher. The year 1947 saw the publication of a first selection of the works by the Communist writer Jura Soyfer, who had died in Buchenwald concentration camp in 1939. Authors such as Karl Bruckner (*Die Spatzenelf* [The Sparrow Eleven]) and Mira Lobe (*Der Tiergarten reißt aus* [The Zoo Runs Away]) made their breakthroughs with books published by KPÖ presses. By the late 1940s, Globus-Verlag had published several novels examining Austria's National Socialist past. From 1948 onwards, Globus-Verlag could draw on its own community of readers, the Buchgemeinde (Book Community), which secured a guaranteed customer base.

The RAVAG *Russische Stunde*

The task of the RAVAG's *Russische Stunde* (Russian Hour) radio series, established in June 1945, was to provide information on the political, socioeconomic, and cultural situation in the Soviet Union. Particular emphasis was placed on Russian or Soviet literature and music. While the *Russische Stunde* was not a KPÖ mouthpiece, from 1947 onwards the programme was put together by Communist staff. Within RAVAG, the *Russische Stunde* was a protected area, a "programme within a programme" in which the KPÖ had control over hiring policy. In 1950, the programme was expanded and became the domain of Communist editors who had a party-line understanding of their work. Up to the hour's disbandment in 1955, round twenty-five members of the KPÖ were employed full time at three departments involved in making the programme: the political department, the literature department (the "Radio Play Department"), and the music department – and also played role in the show's administration. The series also provided both

---

13 Christina Köstner: Das Salz in der Suppe. Der Globus Verlag, in: Gerhard Renner, Wendelin Schmidt-Dengler, Christian Gastgeber (eds.), Buch- und Provenienzforschung. Festschrift für Murray G. Hall zum 60. Geburtstag, Vienna 2009, 129–144.

regular and ad-hoc work for dozens of freelancers and external writers with KPÖ connections or leanings.[14]

After Felix Kreissler took over from Franz Bönsch as head of the programme in 1950, the *Russische Stunde* became "politicized" along KPÖ lines. This was reflected not only in the political information broadcasts but also in the fields of literature and music: the literary programmes were no longer devoted solely to Soviet topics, but also examined the socialist countries or progressive world literature as a whole, including Austrian writers. The music broadcasts now comprised entertainment music in shorter programmes, symphonic concerts, (from 1951 onwards) works concerts staged in the halls of large factories belonging to the USIA, opera studio performances, and programmes with amateur orchestras and folk art groups close to the KPÖ (such as the choirs of the FÖJ, the Raxwerke rolling stock factories in Wiener Neustadt, and the Glanzstoff fabric factory in St. Pölten or the folk art group Kremser Volkskunstgruppe).

Between 1949 and 1952, the *Russische Stunde* broadcast several festival concerts organized by the conductor Gottfried Kassowitz and termed "workers' concerts". Along with works by Russian and Soviet composers, they included new compositions by Marcel Rubin, such as the *Österreichische Arbeiterkantate* (Austrian Workers' Cantata) entitled *Wenn wir nicht wollen, gibt's keinen Krieg* (If We're Not Willing, There's No War; libretto by Otto Horn) in 1951, as well as Austrian and international socialist workers' songs. Works by Hanns Eisler, such as a radio version of his cantata *Die Mutter* (*The Mother*), were first introduced to Austria in 1949 by the *Russische Stunde*, sometimes conducted by the composer himself.

Soviet Information Centres

On 16 September 1950, the Soviet Information Centre (Sowjetische Informationszentrum, SIZ) opened in the Porr-Haus in Karlsplatz[15] with the aim of becoming a "centre for education about Soviet culture, art, and science".[16] The SIZ housed a free lending library, a reading room with newspapers and mag-

---

14 Cf. Manfred Mugrauer: Die Personalpolitik der KPÖ in der Russischen Stunde der RAVAG, in: Anita Mayer-Hirzberger, Cornelia Szabó-Knotik (eds.): Zur Russischen Stunde der RAVAG (1945–55). Ein Kapitel österreichischer Radiogeschichte (Anklaenge. Wiener Jahrbuch für Musikwissenschaft 2022/2023), Vienna 2023, 47–76.
15 Wolfgang Mueller: "Leuchtturm des Sozialismus" oder "Zentrum der Freundschaft"? Das Sowjetische Informationszentrum im Wiener "Porr-Haus": ein Instrument der Besatzungspolitik zwischen Volksbildung und Propaganda, in: Wiener Geschichtsblätter 55 (2000) 4, 261–285.
16 Heute feierliche Eröffnung des neuen sowjetischen Informationszentrums, in: Österreichische Zeitung, 16 September 1950, 3.

azines, and theatre, lecture, exhibition, and cinema halls. In 1952/53, six more information centres followed in Vienna-Floridsdorf, Vienna-Stadlau, Wiener Neustadt, St. Pölten, Linz-Urfahr, and Eisenstadt. The information centres presented political speeches and popular science talks, exhibitions, film screenings, theatre and cabaret performances, and musical events. The programmes were devised in consultation with the agitprop department of the KPÖ's Vienna city administration.[17]

The information centres also provided work for artists with KPÖ connections. The SIZ in the Porr-Haus was run by Camillo Heger, who had joined the KPÖ in 1947 – after returning from a Soviet prisoner of war camp, where he had attended an Antifa school. (After 1955 he joined the ÖVP.) In 1951, twenty-eight out of the SIZ's staff of thirty-two (eighteen workers and ten employees) were members of the KPÖ.[18] The composer Joseph Laska, a member of the KPÖ until he left it in 1953, conducted a series of orchestral concerts with works by Russian and Soviet composers. The violinist Karl Brix headed a small orchestra formed at the SIZ in 1954. Besides Brix, Kurt Blaukopf and Charlotte Eisler also presented record concerts the venue.[19] A theatre ensemble performed not only at the SIZ, but also in USIA factors and workers' clubs. Klara Kiss served as a set designer. Hanna Berger ran a children's drama group. Kurt Sobotka founded the cabaret group *Das junge Ensemble* and staged Jura Soyfer's *Der Lechner Edi schaut ins Paradies* (Edi Lechner Looks into Paradise) in March 1951. The cabaret programmes were written by Helmut Pucher, known as Wesp (Wasp). The music for the programme *Scherz ist Trumpf* (Joking is Trumps, 1952) was penned by Karl Heinz Füssl. Wesp also ran the *Wiener Ironiker*, founded in 1954, which also performed at the SIZ until the latter closed down.

Wien-Film on the Rosenhügel

The film studios on the Rosenhügel hill were classified as German Property and operated under Soviet administration from 1946 onwards.[20] In 1948, the KPÖ leadership asked the occupation authorities if it could create a "democratic

---

17 ZPA der KPÖ, Beschluss des Büros der Wiener Stadtleitung über die Verbesserung der Zusammenarbeit zwischen Stadtleitung und Sowjetischem Informationszentrum, 18 June 1953, 1.
18 ZPA der KPÖ, Bericht der Betriebsorganisation SIZ an den 15. Parteitag der KPÖ, 19 August 1951.
19 Barbara Dissauer: "Kampf für die Wahrheit, Kampf für den Frieden." Die Sowjetischen Informationszentren in Wien von 1950 bis 1955 im Spiegel ihrer Programmplakate. Eine diskursanalytische Untersuchung, Diplomarbeit, University of Vienna 2007, appendix.
20 Oliver Rathkolb: Die "Wien-Film"-Produktion am Rosenhügel. Österreichische Filmproduktion und Kalter Krieg, in: Hans Heinz Fabris, Kurt Luger (eds.): Medienkultur in Ös-

company for film production" in which it could deploy "persons close to us politically" – directors, screenwriters, and actors – and to "bring out useful films and make a financial profit".[21] Ultimately, however, the company did not start making its own films until 1950 – for instance Bertolt Brecht's *Herr Puntila und sein Knecht Matti* or the musical film *Gasparone* (based on an opera by Carl Millöcker), with a score by Hanns Eisler and directed by Karl Paryla. From 1952 onwards, another member of the KPÖ, Ruth Mayenburg, served as chief dramaturg at Wien-Film. In 1951, sixty-seven of the staff of 292 were members of the KPÖ.[22] Universal-Film was responsible for distribution of the films produced on the Rosenhügel; the company had been founded in 1949 as a subsidiary of the Soviet distributor Sovexportfilm. Both companies were run by the KPÖ members Karl Röder, Franz Bönsch, and Günter Eulau.[23]

Cultural Work in the USIA Factories

The KPÖ received massive support in its cultural policy and propaganda work from cultural officers employed in USIA and SMV factories, who were gathered in a Central Cultural Division (Zentrales Kulturreferat) of factories under Soviet administration in 1948.[24] The cultural officers were paid by the administration of the Soviet factories, but they were selected by the KPÖ. Their task was to publish works newspapers, stage talks, and organize cultural and sporting activities. At the individual Soviet factories, workers' clubs, sports facilities (especially football pitches and volleyball courts) and libraries were created; some of them also received cinemas and kindergartens.[25] Works orchestras, choirs, and theatre groups also became active. In February 1952, the Central Cultural Division was

---

terreich. Film, Fotografie, Fernsehen und Video in der Zweiten Republik (Kulturstudien. Bibliothek der Kulturgeschichte, Vol. 11), Vienna/Cologne/Graz 1988, 117–132, here: 124.
21 Bericht der Propagandaverwaltung des ZK der VKP(B) an den Sekretär des ZK der VKP(B) M. A. Suslow über das Filmstudio "Wienfilm", 15 April 1948, doc. no. 49, in: Wolfgang Mueller, Arnold Suppan, Norman M. Naimark, et al. (eds.): Sowjetische Politik in Österreich 1945–1955. Dokumente aus russischen Archiven (Fontes Rerum Austriacarum. Österreichische Geschichtsquellen, 2. Abteilung: Diplomataria et Acta, Vol. 93), Vienna 2005, 465–467, here: 467.
22 ZPA der KPÖ, Bericht der Betriebsorganisation Wien-Film an den 15. Parteitag der KPÖ, 20 August 1951.
23 Wolfgang Mueller: Sowjetische Filmpropaganda in Österreich 1945–1955, in: Karin Moser (ed.): Besetzte Bilder. Film, Kultur und Propaganda in Österreich 1945–1955, Vienna 2005, 86–118, here: 98.
24 Zum Geleit!, in: Mitteilungsblatt des Zentralen Kulturreferates der USIA, 1 (1948) 1, 1–2.
25 Soziale und kulturelle Leistungen der USIA- und SMV-Betriebe, in: Der Funktionär 5 (1955) 7, 126–127.

run directly by the Party's Central Committee. At this point, the division employed a staff of 238.[26]

Cultural Cold War

While the years 1945 to 1947 were characterized by a basic anti-fascist stance, a decidedly militant anti-communism developed in cultural life. The "cultural-political fronts" were now determined "along the ideological demarcation line".[27] Theatre, film, radio, and literature became theatres of the Cold War and sites of the oppression and ostracizing of communist artists – for instance, the actors at the Scala, the RAVAG *Russischen Stunde* team, or artists working for Wien-Film. The Scala was denigrated as a "propaganda instrument in cultural camouflage",[28] and its programme was never mentioned. The *Russische Stunde* was considered Communist radio propaganda and was confronted with calls for listeners to boycott it from the government parties. Distribution companies boycotted the productions of Wien-Film. In the 1950s, the US broadcasting group Rot-Weiss-Rot (Red, White, and Red) had a "blacklist" of names of artists active in the above areas, which resulted in their being banned from working for Rot-Weiss-Rot. Such blacklists "existed de facto in the entire cultural scene".[29]

After the conclusion of the State Treaty, the Soviet Information Centres were closed, and the *Russische Stunde* was cancelled. The return of former German Property to the Austrian state meant the end of the Central Cultural Division of the Soviet-administered factories. For the Communist staff at these institutions, this amounted to their dismissal. In 1956, the Scala also had to close due to do a lack of state subsidies. For actors such as Karl Paryla and Hortense Raky, it was then difficult to find work in Austria, and hence they left for the GDR, where they had opportunities in theatre and film.

---

26 Cf. ZPA der KPÖ, Protokoll der Sitzung des Sekretariats des ZK der KPÖ am 18.12.1951, 2; Josef Stückler an das Zentralkomitee der KPÖ, Betr.: Reorganisierung des Zentralen Kulturreferats, 2 January 1952, 1.
27 Oliver Rathkolb: Die paradoxe Republik. Österreich 1945 bis 2015, Vienna 2015, 320.
28 j.h.: Die Scala, in: Arbeiter-Zeitung, 25 February 1956, 1–2, here 1.
29 Rathkolb: "Wien-Film"-Produktion, 127.

Oliver Rathkolb

US Occupying Cultural Policy between Denazification, Cold War, and Democratic Reorientation

As in other political areas of political post-war planning by the Department of State, the Office of War Information, and the military planning staffs, the authors of the directives for the cultural sphere assumed that National Socialism had afflicted German and Austrian society like a disease and had perverted it for ideological ends.[1]

In order to overcome National Socialism after the war, in line with this social-psychological approach the traditional military-authoritarian elites were to be replaced by democratic ones.[1] In addition to extensive "denazification", two other measures – "demilitarization" and "deindustrialization" – would guarantee that military aggression could never again emanate from Germany and Austria.

At the same time, parliamentary democracy was to be rebuilt over a longer phase of military control and re-education. Since the entire cultural and media sphere had been a key ideological instrument during the totalitarian rule of National Socialism, here too the replacement of the elites and reorientation in content were to support the development of democracy.

The culture that was to be renewed was defined along traditional lines, mainly with an eye on high culture and modern instruments of entertainment and mass influence such as radio, film, spoken and musical theatre, literature and publishing houses, and all forms of print media and news agencies.

Hence the first measure after the defeat of the National Socialist regime was the implementation of Decree No. 10 and Information Control Regulation No. 1, according to which all newspapers, radio stations, cinemas, publishing houses, and printers in the US Zone in western Austria were to be shut down immediately. Their owners or managing directors, like those at the venues for theatre, opera, cabaret, and even puppet plays, had to undergo checks by the US military au-

---

[1] See the recent general survey by Mikkel Dack: Everyday Denazification in Postwar Germany: The Fragebogen and Political Screening during the Allied Occupation, Cambridge 2023.

thorities before they could reopen for business.² After precise political vetting, a permit could be granted to suitable – that is, democratically-minded – cultural managers and media personnel without a National Socialist past; such a licence was mandatory for anyone wishing to work in this field.

Even newspapers and a radio station belonging to resistance groups in western Austria had to close. It would be almost a month before newspapers published by US propaganda units could be published in Salzburg in collaboration with Austrian journalists, for instance *Österreichischer Kurier*, followed by *Salzburger Nachrichten* or, in the Upper Austrian zone, *Oberösterreichische Nachrichten*.³

A serious lack of journalistic independence and professionalism was clearly evident after decades of dictatorial and totalitarian suppression of independent media and cultural work, which had begun in Austria in 1933 with the chancellor dictatorship under Engelbert Dollfuss and had intensified appreciably under National Socialism. Moreover, Austrian journalists proved more willing to adapt and more servile than their Italian colleagues, for instance, with whom the units of the Psychological Warfare Branch (PWB) stationed in western Austria had gained experience after the liberation of Italy.⁴

Although Austrian publishers had had to wait until 1 October 1945 to be granted newspaper licences, the originally strict directives preventing permits being given to formerly active representatives of the Dollfuss–Schuschnigg regime could not be enforced. Hence Gustaf Adolf Canaval, formerly press secretary of the paramilitary Heimwehren in Lower Austria and editor-in-chief of the organization's weekly paper *Sturm über Osterreich* (Storm over Austria),

---

2 For more detailed information on the practice of the initial US propaganda measures, cf. Alfred Hiller: Amerikanische Medien- und Schulpolitik in Österreich 1945–1950, doctoral thesis, University of Vienna 1974; Gabriele Hindinger: Das Kriegsende und der Wiederaufbau demokratischer Verhältnisse in Oberösterreich im Jahre 1945 (Publikationen der Österreichischen Gesellschaft für Zeitgeschichte 4), Vienna 1968, 125 ff.; Oliver Rathkolb (ed.): Gesellschaft und Politik am Beginn der Zweiten Republik. Vertrauliche Berichte der US-Militäradministration aus Österreich 1945, Vienna 1985; and Michael Schönberg: Amerikanische Informations- und Medienpolitik in Österreich 1945–1950, Hauptband und Dokumentation I, doctoral thesis, University of Vienna 1975. For a recent extensive study of the aims and implementation of denazification and re-education strategy, cf. Christian Stifter: Zwischen geistiger Erneuerung und Restauration. US-amerikanische Planungen zur Entnazifizierung und demokratischen Neuorientierung österreichischer Wissenschaft, Vienna 2014.

3 On the history of print media, cf. Andy Kaltenbrunner: Geschichte der Tagespresse und Magazine nach 1945, in: Matthias Karmasin, Christian Oggolder (eds.): Österreichische Mediengeschichte, Vol. 2, Wiesbaden 2019, 175–197; Wolfgang Mueller: Informationsmedien in der "Besatzungszeit", in: Karmasin, Oggolder, Mediengeschichte 2, 75–98; and Marion Krammer, Margarethe Szeless: Berufsfeld Pressefotografie, in: Karmasin, Oggolder, Mediengeschichte 2, 99–123.

4 James M. Minifie: "At an Alarming Rate", in: The Saturday Review of Literature, 19 October 1946, 10 f.; moreover, the press officers had been "inundated" with 600 applications for a licence in Rome alone.

received a licence to edit *Salzburger Nachrichten*, then the newspaper with the largest circulation in western Austria. Despite internal US opposition, his time as a prisoner at Dachau and Flossenbürg concentration camps from 1938 to 1945 "offset" his record, and after a few weeks' delay he received a permit.[5]

In Vienna, on the other hand, the US forces retained direct control of their German-language newspaper and its largely Austrian editorial board until 1954. *Wiener Kurier*, first published on 27 August 1945 and in 1946/47 the most widespread daily in Austria, with a circulation of 300,000 copies, was distributed even to the neighbouring countries. The "western" radio stations belonging to the radio group Rot-Weiss-Rot in Salzburg and Linz (from 6 June 1945) and Vienna (from 17 November 1945) also remained under US control and administration with Austrian staff.[6]

The originally stringent denazification of artists who as party members or sympathizers had produced propaganda for the National Socialist regime and had hence been banned from working and performing would soon soften, however. Since the mechanism for automatically banning former members of the NSDAP did not work and also ran contrary to the Anglo-American sense of justice, from the autumn/winter of 1945 decisions were left to Austrian commissions. However, these decisions had to be ratified by the US Information Services Branch (ISB), the US military authority in charge of cultural and media affairs. Evidently, the ISB soon handed this unpleasant task to Austrian authorities, especially in Salzburg, but it had not reckoned with the new (old) Austrian decision makers keen to hand out "Persilscheine" (certificates of exculpation) and more interested in a quick cultural revival than in dealing with the past. In the Soviet Zone and in Vienna too, artists' celebrity and usefulness were more important than denazification and potential involvement in National Socialism.[7]

It was not until the Allied Commission in Vienna began to concern itself with such questions from September 1945 that the US authorities returned to a more restrictive approach in early 1946 – a phenomenon that did not correspond to the general practice of denazification by the US authorities in Austria in 1945/46.[8]

---

5 Rathkolb 1981, 77 ff.; cf. also Fritz Hausjell: "Die gescheiterte Alternative. Sozialisierung der Betriebsgewinne der Salzburger Nachrichten (1945–1960)", in: medien & zeit 2 (1987), 17 ff.
6 On radio, cf. Wolfgang Pensold: Auf rot-weiß-roter Welle, in: Matthias Karmasin, Christian Oggolder (eds.), Österreichische Mediengeschichte, Vol. 2, Wiesbaden 2019, 151–173.
7 On "cultural denazification", cf. Rathkolb 1981, 351 f., and Oliver Rathkolb: "… für die Kunst gelebt", in: Anton Pelinka, Erika Weinzierl (eds.): Das große Tabu. Österreichs Umgang mit seiner Vergangenheit, Vienna 1987, 60 ff.
8 Cf. Oliver Rathkolb: "US-Entnazifizierung in Österreich zwischen kontrollierter Revolution und Elitenrestauration", in: zeitgeschichte 9/10 (1984), 302 ff.

After the elections in November 1945 and the poor performance by the KPÖ, the originally uninterested Soviet denazification policy also changed, however.[9]

Besides this democratization through denazification, the aim was also to propagate a positive image of America in order to dismantle National Socialist propaganda's stereotype of the uneducated, "cultureless" American, although it was overlooked that this form of anti-Americanism was rooted more deeply in the decades before 1938.

The instruments chosen for exerting this positive influence on Austrians were preferably nonfiction, idealizing books, films, and pieces of music from the USA. Such a programme was implemented only partially, if at all – mainly in the US Information Center's lending libraries, which would later become known as Amerika-Häuser (Houses of America). On the radio, these "pure" US programmes had to be dropped due to a lack of listeners; it was not until the cultural Americanization of youth in the early fifties that US music and clothing took hold.[9] Via "Coca-Colonisation" (Reinhold Wagnleitner) – that is, a modern style of leisure and entertainment shaped by the USA – the entertainment and consumerism industry had ultimately changed the image of the USA in Austria much more profoundly than the ISB assumed possible in the early years of occupation.

Ultimately, a main focus of the Allied media and propaganda would soon be the Cold War, the ideological conflict with the Soviet Union and communism in general. It is often overlooked, however, that US High Commissioner General Mark W. Clark himself remained committed to "brotherhood in arms" with the Soviet officers until early 1946, taking note of reports of requisitioning, rapes, and so forth but not attaching any political significance to them, as is evident from his private correspondence.[10] It was not until February 1946 that the high commissioner began to show the first signs of conflict.

From April/May 1946, open East–West propaganda became evident on the level of the ISB too. On the one hand, this reversal of propaganda instruments was only gradual, although the ISB headquarters had already developed a general coordination department in 1947 in order to ensure "optimal" anti-communist press and radio propaganda, including the use of information obtained by the secret services, and to steer this propaganda in such a way as to avoid overreaction and maintain the illusion of objectivity.[11]

---

9 Reinhold Wagnleitner: Coca-Colonisation und Kalter Krieg, Vienna 1991; for a general survey, cf. also Gerhard Jagschitz, Klaus-Dieter Mulley (eds.): Die "wilden" fünfziger Jahre. Gesellschaft, Formen und Gefühle eines Jahrzehnts in Osterreich, St. Pölten 1985.
10 Office of the Presidential Libraries (National Archives), Washington, D. C., Microfilm No. 5, General Mark W. Clark Papers, Citadel Military College (South Carolina).
11 Oliver Rathkolb: "US-Medienpolitik in Österreich 1945–1950. Von antifaschistischer 'Reorientierung' zur ideologischen Westintegration", in: Medienjournal 3(1984), 4ff.

At the same time, the ISB also supported a project of the news agencies Associated Press (AP, based in New York) and Reuters (London), enabling the returning émigré Alfred Geiringer, the European editor at Reuters, to found the independent news agency APA (Austrian Press Agency) on 1 September 1946[12] with the aim of promoting independent journalist work.

As in the USA, cultural anti-communism became increasingly virulent: actors who had appeared in the RAVAG's *Russische Stunde* (Russian Hour), devised by Austrian Communists, were forbidden from working for the Rot-Weiss-Rot station; introduced in 1950, this policy even led to a "blacklist" and bans in the period from 1953 to 1955.[13] Only particularly renowned performers such as Karl Farkas or Fritz Muliar had their bans lifted.

In the theatre, the cultural ice age, an emphasis on intolerance, and ideological militarization impacted not only on the Communists' Neues Theater in der Scala but also on the American pieces that would be imported to Austria.[14] In the first years after the war, the central US authorities responsible for the occupied territories in Europe and Japan refused to send to Austria plays that were "too critical" or anti-military. For example, Ferdinand Bruckner's drama *Die Befreiten* (The Liberated) was classified as too negative in 1948.[15] Obviously anti-American propaganda plays such as *Die Russische Frage* (The Russian Question) were banned at the Volkstheater in the American Zone.[16]

Austrian culture managers long played a role in this Cold War, as demonstrated by Friedrich Torberg's and Hans Weigl's attacks on performances of works by Bertolt Brecht and Communist artists.[17] Ultimately, however, Torberg and Weigl represented the mainstream culture industry. A good example of how cultural anti-communism was understood by the American immigration authorities in the USA is the case of the director Josef Krips, who had not been allowed to direct plays under National Socialism, having been banned from working as "half-Jew", but was the only director in the country without political baggage after 1945. Upon entering the USA in July 1950, he was interned on Ellis Island in New York, since his name was on one of the many blacklists of artists

---

12 https://apa.at/about/alfred-geiringer-stipendium/; https://medienundzeit.at/alfred-geiringer-a-portrait-written-by-michael-nelson/; and https://www.upi.com/Archives/1996/01/10/Austrian-born-reporter-Geiringer-dies/1153821250000/ (1 June 2024).
13 Archiv des Instituts für Zeitgeschichte, University of Vienna, Akte Vinzenz Ludwig Ostry.
14 Carmen-Renate Köper: Ein unheiliges Experiment – Das neue Theater in der Scala (1948–1956), Vienna 1995.
15 National Archives, Record Group (=NA, RG), 260 Austria, Box 72, Folder: ISB Telecon 1, DA 70 NY und ISB-41. RE DA-10 NY.
16 NA, RG 260 Austria, Box 892, Folder: Music-Theater Reports 1945–47, Lothar an Chief ISB – Monthly Report, 31 October 1947, 2. Cf. also Tagblatt am Montag, 10 and 17 November 1947, 7.
17 Kurt Palm, K. Palm: Vom Boykott zur Anerkennung. Brecht und Österreich, Vienna 1983.

who sympathized with the Communist Party.[18] His concert tour to the USSR commissioned by the Austrian federal government and various concerts for the Soviet occupation authorities in Austria had seen him branded a Communist when in fact he had never been one.

If we examine the US propaganda machinery in Austria after 1950, when it operated as a civil authority under the Department of State within the framework of the US Embassy, it is evident that the methods and instruments had changed. The ideological but also cultural integration into the West had already progressed to the point that Austrian institutions and the US media's Austrian staff made the largest contribution to anti-communism.

The Americans made efforts to push through an Exchange of Persons Program that sent future or established opinion leaders to the USA as VIPs so that they could meet the most comparable US equivalents in their fields and become acquainted with new ways of training and working: journalists, politicians, doctors, scientists, technicians, teachers, and representatives of several other vocations thereby formed a thoroughly positive picture of America.[19]

Due to its intentionally entertaining programming, from popular quiz shows with prizes to the youthful and sophisticated cabaret of a Helmut Qualtinger, the broadcaster Rot-Weiss-Rot had gained a young and also objective image while the RAVAG was considered the "outdated" and "boarding" station. Before becoming very successful later, the writer Ingeborg Bachmann also spent two years working for the Rot-Weiss-Rot script department, which also included a number of directors who would go on to have great success working for the Austrian state broadcaster ORF, such as Walter Davy but also the later ÖVP politician Jörg Mauthe and the culture manager Peter Weiser.

Along with the political-ideological concepts, economic factors also played a large role, as demonstrated by the film industry in particular. While private American film companies had sought to circumnavigate military restrictions since late 1945, the occupiers did not always look favourably on such private capitalist plans.[20] Although censorship had been abolished in 1946, new problems arose in the cause of the Cold War, and it was only after long negotiations that an agreement could be reached with the Soviet authorities concerning quotas for film screenings.[21] A weekly newsreel, *Welt im Film* (World in Film), produced in conjunction with the British in Munich, was disbanded in 1949.[73]

The *Wiener Kurier*, on the other hand, had developed into one of the largest Central European daily newspapers during the early post-war years and did not

---

18 New York Times, 18 February 1951, II 3.
19 NA, RG 260 Austria, Box 101, Exchange of Persons Program.
20 NA, RG 260 Austria, Box 65, Folder 14, Operations Coordinator to Chief of Branch, ISB: Various Matters Discussed with Wolfgang Wolf (MPEA), 17 July 1947.
21 Rathkolb 1981, 192f.

Fig. 1: The Max Reinhardt memorial programme by the Rot-Weiss-Rot broadcasting group: the radio performance of Johann Wolfgang Goethe's *Faust* under discussion at the recording studio in Salzburg. From left to right: Maria Mayer, Felix Steinböck, Inge Konradi, director of programming Geza Rech, Alma Seidler, director of programming Ernst Haeusserman, Raoul Aslan, Ewald Balser, Helene Thimig, Adrienne Gessner, 1947 (ANL/Vienna, US 23.316)

have to pay tax on its profits; until late 1950, it could use them to support other propaganda institutions.[22] While the broadcasting group Rot-Weiss-Rot was closed in 1955, the central offices in Washington DC had decided the previous year to sell at least the name of *Kurier*. The mill owner Ludwig Polsterer, with the financial backing of ÖVP circles, took over the newspaper's name and fifty per cent of its shares, continuing the former US paper as the *Neuer Kurier* from 18 October 1954. As in the case of film, the liaison in the background was the former US cultural officer and remigrant Ernst Haeusserman. Hans Dichand, who had previously applied to take part in an exchange programme, became editor-in-chief and brought on board Hugo Portisch, who had been a member of the first group of journalists to visit the USA, as his deputy and later successor (1958–1967).

---

22 Ibid., 215: Up to 28 February 1947, *Wiener Kurier* made a profit of 10.4 million schillings. From late 1948/early 1949 it operated at a loss, not least due to the currency reform.

The extent of the US cultural and propaganda activities is well illustrated by the ISB's proposed budget for 1950: some 1,295.481 US dollars in addition to constantly sinking "tax-free" profits that amounted to 7,085,610.12 Austrian schillings between July and September 1949.[23] A list of personnel from 1947[24] comprised 63 Americans compared to 707 Austrian employees or staff from groups of displaced persons.

Moreover, the ISB developed for its activities operations diaries tailored to very specific target groups, the most important of which were identified as leading personalities from the middle class: the aim was to reach opinion leaders from the field of education, the press, the economy, and scholarship, but also lawyers and artists. An important role was also assigned to trade union functionaries. Only secondary importance was attached to youth groups, "the solidly rightist rural population", and "small-town, non-intellectual middle-class elements [...] most susceptible to extreme rightist propaganda".[25]

While in 1945 and early 1946 anti-fascist reorientation and extensive democratization were at the forefront of US cultural policy as part of an intentionally rules-based policy combating National Socialism and fascism, a new approach was launched in April 1946 and would prove far more influential on the socio-political level: "reorientation", the cultural integration of Austria into the West. This US propaganda offensive should not be seen as an isolated political activity; rather, it consciously supplemented the country's political and economic Western integration – the latter via the targeted deployment of the Marshall Plan as part of economic reconstruction.

If one wishes to answer the question whether US culturally policy was "successful" in the broadest sense, it certainly was with respect to an ideological Western orientation, and this can be explained by the nuanced and deliberate adaptation to societal circumstances and traditions in Austria, the post-war generation's support for "modern" developments, and the influence of anti-communist attitudes from the pre-1945 era.

Important cultural-political gatekeepers and networkers in spoken and musical theatre in the 1950s and beyond, such as Ernst Haeusserman and Marcel Prawy, began their careers as remigrants working for the culture and film department of the Information Services Branch, Prawy succeeding in establishing the US musical in Vienna. Others, like Haeusserman's father-in-law and boss as theatre and music officer Ernst Lothar, were unable to continue their successful

---

23 NA, RG 260 Austria, Box 889, Folder 33, Estimated Cost, 12 June 1950, 4. NA, RG 260 Austria, Box 862, Folder 92, USFA-ISB, Statement, 3.
24 NA, RG 260 Austria, Box 886, Folder 71, The ISB fields of Interest, 3 March 1947, 1.
25 NA, RG 260 Austria, Box 889, Folder 43, USIE Country Paper, 2 May 1950, 2.

pre-1938 careers after 1945, since they refused to draw a line under the National Socialist past and its post-war continuities.[26]

Fig. 2: "Aus Amerikas Operetten – Streifzug durch die Welt des Musicals" ("From America's Operettas: A Foray through the World of Musicals") by Marcel Prawy, 1955 (ANL/Vienna, US 12.733/29)

---

26 https://literaturgefluester.wordpress.com/2018/02/26/die-zweite-ernst-lothar-neuerscheinung/ (1 June 2024).

Richard Hufschmied

British Cultural Policy in Vienna, 1945–1955. Intentions, Actions, and a Jewish Underground Struggle

After the war, British cultural policy[1] in Austria and its federal capital concentrated on two levels. The first served the self-promotion and projection of Britain. The aim was to ensure that the third Great Power, whose position had already been losing strength and influence before the Second World War, remained a strong player on the international stage.[2] In the European sphere, on the other hand, Britain determined the course of political confrontations in Europe after the war ended in 1945.[3] The second level of British cultural, information, and propaganda policy focused on the "re-education" and "re-orientation" of the Austrian population towards a Western-type democracy. In

---

1 On British cultural policy in Vienna and Austria and on the foundation, intentions, and actions of the British Council in Vienna, cf. inter alia Gerda Treiber: Großbritanniens Informationspolitik gegenüber Österreich 1945 bis 1955: Publicity und Propaganda sowie deren Instrumente in Printmedien und Rundfunk, dargestellt anhand britischer Dokumente, doctoral thesis, University of Vienna 1997; Johannes Feichtinger: Die Kulturpolitik der Besatzungsmacht Großbritannien in Österreich, in: Alfred Ableitinger, Siegfried Beer, Eduard G. Staudinger (eds.): Österreich unter alliierter Besatzung 1945–1955, Vienna/Cologne/Graz 1998, 495–529; Isabella Lehner: Anglo-Austria Cultural Relations between 1944 and 1955. Influences, Cooperation and Conflicts, Diplomarbeit, University of Vienna 2011; Rolf M. Urrisk-Obertyński (ed.): Wien. 2000 Jahre, Vol. 6: Die vier Alliierten 1945–1955, Gnas 2015; Monika Platzer: Kalter Krieg und Architektur. Beiträge zur Demokratisierung Österreichs nach 1945, Vienna/Zurich 2019.
2 This kind of cultural policy can also be seen as a substitute for power or as a compensatory policy for a loss of power. This concept and way of thinking goes back to Lothar Kettenacker. Cf. idem, Die anglo-amerikanischen Planungen für die Kontrolle Deutschlands, in: Josef Foschepoth (ed.): Kalter Krieg und deutsche Frage. Deutschland im Widerstreit der Mächte 1945–1952, Göttingen 1985, 66–87, cit. Feichtinger: Kulturpolitik der Besatzungsmacht Großbritannien, 499. Peter Pirker sees in the British secret service contact with exiled Austrian socialists in London during the war the idea of establishing a left-wing counterweight to the Communists in Austria. Cf. Peter Pirker: Subversion deutscher Herrschaft. Der britische Geheimdienst SOE und Österreich, Göttingen 2012, 33, cit. Platzer: Kalter Krieg und Architektur, 47.
3 Platzer: Kalter Krieg und Architektur, 43.

1947, a third level was introduced with the establishment of a long-term aim to support a Western-looking Austrian foreign policy.[4]

As a reaction to the country's declining power, the British Council had been formed in 1934 as an institution geared towards Britain's self-presentation in coordination with foreign policy. The Austrian branch was set up in Vienna in November 1945. It was not part of the Allied Commission for Austria (British Element), but was rather intentionally tied to the Political Advisor's Office, which had special status within the British administration in Austria, in order to maintain the impression of independence. This was also manifested in its location: the British headquarters had been set up in Schönbrunn Palace, while the British Council used an apartment with twelve rooms at Freyung 1 and the military staff worked at Hotel Sacher.

The British defined and prioritized their Vienna outpost thus: "The three most urgent requirements in Austria are: 1. Books, 2. Music and 3. The establishment of some kind of reading room which might eventually be developed into a British Institute as finance allowed."[5]

In February 1946, Richard Hiscocks[6] became the director of the British Council in Vienna. Expressing his office's aim for 1946 and 1947, he stated, "In a country which was under control for seven years and during that time was cut off from literary and cultural contact with the outside world, top priority in Council work must be given to re-education in the broadest sense."[7]

The British Council's first major cultural mission in Vienna realized one of Hiscocks's goals: the exhibition "Books from England", held in the Council's reading room at Kärntnerstrasse 53 from 15 to 30 March 1946. The exhibition catalogue relates how three cargo flights had taken the books from London to Vienna: "As everyday an event as it looks, these planes had very exciting cargo on board: they were on their way to your capital Vienna with these selected books – with these messengers from Britain, where the freedom of the written word had never been in question; they have now arrived in Austria, which can now enjoy this freedom for the first time in eight years."[8]

---

4 Feichtinger: Kulturpolitik der Besatzungsmacht Großbritannien, 499–501.
5 Cit. Feichtinger: Kulturpolitik der Besatzungsmacht Großbritannien, 508.
6 Hiscocks was a historian and director of the British Council in Vienna from February 1946 to October 1949. In 1954, he published a history of Austria in the first post-war years which contains plenty of information on the British aims: Richard Hiscocks: Österreichs Wiedergeburt, Vienna 1954.
7 Cit. Feichtinger: Kulturpolitik der Besatzungsmacht Großbritannien, 509.
8 Bücher aus England. Eine Ausstellung vom 15.–30. März 1946 in Wien I., Kärntnerstrasse 53, unter der Schirmherrschaft des British Council, Vienna 1946, 2.

Fig. 1: Placard for the exhibition "Bücher aus England" (Books from England), 1946 (Vienna City Library, P-11070)

The catalogue listed these hundreds of books in twenty categories[9] over forty-six pages, and they could be purchased in Vienna bookshops after the presentation was over. Their total value amounted to 500 pounds, and they were made available by the British Council in London.[10]

But it was not just about books. The British Council's cultural work used different media to convey Britain's self-presentation,[11] such as concert tours, exhibitions of British paintings, series of talks on various topics, and performances by famous English theatre and ballet troupes and classical musicians.[12]

The first visual arts exhibition took place at the Academy of Fine Arts from 7 September to 2 October 1946, showing 100 paintings from the Tate Gallery.

---

9 In order to show the weighting of each category, the numbers in parentheses indicate the number of pages in the catalogue: autobiographies (3), biographies (4), essays (5), history (7), children's books (9), books on war (15), textbooks (15), medicine (21), novels (26), philosophy (26), poetry (27), politics (29), travel (30), religion (31), novels (31), plays (36), sociology (37), technology (39), miscellaneous subjects (44), economy (48).
10 Bücher aus England. Eine Ausstellung 1946, 2–48.
11 It is beyond the scope of this discussion to mention more than a few examples of such activities.
12 Feichtinger, Kulturpolitik der Besatzungsmacht Großbritannien, 504.

Along with these paintings, all of them modern for the time, works by the sculptor Henry Moore were on display. Some of his works as a war painter in the Second World War were exhibited – specifically, a row of people in air raid shelters in England. One of these bleak and seemingly hopeless depictions, *A Tilbury Shelter Scene*, was also reproduced in the catalogue.[13] The intention was the confront visitors with the Luftwaffe's bombing raids on England, especially from September 1940 to May 1941, and the suffering of the civilian population.[14] Another art exhibition was held at the Academy of Fine Arts from 22 November to 30 December 1951, presenting watercolours by the English Romantic painter William Turner.[15]

Mention must also be made here of the large architecture exhibition "London – Bild einer Weltstadt" (London – Portrait of a Global City) at the Wiener Messepalast from 12 June to 5 July 1947. Covering some 800 square metres, it was organized by the Österreichischen Institut für Bildstatistik (Austrian Institute for Visual Statistics).[16] Another architecture exhibition, entitled "England im Aufbau" ("Replanning Britain"), was held from 11 October to 15 November 1947.[17]

British self-presentation was also furthered by music and theatre, such as tours by the oboist Leon Goosen, the Sadler's Wells Ballet Company, and the Arts Theatre Company. The Viennese showed great interest in the performances of modern ballet by the Sadlers' Wells Company at the Volksoper. All ten days of the run were sold out.[18]

In the June of 1946, it was not the British Council but the British occupation authorities that presented the population of Vienna with a festival: "after years of severe psychological strain, the first big festival on Viennese soil – a festival the like of which Vienna had yet to experience".[19] The "Vienna Searchlight Tattoo" was performed in the evenings from 24 to 29 June every year, with the proceeds

---

13 Cf. the exhibition catalogue Tate Gallery, Schau in der Akademie der bildenden Künste Wien im Jahr 1946, London, n.d.
14 The British referred to this German military operation as the Blitz. Some 42,000 lost their lives to the bombing campaign.
15 Cf. the exhibition catalogue Turner: 1775–1851, Aquarelle, n.p. 1951.
16 Cf. the exhibition catalogue British Information Service Branch (ed.): London, Bilder einer Weltstadt, Vienna 1947.
17 Platzer: Kalter Krieg und Architektur, 50. A travelling touring exhibition, it toured several cities in Europe, Turkey, and Australia from 1946 to 1949.
18 Feichtinger, Kulturpolitik der Besatzungsmacht Großbritannien, 516.
19 "Tattoo" in Schönbrunn – ein Erlebnis, in: Weltpresse, 24 June 1946, 6. Performances by British military music bands were given predominantly between 1945 and 1946. For instance, on 7 and 14 October 1945, the military orchestra of the 4th Queen's Own Hussars Royal Norfolk Regiment played the Raimundtheater. In late 1945 and early 1946, there were performances by the military musicians of the Royal Dragoons Regiment at the Burgtheater, the Löwen-Kino cinema, the Weißer Engel in Hietzing, the Kleiner Sofiensaal, and the American Rex-Theater. Cf. Rolf M. Urrisk-Obertyński (ed.), Die vier Alliierten, 304.

Fig. 2: Federal President Karl Renner visiting the exhibition "London – Bild einer Weltstadt" (London – Portrait of a Global City) at the Messepalast in Vienna, 11 July 1947 (photo: Lothar Rübelt, ANL/Vienna, 007_47_040_01_046_B_1A_15A)

going to Vienna's children[20] via the administration of the Municipality of Vienna.[21]

On 21 June, an afternoon performance was given for children. Some 6,400 are thought to have attended this performance in the presence of Verney and the mayor of Vienna, General (Retd) Theodor Körner.[22] The performances for adults all began at 9:45 p.m. and opened with daring displays by sixteen military motorcyclists from the Royal Reconnaissance Corps. The shows featured British military bands and the pipes and drums corps of the 1st Royal Dragoons, the 2nd Battalion of the Warwickshire Regiment, and the Coldstream Guards.[23] The performances were enhanced by searchlights, and the spectacle always ended with a firework display.[24]

---

20 "Tattoo" in Schönbrunn – ein Erlebnis, in: Weltpresse, 24 June 1946, 6.
21 Zapfenstreich auf englisch – Tattoo, in: Das kleine Volksblatt, 25 May 1946, 5.
22 Zapfenstreich auf englisch – Tattoo, in: Das kleine Volksblatt, 25 May 1946, 5; "Tattoo" in Schönbrunn – ein Erlebnis, in: Weltpresse, 24 June 1946, 6.
23 "Tattoo" in Schönbrunn – ein Erlebnis, in: Weltpresse, 24 June 1946, 6.
24 Ibid. On the precise order of the performances and the troupes involved, cf. Vienna Searchlight Tattoo, Programm. For the memories of the contemporary witness Tom Canning, who as a member of the British occupying forces was stationed in Schönbrunn and played a monk in the stagecoach scene, cf. Robert M. Tidmarsch: Mein Leben in Schönbrunn. / My Life in Schönbrunn. Eine andere Art, Geschichte zu erzählen / Another way of telling history, Vienna 2012, 77–79.

These events were intended to lavishly present the "British way of military life", both past and present, thereby underlining the union's political power in Vienna. The British occupation authorities' newspaper, *Weltpresse*,[25] stated that the Vienna Searchlight Tattoo's mission was "the great task of reconciliation".[26]

The performances raised over 400,000 schillings. The British supreme commander handed the sum to Mayor Körner in the form of a cheque at a ceremony at Vienna City Hall on 26 October 1946.[27] This contribution enabled the City of Vienna to provide a six-week holiday for around 2,400 children. Similar events were staged in the following years.[28]

In what follows, the focus is not on aspects of British cultural policy in Vienna, but on outright attacks on British cultural institutions in the city. These developments were rooted in the international political scene. A large number of Jews who had survived the Shoah attempted to get to Palestine, including via Austria. The British, as the mandate power, tried to prevent this in order to shape the balance of power in Palestine in line with their colonial ideas. As a response, a Jewish underground struggle[29] developed, culminating in a bomb attack on the King David Hotel in Jerusalem, which was partly used by the British, on 22 July 1946. Ninety-one people were killed and forty-five were injured. Various operations were undertaken in Vienna and Austria too, ranging from attacks with explosives to pamphlet drops. On 4 August 1947, Hotel Sacher, used by high-ranking British officers, was attacked.[30] The bomb caused minor damage.[31]

The severest attack by Jewish underground fighters took place on the evening of Friday 19 March 1948 and targeted Parkhotel Schönbrunn, where British nationals had been billeted since 1945, in the British-occupied 13th District. The

---

25 The first edition of *Weltpresse*, the newspaper of the British occupation authorities, appeared on 18 December 1945. It was printed in the socialist press Druck- und Verlagsanstalt Vorwärts in Vienna. On 1 September 1950, the paper was taken over by the Welt am Montag Zeitungsverlags GmbH, owned by the Socialist Party of Austria (SPÖ). Cf. Richard Hufschmied: Wien im Kalkül der Alliierten. Maßnahmen gegen eine sowjetische Blockade, Vienna/Graz 2002, 87.
26 "Tattoo" in Schönbrunn – ein Erlebnis, in: Weltpresse, 24 June 1946, 6.
27 National Army Museum London, Archive, Presentation of the Proceeds from the Searchlight Tattoo to the Burgermeister for the Children of Vienna, brochure, Vienna 1946, two pages, here: 2.
28 Tidmarsch, Mein Leben in Schönbrunn, 77.
29 The following groups fought for a "Jewish state" in Palestine: Haganah, which had existed since 1920 and formed the nucleus of the later Israeli army and stood for moderate Jewish self-protection, and the radical groups Irgun Zvai Leumi and the Stern Gang.
30 For an overview of these attacks and operations, cf. Rudolf Jeřábek: Zur Tätigkeit von "Partisanen" in Österreich nach dem Zweiten Weltkrieg, in: Erwin A. Schmidl: Österreich im frühen Kalten Krieg 1945–1958: Spionen, Partisanen, Kriegspläne, Vienna/Cologne/Weimar 2000, 137–170, here: 155–159.
31 Bombenattentat im Hotel Sacher. Nur geringer Sachschaden der Explosion, Wiener Kurier, 5 August 1947, 2.

explosion was timed for the evening, when the weekly dance for families of the British occupying forces and their guests was underway. Charles Noble,[32] public safety officer in Vienna, described the dramatic moments in his witness report:

> On 19 Mar 48 I attended the Park Hotel on the occasion of the weekly dance. I arrived there shortly after 22.00 hrs, went to the bar and then to the dance hall, sat down on the far side of the hall from the bar, was seated there about 2–3 minutes and heard a violent explosion and a cloud of dust bozed into the hall from the bar. I immediately went to the bar. This would be about 22.15 hrs and the first person I saw in the cloud of dust was Capt. BLACKSTOCK, who told me there had been an explosion. I suggested to him that he got to the band to start playing again, entered the bar and there saw Mr. WILKINSON lying seriously injured and I attended [sic] to him.[33]

It is doubtful whether the band actually did start playing again, since the detonation did considerable damage those present and to the building. Bomb disposal specialists thought that the ignition had likely been the same as in the attacks in Mallnitz[34] and on Hotel Sacher. The bomb had an explosive charge of 35 to 40 kilos and used a commercially available explosive such as Donarit.[35]

The attack cost one person her life: the twenty-five-year-old Argentinean and German national Dolores Beatrix Friedrich, who had begun working at Parkhotel Schönbrunn two weeks earlier and was in the office at the time of the explosion.[36]

The proclamation of the State of Israel on 14 May 1948 ended this form of Jewish underground struggle in Austria.

Conclusion

In summary, after the war ended in 1945, the British occupation authorities' cultural policy in occupied Austria and Vienna aimed at self-presentation, re-education, and re-orientation. The corresponding events were organized mainly by the British Council, but also by the British military. From 1947 onwards,

---

32 As a member of the British occupying forces, Charles Noble, 1903–1984, was billeted in a villa in Schlöglgasse in the 12th District. He was 1.93 metres tall and hence nicknamed "Tiny" by his friends. Cf. Richard Hufschmied: Simmering im Spiegel britischer Akten, in: Simmeringer Museumsblätter, 73/74, Vienna April 2005, 26–36, here: 34.
33 The National Archives of the UK, Kew, Richmond (TNA), FO 1020-655, Park Hotel (British Officers' Club Vienna) incident (Bomb explosion) and detail of injuries (19 March 1948), Statement of Charles Noble, Public Safety Officer, 1 April 1948.
34 In the vicinity of Mallnitz, in Carinthia, a train carrying British holidaymakers was blown up on 10 August 1947. The explosion derailed six wagons and caused minor injuries to a soldier.
35 TNA, FO 1020-3143, Park Hotel bomb attack with photographs 1948, Sachverständigengutachten des Bundesministeriums für Inneres, Generaldirektion für die öffentliche Sicherheit, Entminungsdienst, 20 March 1948.
36 Ibid.

British (cultural) policy focused on support for Austria's orientation towards the West. Departing from exclusively presenting British culture and art imports, the British Council's work soon concentrated on "functional work", for instance in the form of language training for compulsory and middle school teachers. As early as 1948, Richard Hiscocks considered educational work the most important of the British Council's activities in Vienna.[37] Ultimately, fulfilling these tasks soon became routine. The post-war years up to around 1948 brought the greatest transformations to British cultural policy. While the British Council events were attended only by elitist, intellectual circles and did not cater to the masses,[38] the popular presentations by the British Forces were staged as large-scale events.

---

37 Feichtinger, Kulturpolitik der Besatzungsmacht Großbritannien, 524–525.
38 Ibid., 519–520.

Johanna Lerchner

The Allied Topography of Vienna

From a Viennese perspective, the Soviet troops' conquest of Vienna on 13 April 1945 was the beginning of a ten-year era of occupation. Austria's decade under the occupation of the four victorious Allied powers lasted until the State Treaty of 15 May 1955.[1] During this time, Vienna was, as Manfried Rauchensteiner aptly puts it, a "special case in a special case",[2] and one worthy of closer examination. The city's districts were divided between the Allied occupation authorities, with the 1st District under joint Allied administration.[3] This jointly administered district, known as the Inter-Allied Sector, offered a unique encounter among the four occupying forces that made post-war Vienna at the height of the Cold War a "stomping ground of the secret services".[4]

On 1 September 1945 – almost four months after the conquest of Vienna – the four high commissioners officially took over the administration of their allocated districts. Barracks had to be confiscated for the arriving troops, along with residential accommodation, administrative offices, and leisure areas, for civilian personnel. To accommodate the occupying personnel, a total of 7,800 apartments, villas, shops, and hotels had been confiscated by the end of 1948,[5] including the Austrian National Bank, known as the "Bank Building", which served as the headquarters of the United States Forces Austria until 1951.[6] The British occupation authorities confiscated villas in the 13th District for its own military

---

1 Karl Vocelka: Geschichte Österreichs. Kultur – Gesellschaft – Politik, Graz/Vienna/Cologne 2002, 325.
2 Manfried Rauchensteiner: Der Sonderfall. Die Besatzungszeit in Österreich 1945 bis 1955, Graz/Vienna/Cologne 1979, 251.
3 Vocelka, Geschichte Österreichs, 318.
4 Wolfgang Lackner: Wien als Drehscheibe internationaler Geheim- und Nachrichtendienste im Kalten Krieg, Graz 2010, 72, 198.
5 Peter Csendes, Ferdinand Opll (eds.): Wien – Geschichte einer Stadt, Vol. 3: Von 1790 bis zur Gegenwart, Vienna/Cologne/Weimar 2006, 556.
6 Rolf M. Urrisk-Obertyński (ed.): Wien. 2000 Jahre Garnisonsstadt, Vol. 6: Die vier Alliierten 1945–1955, Gnas 2015, 38.

leadership.⁷ For France, on the other hand, the 6ᵗʰ District, Mariahilf, was of great importance, since it was where the Stadtkommandantur and various administrative and leisure facilities were located.⁸ The Soviet Union also requisitioned industrial works and shops, so-called "reichsdeutsche Kriegsindustrie" (Reich German war industries),⁹ and incorporated them into the Soviet system. Notable examples are the "USIA shops",¹⁰ small grocery stores run by the Soviet military government, where the Austrian population could buy everyday goods and provisions 50 per cent cheaper.¹¹ The exact number of such USIA shops is unknown, since not all shops were registered under the official name of the USIA administrative apparatus. However, it is estimated that there were around 200 such shops and small grocery stores.¹²

At the start of occupation, each of the occupation authorities attempted to influence the zone under its administration via its own way of life, ideology, and politics. As Manfried Rauchensteiner writes, each occupation authorities was "representative and a promoter of its own ideology and [attempted] to make its own mark on the territory it occupied and controlled".¹³ The four occupation authorities differed not only from a cultural perspective but also in terms of the four infrastructures of occupation, which displayed individualized characteristics. Such differences are also evident in the American snack bars and ice cream parlours, which were set up by the US military government to provide the American troops stationed there with a "connection to home".¹⁴ These special leisure facilities could only be found under the American authorities and can be interpreted as a topographical differentiating feature of the US occupation infrastructure.

This question of the topographical features of the Allied occupation infrastructures is the focus of my Master's dissertation entitled "The Allied Topography of Vienna, 1945–1955". The study focuses on the dwellings, hotels, barracks, public administrative buildings, shops, and industrial works con-

---

7 Austrian State Archives (Österreichisches Staatsarchiv, henceforth ÖStA), BKA/Alliierte Verbindungstelle, Britisches Oberkommando, box 133.
8 ÖStA, BKA/Alliierte Verbindungstelle, Französisches Oberkommando, box 131–132.
9 Otto Klambauer: Die USIA-Betriebe (Vienna 1978) 80.
10 Klambauer, Die USIA-Betriebe, 249. USIA stood for Upravlenie sovetskim imshchestvom v Avstrii (Administration for Soviet Property in Austria).
11 Florian Gimpl: Die USIA-Betriebe und der Streik 1950 in Wien und Niederösterreich, Vienna 2017, 32.
12 Gimpl, Die USIA- Betriebe und der Streik 1950 in Wien und Niederösterreich, 33.
13 Manfried Rauchensteiner: Das Jahrzehnt der Besatzung als Epoche in der österreichischen Geschichte, in: Alfred Ableitinger, Siegfried Beer, Eduard G. Staudinger (eds.): Österreich unter alliierter Besatzung 1945–1955, Vienna/Cologne/Graz, 26.
14 Hubert Prigl: Clubs und Einrichtungen der amerikanischen Besatzungsmacht, in: Hubert Prigl (ed.): "off limits" – Amerikanische Besatzungssoldaten in Wien 1945–1955, Vienna 2005, 43, 50.

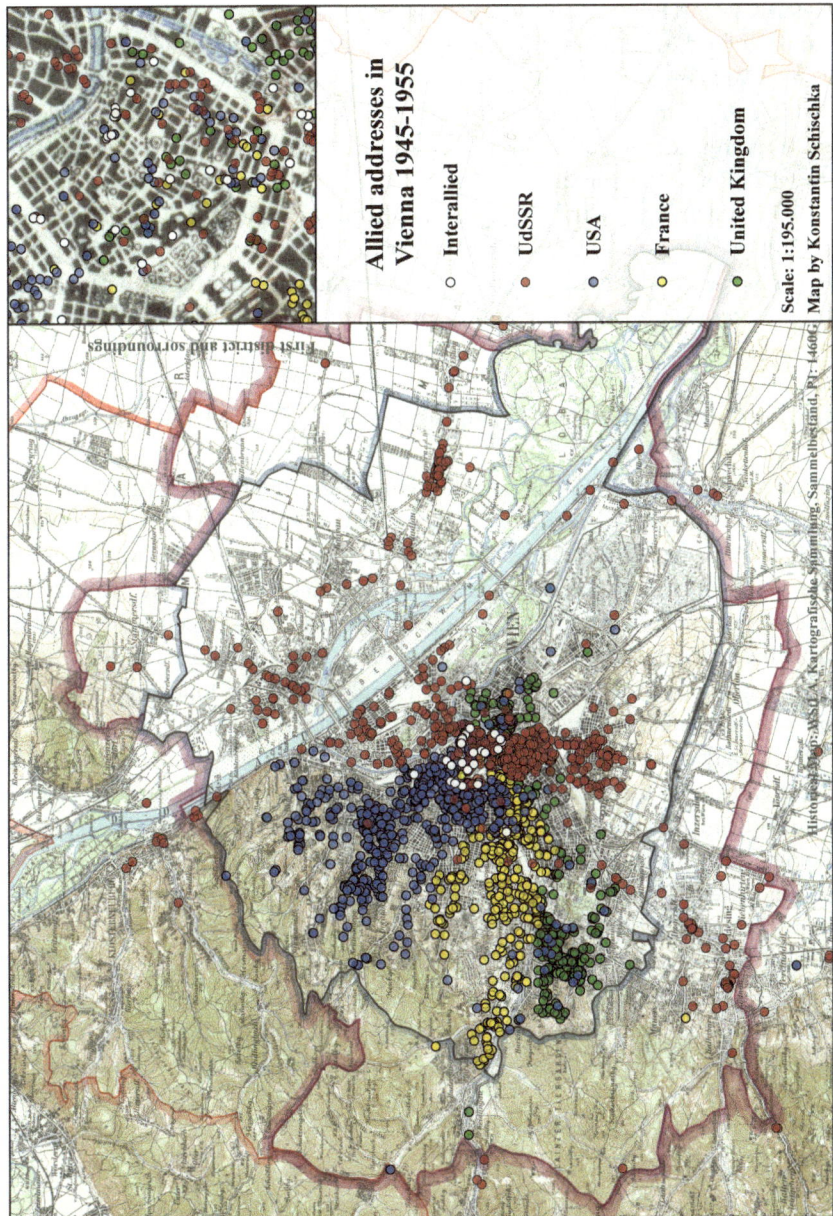

Fig. 1: Allied addresses in Vienna, 1945–1955 (map by Konstantin Schischka)

fiscated by the Allies. Using addresses, it provides the first survey of the occupation infrastructure and topography of the Allied confiscations of buildings. The research on this extensive project began in March 2023. Within a year, it was possible to establish around 1,800[15] addresses confiscated by the Allies. Building on these results, a map of Vienna is under development, providing the first visualization of the buildings confiscated during the decade of occupation.

This contribution to the catalogue will provide initial insights into preliminary studies, focusing on the relevance of confiscated buildings in the 16th District for the French occupation infrastructure before turning its attention to a case study: the US occupation authorities' confiscation and use of Hotel Regina.

Insights into the French Topography: The 16th District, Ottakring

The 6th, 14th, 15th, and 16th Districts of Vienna were under French administration from September 1945, in addition to the jointly administered 1st District. From 1946 to 1955, the headquarters of the Mission Française for Vienna was located in the Breitenseer Kadettenschule, in the 14th District, Penzing. The actual headquarters of the French occupation was in Innsbruck, which received instructions from the high commissioner in Vienna, however.[16] Due to the necessary brevity of this chapter to the catalogue, the insight into the French topography of occupation must remain a small one. It centred on Ottakring, the 16th District, which, interestingly, has only received marginal attention in prior studies, as well as in the literature on the French occupation. In Ottakring, the French military government only confiscated the barracks at Panikengasse 2, set up the Bezirkskommandantur for the 16th District at Schuhmeierplatz 17, requisitioned a garage at Sandleitengasse 38, and confiscated a small number of residential properties and single rooms.[17]

The French had taken over the barracks at Panikengasse 2 from the Soviet military government in September 1945 and named it "Quartier General al Barbot". Until the State Treaty was concluded, it housed the Gendarmerie or the Police Militaire before finally being returned to the Austrian Bundesheer in 1955.[18]

---

15 The research phase of the Masters' dissertation was not quite complete when this contribution to the catalogue was written; the number of addresses may yet increase.
16 Margit Sandner: Die französisch-österreichischen Beziehungen während der Besatzungszeit von 1947 bis 1955, Vienna 1985, 13.
17 ÖStA, BKA/Alliierte Verbindungsstelle, Französisches Oberkommando, boxes 131–132.
18 Urrisk-Obertyński (ed.), Die vier Alliierten, 154.

The Bezirkskommandantur, or Gouvernements d'arrondissements,[19] was located at Schuhmeierplatz 17 from 1946 to 1947. The National Socialist Workers' Party had used it as a Gauhaus from 1941,[20] and the French occupation authorities used it after taking over the sector. Its closure in 1947 coincided with the conclusion of the Second Control Agreement of 28 June 1946, in which the victorious Allied powers agreed to hand responsibility to the Austrian administration, no longer exercising direct administrative functions and henceforth taking on a monitoring role.[21] As a consequence, the two Bezirkskommandanturen in the 14th District, Penzing, and the 15th, Rudolfsheim, were merged to form a central control authority, the Détachement de Contrôle des Arrondissements du Secteur Francais de la Ville de Vienne. This centralized controlling body was located at Breitenseerstrasse 82a, in Penzing, from 1947 onwards.[22] The Bezirkskommandantur in Schuhmeierplatz was most likely incorporated into this new authority the same year.

The first official return of confiscated Ottakring residential property to the Austrian government took place in July 1949. The apartment at Starkenburggasse 45 had been inhabited by a French official and his family. In March 1949, Austrian federal chancellor Leopold Figl wrote to Jean Dutheil, the French governor and cabinet director to the French high commissioner, requesting the dwelling's release, which was not granted until the late July, however, since a suitable alternative accommodation could not be found for the French official and his family. In July 1949, the official was transferred to Germany, which meant that the apartment could finally be returned to the previous owner.[23] In the following years, from 1949 to 1954, a total of only fifty-two further apartments and a handful of single rooms were released. The abovementioned garage at Sandleitengasse 38 was returned in July 1951.[24]

Comparison with the confiscations of buildings in the 6th District, Mariahilf, demonstrates that Ottakring was not of central importance to the French military infrastructure. In Mariahilf, the smallest of the four French-occupied districts, as many apartments were confiscated as in the other three districts combined,[25] in addition to the large number of hotels confiscated and administrative buildings set up.[26] The confiscated buildings in Ottakring thus invite the initial inference

---

19 Stefan Vogel: Frankreich und die alliierte Besatzung in Wien 1945–1955, Vienna 1997, 102.
20 dasrotewien.at, Weblexikon der Wiener Sozialdemokratie, Ottakring, https://www.dasrotewien.at/seite/ottakring (1 June 2024).
21 Vogel, Frankreich und die alliierte Besatzung, 113.
22 Ibid., 114.
23 ÖStA, BKA/Alliierte Verbindungsstelle, Französisches Oberkommando, boxes 131–132, Zl. 3317/HC/CAB/I.
24 ÖStA, BKA/Alliierte Verbindungsstelle, Französisches Oberkommando, boxes 131–132.
25 Vogel: Frankreich und die alliierte Besatzung, 132.
26 Urrisk-Obertyński (ed.), Die vier Alliierten, 9.

that from a topographical perspective, the French military government accorded it less significance.

Hotel Regina: American Confiscation

Upon the conquest of Vienna in April 1945, most of the hotels, inns, and private guesthouses that had escaped damage in the war were used to accommodate occupying soldiers and refugees or as military hospitals and administrative offices.[27] The same held for Hotel Regina, which served as accommodation for Soviet officers in the first summer months.[28] After the First Control Agreement of 9 July 1945, the 9th District, Alsergrund, came under the administration of the American military government.[29] Hotel Regina was used by the American occupation authorities from 23 July 1945[30] to 14 July 1952.[31] During these seven years, it was one of the main locations for accommodating American occupation personnel, housing the Officers' Club Regina Rathskeller in its cellar, a "Hotel Billeting Office",[32] and officers' and civilian messes. The Regina Rathskeller was reserved for American officers and, like the officers' club at Hotel Bristol, it was one of the last two to remain open without interruption until April 1955.[33] The Hotel Billeting Office for "transients & dependents" was also based there from 1949 to the end of its confiscation in 1952. This office was for soldiers who did not belong to military unit and for family members who were not doing active military service but nevertheless received accommodation from the US occupation authorities.[34]

With its countless rooms, Hotel Regina offered the occupiers a place ensuring leisure, accommodation, and provisions for arriving officers and troops. Especially at the beginning of the occupation, when the American military government pursued a policy of "non-fraternization", such accommodation was particularly popular with the US forces. Such buildings bundled "all the comforts of

---

27 Brigitte Entner: Vom Besatzer zum Urlaubsgast, in: zeitgeschichte 23/1–2 (1996), 17.
28 Andreas Augustin, Carola Augustin: Hotel Regina Wien, 2016, 69.
29 Rauchensteiner, Der Sonderfall. Die Besatzungszeit in Österreich von 1945 bis 1955, 107.
30 Archived files of Wolfgang Kremslehner, handwritten copy of Schadensakt ZL.: II/2250/52 (24 December 1952).
31 Archived files of Wolfgang Kremslehner, handover certificate for Mietakt no. H/155 (14 July 1952).
32 Archiv des Instituts für Zeitgeschichte, University of Vienna, estate of Dr. Albert Loewry, Vienna Telephone Directory inventory no. 673/2542 (15 October 1949), 48.
33 Prigl, Clubs und Einrichtungen der amerikanischen Besatzungsmacht, 43.
34 Archiv des Instituts für Zeitgeschichte, University of Vienna, estate of Dr. Albert Loewry, Vienna Telephone Directory inventory no. 673/2544, 1 July 1951, 38.

Fig. 2: The American Military Police's traffic information point. Hotel Regina in the background. View from Freiheitsplatz (later Rooseveltplatz), 1 March 1946 (photo: Hans Siegenfeld, ANL/ Vienna, CL 84, 8)

home"[35] and reduced the initial encounters between American personnel and the Austrian population to a minimum.[36] As the example of Hotel Regina makes evident, accommodation, supplies, and leisure were concentrated in one spot and thus perfectly met the Americans' requirements.

Hotel Regina had largely escaped damage during the war and had some eighty hotel rooms, inhabited by thirteen high-ranking officers in December 1945.[37] It was confiscated unusually early, however, in the July, before the Allied troops officially entered and took over the sector. The timing and the first accommodation of high-ranking officers are in keeping with the infrastructural preparations undertaken by the American occupation authorities; July 1945 was when the "vanguard", those responsible for making contact with the Russian staffs and Austrian government posts, arrived in Vienna. These personnel took care of the

---

35 Lee Kruger: Logistics matters and the U.S. Army in occupied Germany, 1945–1949, Cham 2017, 105.
36 Ibid., 106.
37 Archiv des Instituts für Zeitgeschichte, University of Vienna, Nachlass Dr. Albert Loewry, Vienna Telephone Directory inventory no. 673/2539 (no. 9, 1 December 1945).

final preparations for setting up the Allied Council and prepared the occupation infrastructure for the arrival of the highest American staff in the September.[38]

The composition of those billeted transformed fundamentally after 1946; Hotel Regina was now reserved not only for officers but also for female occupation personnel. In July 1948, the highest number of people were accommodated there, eighty-seven, some seventy-six of them unmarried or married women working in the nearby US administrative buildings such as the "Allianz Building", the "Service Building", or the "Petroleum Building".[39] The available hotel rooms were also predominantly inhabited by female occupation personnel in the years that followed, until 1951.[40]

In 1949, these eighty-seven were halved to forty-two. In July 1951, just twenty-seven were registered under the address Hotel Regina. This reduction allows conclusions to be drawn concerning the general presence of American troops in Austria or Vienna. With the Second Control Agreement in 1946[41] and the transformation of military high commissions into civilian ones in 1950, the number of troops stationed continued to decrease.[42] This reduction in stationed American personnel is reflected by the number of confiscated hotel rooms. In 1952, the hotel was finally cleared and used to for foreign tourists, since the rooms were no longer needed or the personnel could be billeted in other confiscated buildings.

---

38 Günter Bischof: Die Amerikaner als Besatzungsmacht in Österreich, in: Manfried Rauchensteiner, Robert Kriechbaumer (eds.): Die Gunst des Augenblicks, Neuere Forschungen zu Staatsvertrag und Neutralität, Vol. 24, Vienna/Cologne/Weimar 2005, 82.
39 Archiv des Instituts für Zeitgeschichte, University of Vienna, estate of Dr. Albert Loewry, Vienna Telephone Directory inventory no. 673/2540 (1 July 1948).
40 Archiv des Instituts für Zeitgeschichte, University of Vienna, estate of Dr. Albert Loewry, Vienna Telephone Directory inventory no. 673/2544 (1 July 1951). 1949: forty-two people, forty-one of them women; 1951: twenty-seven people, nineteen of them women.
41 Entner: Vom Besatzer zum Urlaubsgast, 24.
42 Rauchensteiner: Das Jahrzehnt der Besatzung als Epoche in der österreichischen Geschichte, 28.

Wolfgang Duchkowitsch

The Allies and the Press, 1945/46

1   Press Policy in the Four Occupation Zones

When Austria was liberated from National Socialism, all existing newspapers were banned. Afterwards, the Allies founded their own publications. At the start of the occupation period, the Allied powers had similar intentions in at least two closely related areas: National Socialism, its aims, and its impact were to be publicly condemned and countered, and Austria's conclusive separation from Germany and its concurrent re-orientation as an independent state had to be perceived by the country's national consciousness. There were differences between the Allies on the level of terminology, however. Propaganda was not a pejorative term for the Soviet occupation authorities, while it was in the other occupation zones. Instead of propaganda, the concept of "information" – often in connection with "re-education" – was propagated. To this end, Britain and the USA set up the British and American Information Services Branch (ISB) and the American Information Coordination Branch, while in the French zone the Division Information was founded. In the political Main Administration of the Red Army (GlavPURKA), Department 7 was responsible for propaganda.[1]

1.1   American

During the first phase of its plan of action, in May 1945 the American Military Government shut down the following newspapers founded on Upper Austrian soil: *Welser Zeitung, Mondseer Nachrichten, Lambacher Nachrichtenblatt,* the *Innviertler Volkszeitung,* and *Salzkammergut-Stimmen.* The American Military Government's aim was to obtain total control over all media in its sphere of influence. A corresponding decree regulated control not only of print media,

---

1 Karin Moser: Propaganda und Gegenpropaganda. Das "kalte" Wechselspiel während der alliierten Besatzung in Österreich, in: medien & zeit 1 (2002), 27–42, here: 27–29.

radio, and film, but also of theatre and film.² These activities were built on by phase two, which was intended to usher in a certain liberalization under American leadership and guidance, including the removal of all Austrians with National Socialist, fascist, or Greater German attitudes from positions in the information space. In this second phase, the following newspapers were founded: *Salzburger Nachrichten* (7 June 1945), *Oberösterreichische Nachrichten* (11 June 1945), and the *Tiroler Tageszeitung* (21 June 1945), which was soon placed under French supervision in line with the new zonal borders. The supreme authority for rewarding the respective permits was the Publications Board. During the following third phase, the aim was to return the media entirely to Austrian hands while still retaining Allied control over it.³ The priority was to completely eliminate National Socialism, militarism, and all German influence and to prevent the spread of doctrine and propaganda by German or Austrian National Socialists, fascists, and German-Nationals (Pan-Germans).⁴

1.2   British

In May 1945, the British Military Government declared via decree the closure of the courts, post office branches, the telegraph administration, all organizations and associations involved in the collection, printing, and distribution of propaganda material. Article III stated in detail: "Without the appropriate approval of the Military Government, it is forbidden a) to overprint existing postage or revenue stamps or to issue new ones b) to operate any telephone or telegraph or wireless broadcasting transmitters, c) to maintain or distribute correspondence, d) to publish or distribute any kind of newspapers, leaflets, newsletters, or placards, e) to use, damage, destroy, or remove from their location printing presses, type (sets), newspapers or other papers for printing."⁵ The British Military Government informed the population of Carinthia about its arrangements by radio and later, from 12 May 1945, via the daily newsletter *Mitteilungsblatt*. This publication was printed on one side only, so that it could also be pinned to walls. On 16 May 1945, the Psychological Warfare Branch (PWB) of the

---

2 Rudolf Tschögl: Tagespresse. Parteien und alliierte Zeitungen. Grundzüge in der unmittelbaren Nachkriegszeit 1945–1947, doctoral thesis, University of Vienna 1979, 88.
3 Oliver Rathkolb: Politische Propaganda der amerikanischen Besatzungsmacht in Österreich 1945–1950. Ein Beitrag zur Geschichte des Kalten Kriegs in der Presse-, Kultur- und Rundfunkpolitik, doctoral thesis, University of Vienna 1981, 47.
4 Michael Schönberg: Die amerikanische Medien- und Informationspolitik in Österreich von 1945–1950, doctoral thesis, Vienna 1975, Dokumentation 1, 76.
5 Handbook: Military Goverment Legislation. Handbuch der Militärregierungs-Gesetzgebung. O.O. 04. 04. 1946. 2–3, 5.

8th Army first published the daily newspaper *Kärntner Nachrichten*. It was printed by the former *Gau* publishing house. After British troops took over the Soviet-occupied part of Styria on 10 May 1945, the *Neue steirische Zeitung* was founded in Graz on 10 May 1945. This edition published the above decree, which extended the total ban on printing to Styria and meant that the *Weststeirische Volkszeitung*, edited by the West Styrian Freedom Fighters (*Freiheitskämpfer*) had to be disbanded, along with the *Demokratisches Volksblatt*, the organ of Styrian democrats. The *Obersteirisches Tagblatt* was also shut down. However, the PWB soon relaunched its publication, which appeared twice a week. The Military Government combated not only the publishing activities of Freedom Fighters, but also their organizations. This stance prevailed until shortly before the National Assembly elections in November 1945.[6]

1.3 French

In addition to Vorarlberg, the French troops were able to liberate and occupy only part of the Tyrol. They took over the rest of the Tyrol, which was under American occupation, in July 1945. The first periodical publications in Vorarlberg – commune papers – were not yet under the control of the French Military Government; they were the responsibility of the respective commune councils. In cooperation with the French, *Vorarlberger Nachrichten* appeared on 1 September 1945. The Austrian People's Party (ÖVP) and the Socialist Party of Austria (SPÖ) each had a representative on the editorial board, while the Communist Party of Austria (KPÖ) had to content itself with contributing articles. Having a free hand in publishing in the province was very much in line with the self-image of *Vorarlberger Nachrichten*. Its founding issue expressed its appreciation: "It shows the occupying authorities' trust in the healthy sense of our population that they didn't take it upon themselves to publish a newspaper but rather permitted Austrians to edit a paper for Austrians." *Vorarlberger Nachrichten* confidently told its readers that "[o]ur paper is not the organ of a party or an orientation – it is Austrian. It aims to help rebuild our beautiful homeland in words and texts, in non-party fashion, to the best of its knowledge and with the best conscience." Only the editorial and economic bulletins had to receive a "vue favourable" and be stamped as such by the French Military Government before going into print.[7] The Tyrol was without a newspaper for many weeks. This situation did not change until 21 June 1945, when the Information Services Branch edited the *Tiroler Tageszeitung*. On 8 July, it handed the newspaper over to the French

---

6 Tschögl, 81.
7 Ibid., 96.

troops. In contrast to the American editors, the French allowed Austrian journalists and politicians to write articles.

1.4 Soviet

Soviet press policy's intention of creating a unified newspaper came to fruition on 23 April 1945 with the foundation, in conjunction with the KPÖ, of *Neues Österreich*, an "organ of democratic unity", as the subtitle proclaimed. Ernst Fischer, the editor-in-chief of *Neues Österreich*, who had previously spent some time leading propaganda work for Austria in the USSR, celebrated in the founding issue: "Finally there can appear in Austria a newspaper that is not the tool of coordinated [German: gleichgeschaltete[8]] lies but is rather the mouthpiece of democratic truth." On 10 May 1945, the *Grazer Volkszeitung* appeared after Russian troops had marched into Graz the day before. It was replaced on 29 May by the *Neue steirische Zeitung*, which was published under Soviet leadership until 22 July 1945.

2 Allies' newspapers

2.1 American

The American forces published the *Wiener Kurier*. Aimed at the population of Vienna, it first appeared on 27 August 1945. The founding issue programmatically announced at the top of the page its "fight for freedom and independence". Below it ranked the "fight for the democratic unity of the state and the people". The paper's underlying ethos promised to stand up for "human worth and dignity", followed by affirmation of its resolve to go into battle to "strengthen and protect Austria's hard-won democracy". It then stated brightly that it sought to stand up "[f]or acts and works of peace" and to promote "joy in responsibility and civil courage", crowned by two bold aims: "The rise of youth and its education for a culture of the heart and the mind" and "openness to the world and Austria's bond with the free nations of the earth". The *Wiener Kurier* assured its readers it would combat any "attempts by the last vestiges of National Socialism and fascism to return to power", any "totalitarian pretentions", and "any pacts with the forces of megalomania and racial fanaticism". Reminding its readers of the "Nazis' cowardly way of attempting to play off the generations against one another in order to divide our people", the paper now saw the danger of "cosy

---

8 Gleichgeschaltet: brought into line with National Socialist policy and ideology.

irresponsibility" and a "cowardly irresponsibility in the face of violence". It promised that Austria would have a great future if it did not chose the path of "intellectual and economic autarchy".

The American editor-in-chief of the *Wiener Kurier* was Henry Reichert.[9] He was supported by Oskar Maurus Fontana as the Austrian editor-in-chief. In the founding issues, Fontana added to his declaration of the line the paper would be taking an assessment of the Austrian people disseminated by the prominent nineteenth century essayist and journalist Walt Whitman: "You sturdy Austrian!" Fontana branded this designation, rendered in Hans Reisiger's German translation[10] as "standhaft" – "steadfast" – as "America's greeting to us"; steadfastness was indeed "our best strength". In his use of language, Fontana seems not to have adopted such a stance himself under the "Third Reich"; he was summarily dismissed as editor-in-chief of the *Wiener Kurier* by the Office of War in February 1946 for political collaboration with the National Socialism.[11] Soon thereafter, he managed to become editor-in-chief of the *Welt am Montag*, set up by the French Military Government. In the founding issue of the *Wiener Kurier*, General Mark W. Clark, US high commissioner to Austria, penned an address aimed at the population of Vienna. The "Cold War" had not yet broken out: the publication of this newspaper provided "new evidence" of the "good waves of the Allies" in providing the Austrian people "with every assistance in the transitional phase" in order to "pave the way for the creation of a free and democratic nation" that no "Nazi threat" would "dare" to challenge. In late 1945, the paper became a tabloid, as Kurt Paupiè observed in his study of newspapers, but it continued to attempt to use news to exert political influence on its readership.[12]

2.2   British

On 18 September 1945, the British Information Services Branch published a paper entitled *Weltpresse*. It featured a preface by Lieutenant General Sir R. L. MacCreery, supreme commander of the British forces. He appealed to the Austrian people, assuring them that they had come as victors and liberators to free them from the "deadly pressure of seven years of total propaganda". The aim of *Weltpresse* would be to present events, opinions, and facts from all around the world for "your judgement". It would "report from all positions clearly and

---

9 Kurt Paupiè: Handbuch der österreichischen Pressegeschichte. Vol. 1, Vienna 1960, 190.
10 "Du standhafter Österreicher! [...]"; Walt Witman, Salut au monde, in: Walt Witmans Werk, trans. Hans Reisiger, Berlin 1922, 122–132, here: 129.
11 Fontana did not have a National Socialist past. Oliver Rathkolb: U.S.-Medienpolotik und die neue Österreichische Journalistenelite, in: medien & zeit 2 (1987), 3–16, here: 5.
12 Paupié, 191.

objectively, providing not only the political declarations of the great and small powers but also reports that contain criticism". He fundamentally declared that, carried by the spirit of British information policy, *Weltpresse* would not push any propaganda. "Apart from in one sense: it will profess the principles of democracy and their exercising in practice for which the British people have fought." He looked far into the future when he also stressed, "It will take an enormous effort to overcome the devastation of the war and to create the foundations of lasting peace." He then urged, "We will seek to make this clear to the reader. If he follows us, then he will gain a sense of the titanic efforts for peace all nations of the world make over the course of time." *Weltpresse* was Austria's only evening newspaper. Another unique aspect was that it was connected to the "special service" of *The Times*, *The Manchester Guardian*, and *The Observer*. Initially, the flongs were taken on lorries to Graz by the British occupation authorities. There, they were given their own local and advertising sections. From October 1946 onwards, a 3 p.m. edition was added to the daily issue, which was also published predated in rural areas.[13]

In Vienna, the Information Services Branch published the *British Morning News*. It first appeared on 21 November 1945, serving merely as a news bulletin for the British occupying troops in Austria and for English speakers in Austria, the CzSSR, Hungary, and Italy. Its presentation was reminiscent of English newspapers such as the *Daily Mirror* and the *Daily Sketch*.[14] In its content and external form, the experiment British Morning News had very little in common with the Austrian press.[15]

---

13 Ibid., 192-193.
14 Ibid., 195.
15 Tschögl, 158.

The Allies and the Press 81

Fig. 1: Front page of *Wiener Kurier*, 27 August 1945 (ANNO, ANL/Vienna)

Fig. 2: Front page of *Weltpresse*, 18 September 1945 (ANNO, ANL/Vienna)

Fig. 3: Front page of *Welt am Abend*, 1 October 1946 (ANNO, ANL/Vienna)

Fig. 4: Front page of the *Österreichische Zeitung*, 15 April 1945 (ANNO, ANL/Vienna)

2.3 French

The French information service did not launch a newspaper until much later, founding *Welt am Abend* on 1 October 1946. The Austrian Foreign Minister Karl Gruber provided the introductory address, conveying the message of the supreme commander of the French troops in Austria, General Bethouart, that they had come as liberators and not as occupiers. He wrote that Bethouart was certain "that in Austria there are already a sufficiently large number of democrats [for us] to let the Austrians finish on their own the job the Allies started".

2.4 Soviet

On 15 April 1945, the *Österreichische Zeitung* was first published as an instrument of the Soviet occupation authorities, bearing the subtitle "Frontzeitung für die Bevölkerung Österreichs" – "Front Newspaper for the population of Austria". In the founding issue, Fyodor I. Tolbukhin, commander of the troops of the 3rd Ukrainian Front and marshal of the Soviet Union, asserted that the Red Army had set foot on Austrian soil "not to conquer Austrian territory" but "to cleanse Austria of the German-fascist troops completely and utterly, as soon as possible". He appealed to readers, "Support the Red Army in arresting Hitler's agents, provocateurs, spies, wreckers, and all of the elements preventing Austria's swiftest cleansing of Germans and working against the measures of the Red Army." He promised that "[t]he peaceful population of Austria has nothing to fear". The newspaper's main objective was to emphasize Austria's independence from the German Reich. The editorial board comprised Austrian Soviet staff. The editor-in-chief and the heads of the different sections were members of the Red Army.

3 The Declaration on the Freedom of the Press in Austria

Preparatory work on the Declaration began as early as June 1945, when General Mark Clark was instructed to "come to a corresponding agreement with the three other occupying elements regarding control of the public news media and press censorship that should apply to all of Austria."[16] On 25 September, a committee proudly announced, "The report of the Chiefs of the Political Division was approved and recommended to the Allied Council for adoption."[17]

---

16 Schönberg, 47.
17 Proceedings of the Executive Committee. Agenda 4, 3.

The Declaration on the Freedom of the Press was made on 1 October 1945. In the preamble, the Allied Council stressed the importance of the press: for rebuilding the country, for reinforcing democratic freedom, and for restoring a free, independent, and democratic Austria.[18] The democratic press would be given as much freedom as possible, declared Article I. Democratic principles were to be maintained, and a "resolute battle" was to be fought "against all the National Socialist, Greater German, and military ideologies and doctrines in all their forms and aspects in political, social, cultural, and economic life". This commitment was further specified by the following tasks: the democratic press "should refrain from publishing material with the potential to endanger the military security of the occupying troops or all or one of the occupation authorities, abstain from malicious material targeting one of or all of the occupation authorities with the aim of sowing discord between the Allies or breeding mistrust and hostility towards one or all of the occupation authorities or their troops in Austria among the Austrian people, [and] abstain from material with the potential to disrupt the existing public order".

Article II stressed the Declaration's validity in all occupation zones. Article III established that "newspapers and magazines are not subject to censorship".

On 6 October 1945, the restoration of freedom of the press was announced with great fanfare in Linz's provincial theatre (Landestheater). The newspaper publishers in attendance were presented with the publishing permits for their papers. The next day, the *Wiener Kurier* announced triumphantly, "The festive format of this hour alone indicates what great significance the Americans accord to the restoration of freedom of the press in Austria and what immense responsibility is thus being taken on by those whose task it will henceforth be to preserve and cultivate this hard-won, precious commodity".

In January 1946, the Declaration was published in the *Amtsblatt der österreichischen Bundesregierung* (Official Gazette of the Austrian Federal Government), including an explanation of the consequences in place for transgressions of the conditions set out in Article I: they could result in the temporary or permanent closure of the offending newspaper or magazine.

---

18 It is possible that the preamble had some influence on negotiations between the Ministry of Education and the University of Vienna in the autumn of 1945 over whether to continue the Department of Newspaper Studies (Institut für Zeitungswissenschaft), which had been closed due to the war; both the ministry and the university agreed that a free and strong press were indispensible and that the university should now have a department devoted to its scholarly analysis.

4 Press Reactions

The Austrian newspaper's response to the Declaration of Freedom of the Press was predictable, reflecting Oskar Pollak's assessment as editor-in-chief of the *Arbeiter-Zeitung* on 5 October 1945: "[…] one will try to justify the trust that the press is aware of its democratic order". The question as to "whether it really is" was met with suspicion: "Today's journalism seems not to notice at all how little freedom of the press is really at home in the daily workings of the Austrian newspapers." On 20 March 1946, Oskar Pollak examined the guidelines prescribed by the Declaration: the Austrian press was impeded in fulfilling these obligations due to "manifold circumstances". As an alternative to Allied control, he argued vehemently for a "self-monitoring of Austrian democracy in the field of newspapers".[19]

5 Monitoring the Declaration

Before the Declaration, the Allies had controlled the press directly, for instance by banning certain newspapers, by the provision of news, by allocation of paper supplies, and by monitoring circulation. The Declaration enabled intervention by the high commissioners and the imposition of sanctions by the Allied Council and the Executive Committee of the Allied Commission. It was legally contentious to shut down newspapers about which the Allies had no concerns but which contravened the Austrian constitution. However, de facto, the Austrian government recognized this restricted freedom of the press.

Between late October 1945 and mid-January 1946, some eighteen breaches of the Declaration were registered, nine of them by the *Arbeiter-Zeitung*. Soviet High Commissioner Ivan S. Konev called for strict punishment in the Allied Council: "It is quite impossible to let the press public Fascists' doctrines. The Austrians have forgotten their responsibility in this matter."[20] He demanded the suspension of the *Arbeiter-Zeitung*, but the Americans and the British rejected his proposal. As a compromise, a letter was written to Austrian Federal Chancellor Leopold Figl and another was sent warning all Austrian newspaper publishers. The following year, the Allied Council discussion of the freedom of the press continued in a similar vein.

---

19 Cf. Rathkolb, 162 ff.
20 Cit. Tschögl, 214.

Marion Krammer / Margarethe Szeless

Press Photography in the Cold War. Photo Policy in Austria, 1945–1955

"The communist story in Hallein is a very touchy bussines [sic], I spoke with the director of the factory and seemed to be very cooperetive [sic]. He will prepare the story for me and will let me know when it is ready for shooting. I am working simultaneously on three stories for the Bilderbeilage."[1] These words were written by the twenty-four-year-old press photographer Robert Halmi in 1950, earnestly and in somewhat broken English, to his American boss Yoichi Okamoto, the head of the American press photo service in Austria. At this point in time, the American occupiers, financially the strongest of the four Allies, had already attained a hegemonic position in Austrian hearts and minds with their Marshall Plan aid and American popular culture, for which there was a rapacious appetite. In this context, Reinhold Wagnleitner coined the catchy term "Coca-Colonization".

Allied press photo policy, which has only recently been the subject of scholarly research,[2] seamlessly fits into the narrative of coca-colonization; when it came to visual propaganda in the Austrian print media, the Americans were again ahead of the other occupation authorities, investing in a professional and nationwide press photo service from the outset. Known as the Pictorial Section, this department of the Information Services Branch[3] not only systematically built up a negative archive with photographic material about American themes for distribution in the Austrian press, but also recruited young Austrians as press photographers. The Pictorial Section's team of photographers operated in all the

---

1 Halmi, Robert: Memo to Okamoto, Yoichi, no date [early July 1950?], National Archives and Record Administration, RG 260, Pictorial Section, Box 1, File 6.
2 This chapter is based on the findings of the Austria Science Fund (FWF) research project "War of Pictures. Press Photography in Austria 1945–1955", which the authors conducted under the principal investigator Prof. Friedrich Hausjell at the Department of Communication, University of Vienna, from 2014 to 2017.
3 The Pictorial Section was a department of the Information Services Branch (ISB, from 1950 onwards United States Information Services, USIS), which was responsible for culture and media policy in occupied Austria.

federal provinces, shooting up-to-date photo reportages for wall newspapers, placards, magazines, and above all for the daily newspaper published by the American occupiers, the *Wiener Kurier*. The American photo service also targeted several other Austrian media and institutions, supplying them with photographic material free of charge. For instance, in 1950 the Pictorial Section provided some twenty-five Austrian media and educational institutions with a monthly output of around 5,000 to 6,000 photographic prints.[4]

By comparison, the press photo agencies of the English and French occupation authorities were much smaller with few staff, as were their photographic production and reach. The British information service operated a press photo service headed by Sybil Kerrison, who cooperated closely with the commercial British and international photo agencies in order to place photos in the Austrian illustrated magazines and the daily newspaper *Weltpresse*, the mouthpiece of the British occupation authorities. For local reports, they commissioned Austrian press photographers such as Johann and Fritz Basch, August Makart, and Alfred Marko.

The French photo service was headed by Robert Moisy, a former war reporter and the personal photographer to General Béthouart, but it was disbanded for financial reasons as early as 1947. An examination of French press output in Austria shows that the emphasis was placed on the written word and high culture – that is, reporting on the fields of literature, fine art, and music. The French occupiers evidently thought up-to-date photographic reporting was of less value as a propaganda tool.[5]

Nor did the Soviets succeed in developing an efficient and functional network for distributing press photos in Austria, although they published their own illustrated newspaper, *Welt-Illustrierte*, in Vienna. This structural deficit had a negative impact on Soviet media policy. Whereas the flood of American press photos spread throughout all areas of the Austrian illustrated press market during the occupation era, fostering pro-American sentiment, the photo policy of the three other occupying forces did not make a comparable mark on the domestic media landscape.[6]

---

4 Cf. memo from Yoichi Okamoto to Francis J. Connaughton, Deputy of Chief of Branch, 9 August 1950, in: National Archives and Record Administration (NARA), RG 260, Pictorial Section, Box 2, File 25.

5 Margarethe Szeless: Im Schatten der amerikanischen Bildpolitik, Zur Rolle der Fotografie im britischen und französischen Informationsdienst, in: Alliierte Bildpolitik in Österreich 1945–1955, medien & zeit 1 (2017), 34–51.

6 This assessment is based empirical data from the project "War of Pictures. Press Photography in Austria 1945–1955", collected from five post-war Austrian illustrated publications. Of the 60,000 press photographs collected, some 20,000 appeared without attribution. Of the ca. 40,000 photographs with attribution, some 4,819 are credited to the American photo service, 460 to the Soviet, 338 to the British, and only 90 to the French photo service.

Hence we can already state this much: the American occupation authorities won the pictorial Cold War in occupied Austria. But did this involve open confrontation between the opposing ideologies on the visual level, a kind of Soviet-American exchange of blows? An examination of the photo editorial offices of the two leading visual media, the Soviet *Welt-Illustrierte* and the weekly photo supplement of the American *Wiener Kurier*, reveals the themes and propagandistic accents with which the Cold War was fought in Austria via the medium of press photography.

"The editors have followed the instructions" – Soviet photographic propaganda in the *Welt-Illustrierte*

The weekly newspaper *Welt-Illustrierte* first appeared on 1 September 1946, with a circulation of 80,000, and was run in conjunction with the editorial team of the *Österreichische Zeitung*, the official organ of the Soviet occupation authorities.[7] The editors-in-chief were Josef Lazak, who spoke excellent German, and his deputy, Major Musatov. The press handbook for 1947 lists Walter Staudacher and A. Chasanowitsch as the editors. Overall, seven people were employed at the *Welt-Illustrierte*. In subsequent years, the circulation fluctuated considerably, reaching its zenith of 127,000 copies in September 1947 but dropping to 22,000 in 1949 and 42,000 in 1954. Outside the Soviet Zone, a mere 2,500 copies were distributed. Compared with the weekly photo supplements accompanying the American occupation authorities' *Wiener Kurier*, which had a circulation fluctuating between 150,000 and 300,000 during the decade of occupation, the *Welt-Illustrierte* had far less reach.

The main aims of the *Welt-Illustrierte* were spreading propaganda about the USSR, promoting socialism and its achievements, and launching counterpropaganda, particularly with respect to what editor-in-chief Josef Lazak bemoaned in 1948 as the "Marshallization of Austria".[8]

Opinions were divided concerning the success of the propaganda directives. For instance, in his assessment of the Soviet illustrated magazine in 1949, Major

---

7 The observations on Soviet photo policy in this chapter are based on our research findings; cf. Marion Krammer: Sowjetunion im Bild. Die sowjetische Medien- und Bildpropaganda in Österreich 1945–1955, in: medien & zeit 1 (2017), 52–68 and Marion Krammer, Margarethe Szeless: Occupied Images. Photojournalism and Visual Propaganda in Austria 1945–1955, in: Waldemar Zacharasiewicz, Siegfried Beer (eds.): Cultural Politics, Transfer & Propaganda. Mediated Narratives and Images in Austrian-American Relations, Vienna 2021, 295–326.
8 Josef Lazak: Bericht über die Arbeit der Zeitung der Sowjetarmee für die Bevölkerung Österreichs im 4. Quartal 1948, Foreign Policy Archive of the Russian Federation 451/12/253/3, 72–103.

Komarov not only criticized its ideological flakiness and the lack of Austrian topics, but also explicitly took issue with its "bourgeois" design, such as the apolitical title pages and reporting on stars. In Komarov's eyes, the *Welt-Illustrierte* did not display any distance to the bourgeois press. However, an altogether different assessment was voiced by the Austrian journalist August Beranek[9] in a review of the newspaper: Beranek observed that communist readers did not think the *Welt-Illustrierte* was clear enough in taking a progressive stance, while indifferent bourgeois Austrians considered it politically tendentious propaganda.

Moreover, the *Welt-Illustrierte* could not compete when it came to publishing press photos. When the Russian politician and close colleague of Stalin's Andrei Aleksandrovich Zhdanov died in the late August of 1948, the *Welt-Illustrierte* was the only illustrated publication in Vienna not to provide a photo. The others received photos via foreign photo agencies. Editor-in-chief Josef Lazak lamented in this connection that "[when] current photos reach us, it's with great delay and it no longer makes sense to publish them in the Welt-Illustrierte".[10]

Lazak's complaint is symptomatic; the *Welt-Illustrierte* constantly suffered from a shortage of recent and high-quality pictorial material from the Soviet Union, and there was no Soviet photo service in Austria. Judging by the Soviet themes depicted, most of the photographic material that appeared in the *Welt-Illustrierte* without a photographer's name probably came from the TASS news agency, which had an office in Vienna's Kärntnerstrasse from September 1945 onwards. Between 1946 and 1948, however, the Vienna office did not have a single photo correspondent; around 1950/51, O. Grigorev may have been active as TASS's photo correspondent in Austria. However, the majority of the photos credited to TASS surely came from the Moscow headquarters.

By far the larger part of the photographs *Welt-Illustrierte* credited to an individual were taken by the Austrian press photographer Franz Fremuth, followed by the Sovinformburo. The Sovinformburo, founded in 1941, was the most important channel for disseminating propaganda abroad. In 1950, this organization provided some thirty-six countries with written and pictorial materials and maintained official and unofficial offices in twenty countries, but not in Austria, although the Soviet propaganda department in Austria frequently complained about the Moscow Sovinformburo's uneconomical distribution channels.

In summary, the *Welt-Illustrierte*'s low popularity and lack of impact was due to the following factors: the delayed delivery of high-quality and up-to-date photographic material from the Soviet Union, the scant thematic relevance to

---

9 August Beranek was the last representative of Vienna-based Internationaler Psychoanalytischer Verlag, which was disbanded by the National Socialists in 1938. Beranek later ran the Deutscher Verlag der Wissenschaften, founded in the GDR in 1954.
10 Josef Lazak: Bericht über die Österreichische-Zeitung für Juni-September 1948, 5 October 1948, Foreign Policy Archive of the Russian Federation 451/11a/225/37, 116–119.

Austria, and its operating exclusively in the Soviet Zone. In general, the paper's failure can also be seen as a result of the flawed concept of Soviet media and propaganda policy in Austria. Despite a lack of success and repeated criticism, the Soviet occupation authorities continued to adhere to the adoption of Soviet propaganda concepts and materials. The Soviet authorities' visual propaganda thereby differs diametrically from that of its great "enemy" and competitor, the USA. The latter viewed a focus on Austrian themes and strengthening Austrian photo journalism as an effective means of positive self-presentation.

"We do not ridicule the Russians directly" – American Visual Propaganda Policy at the *Wiener Kurier*

Especially in comparison with the largely insignificant Soviet photo policy, American visual propaganda's recipe for success is most evident: unlike the other occupation authorities, the USA had a much bigger budget at its disposal and invested in the development of a photo archive and local photo service from the outset. Additionally, the American press photographer Yoichi Okamoto's[11] longstanding work as head of the American photo service proved both highly successful and consequential: under his aegis, nineteen young Austrian press photographers were employed and trained by Okamoto himself, learning the reportage style of the successful American magazine *Life*.[12] His work as photo editor led to the professionalization of the Austrian press photo culture, and at the same time the weekly photo supplement he ran, *Bilderbeilage des Wiener Kurier*, became a valuable mouthpiece of America's cultural mission. Yoichi Okamoto was a conscientious, committed, and decidedly confident occupation official who had recognized that permanent reporting on American achievements and the Marshall Plan led to a certain saturation and hence negative feelings on the part of the Austrian population. He thus deliberately laced the pages of the *Bilderbeilage* with photographic material offering pure entertainment or aesthetic and optical appeal.

---

11 Yoichi Okamoto (1915, Yonkers–1985, Washington) served as personal photographer to General Mark Clark, supreme commander of the US armed forces in Austria. After returning to the USA in 1954, he became head of the department for visual materials at the United States Information Agency (USIA) in Washington. In 1963, he became the White House's first photographer under President Lyndon B. Johnson. For detailed biographical details, see Hans Petschar: Der Mann, der Geschichte in Bildern schrieb. Wer war Yoichi Okamoto? in: Marlies Dornig, Hans Petschar (eds.): Bild. Macht. Politik. Yoichi Okamoto. Ikone der Nachkriegsfotografie (Ausstellungskatalog Österreichische Nationalbibliothek), Vienna 2023, 25–62.

12 Cf. Marion Krammer, Margarethe Szeless: Fotograf, Bildredakteur, Besatzungsbeamter. Yoichi Okamotos Einfluss auf die österreichische Pressebildkultur, in: Marlies Dornig, Hans Petschar (eds.), 2023, 85–97.

Fig. 1: The photo editing team at *Wiener Kurier*. Yoichi Okamoto and staff in a meeting, 1952 (photo: Hans Nagl, ANL/Vienna, US 10.087/9)

Regarding the Cold War, Okamoto neatly sums up the stance taken by US propaganda policy's approach to communism: "We do not ridicule the Russians directly, however we will push something like the Berlin airlift to the maximum."[13] The media campaign surrounding the Berlin airlift in June 1948 was an unparalleled success for American propaganda and a milestone in the ideological battle against communism.[14] In the context of the Cold War, then, US propaganda policy in Austria banked not on direct attacks but on pro-Western narratives, events, and symbols in order to strengthen their own position. Agitatory visual counter-propaganda was explicitly eschewed in the *Wiener Kurier*.

Similarly to the photo media success story of the "Berlin airlift", as photo editor Okamoto succeeded in conveying a thoroughly pro-American perspective

---

13 Yoichi Okamoto: Bericht über die Tätigkeitsbereiche der Pictorial Section, no year [November 1949?], NARA, RG 260, Pictorial Section, Box 2, File 20.

14 On the media campaign surrounding the "Berlin airlift" in the German illustrated press, see Sigrid Betscher: Von großen Brüdern und falschen Freunden. Visuelle Kalte-Kriegs-Diskurse in deutschen Nachkriegsillustrierten, Essen 2013, 305–383. The photograph of West Berliners waiting on a pile of rubble as an American "raisin bomber" comes to their rescue overhead, attributed to Henry Ries, became the main iconic image of the "Berlin airlift" and a significant pro-Western symbol during the Cold War.

in extremely subtle fashion through his choice of topics and narratives. In October 1953, the *Wiener Kurier* published extensive illustrated reports on the politically explosive subject of prisoners of war returning from Russian captivity, which fed the Austrian population's anti-Soviet resentment. For their series of photographs of the returning POWs, Jeff Rainer and Franz Kraus, staff at the Pictorial Section, received recognition in the form of the American Christopher Award for International Understanding – presumably at the instigation of Okamoto. Their pictures were subsequently published in American magazines; the subject of returning POWs thus received new publicity and the implicit indictment of the Soviets reaching an even wider audience.[15] It was not least this type of photo policy with which Yoichi Okamoto tapped the full propagandistic added value of press photos in the service of the American occupation authorities. An open East–West confrontation via visual propaganda was avoided in both the *Wiener Kurier*'s photo supplement and the Soviets' *Welt-Illustrierte*. That is certainly not to say that there was no agitatory visual propaganda in occupied Austria, but it took place in much more fleeting presentations in the public sphere and not in the pages of illustrated magazines.

"Pavement propaganda" – the Cold War in Public Spaces

Unlike in the illustrated press, public spaces saw an intensive ideological battle, a kind of Soviet–American sparring, at least from time to time. The wall newspaper display cases holding the Soviet *Welt-Illustrierte* and the American *Wiener Kurier* were regularly papered over or daubed with hostile slogans. In the city, the slogan "Ami go home" was repeatedly on display, often next to placards advertising Marshall Plan aid.[16]

In contrast, the windows of the American Information Center in Vienna were a central scene for anti-communist propaganda. Here, the Americans allowed themselves blatant attacks on communism in words and pictures. In particular, a window display in 1953 attracted plenty of attention, even making headlines in the American magazine *Life*'s issue of 23 November 1953: "Speaking of Pic-

---

15 Cf. Marion Krammer, Margarethe Szeless: The Cold War of Pictures: Framing Returning Prisoners of War in Austria's Illustrated Press, in: History of Photography 42:4 (2018), 376–391.
16 Pictorial testimonies on political agitation in public spaces have survived in the archive of the American photo service, with photographs of Soviet military facilities, anti-communist demonstrations in Vienna, and life in the Soviet Zone. These images were taken in order to keep the enemy under observation and were not intended for publication. Hence all these pictures are marked in the archive with the code NFR (not for release). Cf. "War of Pictures" (https://warofpictures.univie.ac.at/kalter_krieg), online exhibition, curated by Marion Krammer and Margarethe Szeless.

Fig. 2: Communist and anti-American slogan: banner in front of the Karlskirche: "Ami go home! Es lebe ein unabhängiges Österreich" (Americans go home! Long live an independent Austria), 1952 (ANL/Vienna, US 24.082)

tures... American Babes in Vienna woods annoy Russian Bear". The Vienna display showed photographs of two babies pulling exaggerated faces, originally taken by the American photographer Constance Bannister for an advertising campaign. For the Vienna display, captions ridiculing communism were placed under the babies. One caption, next a baby peering wide-eyed from under a bed sheet, read, "Have the secret police gone?". Another baby has its face in its hand and is rolling its eyes, the caption reading "Not another demonstration!" The principle of this combination of text and image is as simple as it is ingenious in propaganda terms: the cute baby photos are transformed into biting satire.

The Soviet side, on the other hand, agitated in the urban space via what was known as pavement propaganda. For instance, Vienna's squares featured displays with bright and striking collages attacking the capitalist system. Screens in the Resselpark from 1952, for example, show collages, statistics, and political slogans regarding the Korean War; their graphic design draws on the long tradition of agitprop in the Soviet Union.

In summary, concerning the pictorial battle in Austria in the context of the Cold War it can be established that both the Soviet and the American occupation authorities strove to propagate a positive image of their political systems and world views in their respective illustrated press publications, in words and pictures. Openly agitatory counter-propaganda did not play a role in either the *Wiener Kurier* or the *Welt-Illustrierte*. In contrast, in public spaces Soviet–American sparring may occasionally have taken place. While ideologically provocative pictorial material was avoided in print media, both sides used temporary installations such as window displays and mobile screens on pavements to advance an unsparing and polarizing visual Cold War rhetoric.

Wolfgang Pensold

Radio between the Zones

In the final days of the war, the former director general of RAVAG, Oskar Czeija, went about reviving the Vienna broadcaster.[1] Despite bomb damage to the broadcasting house and the fact that the transmitters on the Bisamberg hill were no longer operational, having been blown up by the withdrawing SS,[2] on the evening of 29 April a first broadcast was made via a makeshift station. The subject matter was the symbolic act of state represented by the creation of a provisional government under Karl Renner.[3] The audience was only small, however; the station did not have sufficient range and the population did not have radios that worked.

Czeija's efforts were curtailed, incidentally, by his dismissal from his post in November 1945, after the Communist newspaper *Volksstimme* expressed the suspicion he had been a candidate for membership of the NSDAP years earlier, which he denied – in vain.[4]

Separate radio stations nevertheless emerged in the federal provinces. An engineer by the name of Otto Schubert prevented the Vorarlberg transmitter from being blown up, henceforth running it himself. The programme began on 2 May 1945 with Schubert's words: "Here is Austrian radio, Sender Vorarlberg in Dornbirn."[5] The meeting hall of the Dorbirn town hall was repurposed as a concert hall.[6]

In Aldrans, in the Innsbruck district, members of a resistance group improvised a makeshift radio station in a cellar bar after a bomb hit the regular studio facilities in an Innsbruck high-rise. They announced the capitulation of

---

1 Cf. Reinhard Schlögl: Oskar Czeija. Radio- und Fernsehpionier, Unternehmer, Abenteurer, Vienna/Cologne/Weimar 2005, 144.
2 Radio Wien, Sonderheft, 1949, 12.
3 Radio Wien, 1 June 1946, 46.
4 Cf. Wolfgang Pensold: Zur Geschichte des Rundfunks in Österreich. Programm für die Nation, Wiesbaden 2018, 98.
5 Cit. Viktor Ergert: Die Geschichte des Österreichischen Rundfunks, Vol. II, n.d., 15.
6 Funk und Film, 3 May 1946, 6.

the Wehrmacht and the abolition of the greeting "Heil Hitler", calling on the population to raise red, white, and red flags.[7]

Soon afterwards, the stations in Dornbirn and Innsbruck came under the control of the advancing French occupying forces; together, they formed the Sendergruppe West (Broadcasting Group West), which developed its programme independently of Vienna. In the months that followed, the Vorarlberg station enjoyed the support of a remote teletypewriter of the French army, which provided the latest news from Paris. The news service of the Schweizer Depeschen Agentur was regularly collected from the border crossing with Switzerland. Hence the station had good knowledge of international developments but knew hardly anything about events in the rest of Austria.[8]

In the south of Austria, on 8 May a new-era radio station began broadcasting from a tunnel under Klagenfurt's local Kreuzberg mountain after Gauleiter Rainer had announced his resignation by radio. The station now declared, "This is the free Kärtner Landessender Klagenfurt [Carinthian Provincial Broadcaster] speaking."[9] It then came under the control of the British occupation authorities.

In Graz, Gauleiter Uiberreither also resigned via radio on 8 May. The next day, from the Österreichische Freiheitssender Graz[10] (Austrian Liberty Broadcaster Graz) announced itself from the Ferry-Schlössl (Ferry villa) while the Styrian provincial capital was occupied by the Red Army. After three months of Soviet control, the Styrian radio facilities came under British jurisdiction after the shift in the demarcation line in the summer of 1945. The Sendergruppe Alpenland (Alpine Land Broadcasting Group) emerged in Carinthia and Styria. In Graz, the station had a broadcasting house together with the strong Dobl transmitter, which the National Socialist regime had had built in order to broadcast propaganda to Southeastern Europe.

In the north of the country, on 6 June 1945 the Sender Gruppe Rot-Weiss-Rot (Red, White, and Red Broadcasting Group) was launched from the attic of the Salzburg Landestheater (Provincial Theatre). The group was soon supported by a branch in the Landhaus (provincial headquarters) in Linz, and later by another in Vienna's Seidengasse.[11] This last had become necessary after many renowned Austrian cultural figures who had withdrawn to Salzburg after the war gradually returned to Vienna. The aim was to ensure they worked for Rot-Weiss-Rot and not for the Soviet-controlled Radio Wien. Ernst Haeusserman, the former sec-

---

7 Cf. Ergert, Vol. II, 17–18; Funk und Film, 16 August 1946, 6.
8 Cf. Ergert, Vol. II, 81–82.
9 Cit. ibid., 22.
10 Cit. ibid., 24.
11 Funk und Film, 6 June 1947, 15; Funk und Film, 4 June 1948, 3; cf. Ergert, Vol. II, 11–12.

retary of Max Reinhardt, who had had to leave Austria and had returned as an American officer, took over management of the group's programming.[12]

A big problem facing all the stations was the acute shortage of records; appeals went out to the population to donate their own.

The Soviets were the only occupation authorities not to run their own radio station. They were happy with their censorship of Radio Wien and the creation of programmes billed as *Russische Stunde* (Russian Hour).[13] These broadcasts were intended to correct the distorted image of the Soviet Union fascism had spent many years drawing and to make listeners acquainted with "the real Russia".[14] But of course the programmes, devised by qualified Communists, also pursued the aim of beating the propaganda drum for the Soviet Union.

In order to bring radio under its own control, the concentrated government constituted by the Austrian People's Party (Österreichische Volkspartei, ÖVP), the Socialist Party of Austria (Sozialistische Partei Österreichs, SPÖ), and the Communist Party of Austria (Kommunistische Partei Österreichs, KPÖ) following the first elections in late 1945 first re-established a Radio Council (Radiobeirat).[15] This panel, comprising representatives of the three parties, was tasked with advising on all important staffing, economic, financial, and technical measures and to control the administration and funding of Radio Wien. In order to reorganize the news department, a staff of journalists were recruited, itself close to the three governing parties.[16] Radio Wien regained its role as a mouthpiece of the government, this time one that had been democratically elected. Federal Chancellor Leopold Figl was of the opinion that the station should offer representatives of the parties the opportunity to take a position on issues of the day and broadcast compilations of recent contributions from the party newspapers.[17]

The government also attempted to bring together again Austrian radio transmitters and studios, which were spread through all the occupation zones. The Public Administration of Austrian Radio (Öffentliche Verwaltung des österreichischen Rundspruchwesens) with its headquarters at the Vienna broadcasting house was responsible only for the territory of the Soviet Zone in the east

---

12 Cf. Ergert, Vol. II, 124.
13 Cf. Ernst Glaser: Die "Russische Stunde" in Radio Wien (1945–1955). Ein Beitrag zum Problem der sowjetischen Medienpräsenz in Österreich, Wiener Geschichtsblätter 46/1, Vienna 1991, 3–4; Funk und Film, 11 April 1947, 2.
14 Radio Wien, 27 April 1946, 6.
15 Radio Wien, Festschrift 1949, 32.
16 Ergert, Vol. II, 116.
17 Radio Wien, 26 April 1947, 3.

Fig. 1: Press cutting on the *Russische Stunde*, Radio Wien, 17 August 1946, 9 (ANNO, ANL/Vienna)

of Austria.[18] In the other federal provinces, the broadcasting groups worked independently of the respective occupation authorities. A request to the latter to return the radio facilities in the federal provinces to Vienna was not fulfilled, however. The Americans feared that this would enable the Soviets to control all radio stations in Austria.[19] With the outbreak of the Cold War, the front between East and West ran through the country. For the time being, Radio Wien remained an eastern Austrian local broadcaster under the control of Soviet censorship.

It was no coincidence that the programme was oriented around the old RAVAG, many of those responsible having worked in the same role under the corporate state. The station played serious music from operas and concert halls, entertainment music by the radio's orchestra and the Symphonisches Jazzorchester, but also popular folksongs, cabaret, and *Heimatlieder* (homeland songs), and it also broadcast adaptations of plays and radio plays, series of readings of Austrian poetry, and literary programmes. Church choirs were also represented as part of church services. *Radiohochschule* (Radio University) broadcast lectures by scholars, but there were also programmes aimed at workers, *Arbeiterfunk*, and schoolchildren, *Schulfunk*. And, as earlier, there were also news broadcasts supporting the government: *Echo des Tages* (Echo of the Day) delivered interviews, reports, and reportages on contemporary events.[20] A central task of this somewhat conservative programme was cultivating a national identity; especially those young people who had had an Austrian consciousness beaten out of them during the National Socialist years were to be reacquainted with the homeland and given the experience of a common fatherland despite living under occupation.[21]

Radio Wien's strong orientation towards the educated citizen did not go down too well with audiences, even if an attempt was made to offer more "relaxing programmes" with the introduction of a second station, Wien II.[22] Radio Wien was said to cling to the idea that it had to provide the nation with high-quality programming. A modern radio station, however, had to be popular in character and offer its listeners entertainment, up-to-date programmes, and relaxation, as Rot-Weiss-Rot did.[23]

Indeed, the Rot-Weiss-Rot broadcasting group's programming stood in strong contrast with Radio Wien. It offered variety and entertainment, tailored to

---

18 40 Jahre Rundfunk in Österreich, ed. by Österreichischen Rundfunk, Vienna 1964, n.p.; cf. Norbert P. Feldinger: Nachkriegsrundfunk in Österreich: zwischen Föderalismus und Zentralismus von 1945 bis 1957, Munich et al. 1990, 60.
19 Radio-Woche 50/1949, 2.
20 Rudolf Henz: Österreichischer Rundfunk Jahresbericht 1952, Vienna, 62–64.
21 Radio Wien, 8 May 1948, 1.
22 Funk und Film, 27 September 1946, 4.
23 Österreichische Radioschau, 14 July 1955, 181.

the needs of its listeners. Hence accusations of triviality were levelled at it from some quarters. A regular feature was performances by a radio orchestra conducted by Alois Melichar, and there were cabaret shows in the *Brettl* variety tradition; writers included Hans Weigel, and Gerhard Bronner was one of the pianists. The *Schlager* singer Rudi Kamperski also became an audience favourite. *Wer ist wer und was ist wo?* (Who's Who and What's Where?) was the title of a quiz show in which listeners could win prizes. The series *Hörer senden für Hörer* (Listeners for Listeners) also offered them the opportunity to make their own show. There was also a fifteen-minute daily current affairs programme, *Spiegel der Zeit* (Mirror of Time).[24] The series *Wir sind der Meinung...das RWR-Radioparlament*[25] (We're of the Opinion ... the RWR Radio Parliament) offered expert discussion of current affairs. Undoubtedly, the Rot-Weiss-Rot broadcasting group also provided important impetus for the democratization of its audience.

Furthermore, Rot-Weiss-Rot advanced the modernization of radio after the American model, with news bulletins at the top of every hour and precise timings of programme segments. Regular series with well-thought-out titles let audiences know what was on when. Programmes were advertised, and there was also commercial radio advertising. Radio scripts, written by in-house staff, replaced the writing contracts previously awarded to freelance writers, and the radio director took on greater importance; Rot-Weiss-Rot signposted the future of radio.

In the summer of 1946, the first audience survey was held in the American Zone. A quarter of a million questionnaires were distributed, asking "Which broadcaster are you best off listening to?" but also "Which programmes do you like listening to most?" The findings were clear: the overwhelming majority of respondents preferred dance music, light entertainment, and news.[26] It was a vote for the modern American concept of radio.

Music proved most effective. The youth in particular enthusiastically listened to American swing, which had been frowned upon by their parents' and grandparents' generations.[27] Such sounds were primarily on offer from the British and American army stations. In the form of the Blue Danube Network Radio Station WOFA, the Americans ran a station in Vienna fulfilling the musical requests of their soldiers stationed in the city. From 7 a.m. to 1 p.m., music was played at the request of GIs.[28] The programme usually came from the station's

---

24 Funk und Film, 4 June 1948, 3.
25 Funk und Film, 9 December 1949, 2.
26 Cf. Ergert, Vol. II, 125, 132–133.
27 Helga Maria Wolf (ed.): Auf Ätherwellen. Persönliche Radiogeschichte(n), Vienna/Cologne/Weimar 2004, 169.
28 Funk und Film, 8 November 1946, 3.

extensive record archive. The British ran their own Army Broadcasting Service on the Welle 345 frequency as a branch of their main station in Graz. Here too, the programme was based on an extensive record archive.[29] Apart from the soldiers of the two occupying forces, its audience included many Austrian adolescents who loved the new, English-language pop music.

Vienna was a little radio paradise in these years. Listeners could choose between the two Radio Wien channels, the offerings of Rot-Weiss-Rot and the Sendergruppe Alpenland, or the military stations. It was a taste of radio's distant future, which would be characterized by an ever wider selection of programmes.

In late 1949, the programme guide *Funk und Film* (Radio and Film) conducted another survey. In the end, more than 18,000 listeners filled in the questionnaires and sent them to the editors, making one thing clear: by far the most popular programming was that of Rot-Weiss-Rot, which received some 61 per cent of votes, compared to just 17 for Radio Wien, 16 for Sendergruppe Alpenland, and 5 for Sendergruppe West. The most popular programmes turned out to be evening variety shows (*Bunte Abende*) and cabaret. Second was dancing, entertainment, and "farmer's" music, followed by theatre, operetta, and opera performances. A few per cent were keen on radio reportages, interviews, and talks. Concerts, symphonic and literary programmes fared poorly.

In general, listeners wanted programmes to begin earlier in the morning so that those who left home early also had something to listen to. There was a desire for more entertainment programmes in the evening. Respondents also called for better coordination between the broadcasters so that they could change channels and listen to entertaining music all day. And they wanted the stations to do away with pauses in broadcasting during the day and significantly lengthen broadcasting hours on Saturdays and Sundays.[30]

Behind this survey, we can recognize the old conflict between a discerning educational programme and light entertainment. As the public administrator of Austrian Radio (Öffentlicher Verwalter des österreichischen Rundspruchwesens), ÖVP member Siegmund Guggenberger demanded that radio should not give in to the listeners' demand for an "easy cultural commodity" that "serves only to entertain and relax"; rather, those responsible for programming had to be aware of their cultural mission and know how to "raise [listeners] onto a higher intellectual plane".[31] Director of programming Rudolf Henz, who had occupied this role in the fascist corporate state, adopted the same stance, rejecting claims that most listeners merely sought diversion: in an "old country of culture"[32] like

---

29 Funk und Film, 22 November 1946, 3.
30 Funk und Film, 16 December 1949, supplement, 1.
31 Cit. Radio Wien, 11 March 1950, 3.
32 Cit. Radio Wien, 14 January 1950, 5.

Fig. 2: Radio broadcaster Rot-Weiss-Rot's recording van with three members of staff at Palais Auersperg, ca. 1945–1955 (copyright unknown, Wien Museum, inv. no. 224813)

Austria, there was room for *Hörbühne* (Audio Stage) as well as the variety show *Bunter Abend* (Colourful Evening) and the scholarly report as well as dance music. He stood by his credo that "High art will again be part of our programmes. We owe that to Vienna and Austria."[33] He rejected modern influence from abroad: a lot of what other Austrian stations praised as progress was nothing more than a transient fashion. He described contemporary American music as mere "howling and droning".[34]

The programme was also characterized, of course, by the emergent Cold War. The Soviet occupation authorities controlled Radio Wien's programming, and hence it was publicly perceived to be a Russian propaganda station.

The autumn of 1950 proved to be the acid test. In response to the Fourth Wage–Price Agreement, the Communist Party called for a general strike. Adolf Schärf suspected that this was a plan to take over first the trade union and then the government and turn Austria into a people's democracy after the Eastern European model. Public Administrator Guggenberger was urged to broadcast the calls to strike on Radio Wien, which he initially refused to do. However, when the Soviet occupation authorities pressed him, after consulting the government he

---

33 Cit. Radio Wien, 7 October 1950, 3.
34 Cit. Ergert, Vol. II, 132.

decided to broadcast the controversial announcements of the strike committee, albeit followed directly by announcements by the Federation of Trade Unions (Gewerkschaftsbund) and the government. Radio Wien nevertheless came under suspicion. Some newspapers ran with the headlines "Don't believe RAVAG" and "Anyone who wants to listen to the news, switch over to the stations Rot-Weiss-Rot and Alpenland".[35] The fact that the *Russische Stunde* programmes had been extended to sixteen hours a week compounded Radio Wien's poor reputation at this time.[36]

However, in some circumstances, the American occupiers also relied on censorship to suppress undesirable content, and they too of course produced propaganda to advance their own ends. Rot-Weiss-Rot propagated praise for the "American way of life", characterized by a democratic political system, the promise of prosperity, and popular culture,[37] in contrast to Soviet communism, portrayed as a threat.[38] Series such as *Amerika ruft Österreich* (American Calls Austria), *Amerika hilft Österreich* (America Helps Austria), *Das ist Amerika* (This is America), *Amerika in Wort und Ton* (America in Words and Sounds), or *Die Stimme Amerikas* (The Voice of America) were clearly tendentious productions.[39]

American cultural work's task was to suppress the spirit of National Socialism, fight communism, paint a positive image of the United States, and create pathways for flooding the country with American assets.[40] With the outbreak of the Cold War, however, the anti-communist mission was increasingly privileged over denazification, Austria serving as a bridgehead to behind the Iron Curtain – and this also applied to radio. Rot-Weiss-Rot often broadcast also in Hungarian, Serbo-Croat, Czech, and Slovak.[41]

The Cold War also raged in the ether. Investments were made in radio technology in order to improve sound quality, but also to increase range. In the Upper Austrian capital Linz, for instance, the American occupation authorities opened a new studio for their broadcasting group in 1950, consisting of three broadcasting rooms, a large studio for musical performances, a smaller one for radio plays, and an announcer's studio, each with its own control room. Another large

---

35 Cit. Ergert, Vol. II, 149–150.
36 Ergert, Vol. II; 153.
37 Reinhold Wagnleitner: Radio und Kalter Krieg. Die US-Radiopolitik und die Entwicklung des Österreichischen Rundfunks zur Zeit der alliierten Besatzung 1945–1955; in: Theo Mäusli (ed.): Schallwellen. Zur Sozialgeschichte des Radios, Zurich 1996, 182.
38 Thaddäus Podgorski: Die grosse Illusion. Erinnerungen an 50 Jahre mit dem Fernsehen, Vienna 2005, 19.
39 Wagnleitner: Radio und Kalter Krieg, 188.
40 Ibid., 183.
41 Ibid., 185.

room was in preparation for performances by large orchestras. Next door there were tech rooms with the latest American equipment.

In Kronstorf, right on the border with Soviet-occupied Lower Austria, the Americans set up a modern Westinghouse transmitter, which went live on 1 March 1952, with the aim of flooding the Soviet-occupied part of Austria with American-inspired radio programmes. At 274 metres, the tower was the tallest of its kind in Western Europe. There were another two 137-metre towers – as high as Vienna's St. Stephen's Cathedral.[42]

The project came in for strong criticism in the Communist newspaper *Österreichische Zeitung:* the new "agitation broadcaster" served to "further increase the agitation against the people's democratic states that has hitherto been practised by the Rot-Weiss-Rot station. The entire Kronstorf transmitter is thus nothing other than a component of the American preparations for war on Austrian soil",[43] intended to direct the propagandistic voice of American against the Soviet Union and the people's democracies "directly from the demarcation line".[44]

The subordination of the broadcasting groups to Radio Wien was thus a slow process. On 1 September 1953, the Allies lifted the ban on VHF radio,[45] allowing the Austrian government to finally begin to establish a programme for Austria as a whole. A few days later, VHF transmitters went operational on Vienna's Kahlenberg hill and in Klagenfurt. For the first time, the announcement rang out: "This is Radio Österreich!"[46] In this spirit, the official radio magazine *Radio Wien* also changed its title to *Radio Österreich*.[47]

One could not speak of nationwide reception; a large part of the population – especially in the poorly served areas of western Austria – remained out of reach.[48] But the *Radio Wien* magazine announced that broadcasts would soon also be transmitted regularly from Salzburg, Linz, and Graz, as well as from Innsbruck and Bregenz.[49] Another barrier to uniform nationwide radio programming was the fact that the VHF transmitters that had been built were not yet connected by radio link. To enable nationwide broadcasting nevertheless, head of programming Henz devised the following system: he had the Vienna programmes taped and driven around the federal provinces in a weekly cycle.[50] Passed from studio to

---

42 http://www.wabweb.net/radio/radio_a/radio_a3d.htm (20 September 2024).
43 Österreichische Zeitung, 9 September 1951, 2.
44 Österreichische Zeitung, 30 December 1951, 2.
45 E und M. Elektrotechnik und Maschinenbau,11: 25 Jahre Fernsehen in Österreich, 457.
46 Ergert, Vol. II, 181.
47 Ibid.., 182.
48 Radiotechnik 4/April 1953, 115.
49 Radio Wien, 5 September 1953, 3.
50 Das Elektron 9/1953, 262.

studio, they were broadcast by one individual station after another.[51] Hence everyone received the same selection of programmes, albeit not at the same time.

However, since the public was not particularly enthused with this solution, Henz explained to listeners this "provisionally somewhat complicated rotation business". He defended the content of his programming; it provided the best that could be offered "in words and music, in relaxation, merriment, and high enjoyment of art, in recitation and performance".[52] Given the circumstances, he argued, it was naturally impossible to expect up-to-date news broadcasts.

Another reason the new VHF offering, entitled Radio Österreich, was far from reaching all Austrians was that there was a shortage both of transmitters and the modern, expensive receivers required for the higher-quality VHF broadcasts. In order reconcile listeners with the idea of expensive acquisitions, Austrian radio promised that in the future, it would offer programmes that were "not merely new" but also "free from interference".[53] A radio broadcast "going under in the chaos of the European airwaves or being ruined by thunderstorms and electric equipment"[54] would be a thing of the past.

In the meantime, the end of occupation was on the horizon and Österreichischer Rundfunk (Austrian Radio) was finally able to return. In early 1954, the British occupation authorities transferred Sendergruppe Alpenland to Österreichischer Rundfunk. Soon afterwards, the Americans followed the British example and transferred the transmitters in Salzburg and Linz. While the French occupation authorities had already transferred Sendergruppe West's transmitters to the provincial governments, the latter wanted to continue running its radio stations by itself. The dispute was taken to the Constitutional Court,[55] which ultimately rejected the group's proposal. Radio was confirmed as federal business in terms of both technology and programming, and hence the Tyrolean and Vorarlberg radio transmitters also went over to Österreichischer Rundfunk.[56]

A few weeks after the State Treaty was signed, on 27 July 1955 the Rot-Weiss-Rot station also ended its broadcasts in Vienna. The same day, Radio Wien put an end to its *Russische Stunde*. In the ether too, the occupiers' era was now over.[57]

---

51 Radio Österreich, 12 September 1953, 6.
52 Ibid., 7.
53 Radio Wien, 5 September 1953, 2.
54 Radio Wien, 12 September 1953, 6.
55 Ergert, Vol. II, 195–198.
56 Ibid., 206.
57 Cf. Christine Ehardt: Radiobilder. Eine Kulturgeschichte des Radios in Österreich, Göttingen 2020, 138.

Karin Moser

Allied Film Policy between Cooperation, Control, Enlightenment, and Self-interest

At the end of the Second World War, the Allied troops sought to bring everything under their control as quickly as possible for purposes of "re-education" or "reorientation" and propagating their own value and social systems. Film, as a modern medium for entertaining and steering the masses, formed part of an extensive information, cultural, and propaganda policy. At the beginning of this era of Allied control, they initially occupied all the film production companies and studios; in parallel to this, the cinemas were closed, and all copies of German and Austrian films were withdrawn. From July1945, cinemas gradually reopened, and German-language films approved by the Allies could be shown.[1] Ultimately, each power had control over its own film business. The Americans owned the Sievering Filmatelier and the Film-Zentralbüro (Central Film Office) in Siebensterngasse. The Soviets had the Rosenhügelstudios and the local copying facilities. The British confiscated the Schönbrunn-Atelier, and the French ran the film repository and archive in Penzing.[2]

Cooperation and Opposition

In the early days of occupation, the Allied Powers had shared propaganda aims in at least two closely connected areas: firstly, National Socialism, its aims and impact, were to be publicly condemned and combated, and secondly, separation from Germany and reorientation towards an independent Austrian state had to be anchored in the Austrian conscious. To this end, a first step in the field

---

[1] Barbara Porpaczy: Kultur- und Propagandapolitik der französischen Besatzungsmacht, in: Karin Moser (ed.): Besetzte Bilder. Film, Kultur und Propaganda in Österreich 1945–1955, Vienna 2005, 133–154, here: 142. Ulrike Halbritter: Der Einfluss der alliierten Besatzungsmächte auf die österreichische Filmwirtschaft und Spielfilmproduktion in den Jahren 1945 bis 1955. Diplomarbeit, University of Vienna 1993, 124.
[2] Karin Moser: Propaganda und Gegenpropaganda. Das "kalte" Wechselspiel während der alliierten Besatzung in Österreich, in: medien & zeit 17 (2002) 1, 27–42, here: 28.

of cinema and film was securing, confiscating, and holding fascist films. The film commissioners of all four powers compiled lists of productions that were to be banned or destroyed. In February 1947, the Allied film sections stored the confiscated tapes in the film bunker at the Rosenhügelstudios in Vienna's 13th District.[3]

On the level of film, from 1945 to 1947 the Allies also used documentaries about the concentration camps in order to openly confront the Austrian population with the crimes committed during the National Socialist era. These "atrocity pictures", such as *Les camps de la mort/Lager des Grauens* (French: Camps of Death/German: Camps of Horror, F 1945), *Osvencim/Auschwitz* (USSR 1945), or *Death Mills/Die Todesmühlen* (US 1946), were included in the official cinema programme from November 1945. Ultimately, these atrocity films did not prove particularly effective, failing to give rise to feelings of personal or collective guilt, according to American surveys. In the Western zones, these concentration camp films were already withdrawn in early 1947. The Americans in particular expected more from films intended to make Austrians familiar with the rules of democracy.[4] Austria's separation from Germany and the construction of an independent Austrian self-image remained an inter-Allied aim and coincided with the interests of the Austrian federal government.

Initially, the Allies cooperated in the field of film production. For instance, until the spring of 1946, the staff of the Soviet-controlled Rosenhügelstudios were paid by the Americans. In return, the Rosenhügel staff produced copies of films for the American Information Service Branch (ISB) free of charge. Moreover, the Vienna office of the US Film Section supplied all sectors in Vienna, including the Soviet Zone, and took over distribution of the confiscated films in addition to the British and French productions, and even the Soviet ones.[5] Nevertheless, as early as the autumn of 1945, conflicts of interests between the Allied forces became evident. The ISB's Film Section was tasked with representing the interests of the American film industry in Austria, doing its best to prepare and open up the local market for Hollywood productions. Within a short period of time, the ISB confiscated all film holdings and credits owned by film companies in the US Zone, the Film Section took over the newly founded Austria-Film-Verleih- und

---

3 Some 370 copies of feature films and 2,144 short films and newsreels had been earmarked for destruction by the late April of 1947. Cf.: Allied Commission for Austria (British Element), Political Directorate, Report on the Destruction of Withdrawn Fascist and Anti-Allied Literature and on the Withdrawal and Destruction of Cinema Films, 9 April 1947. Cit. Siegfried Beer: Die Kultur- und Informationspolitik der britischen Besatzungsmacht in Österreich 1945–1955, in: Moser: Besetzte Bilder, 119–132, here: 128f.

4 On the "atrocity pictures", cf.: Thomas Tode: KZ-Filme in Wiener Kinos. Überlegungen zu zwei "Atrocity-Filmen" 1945/46, in: Moser, Besetzte Bilder, 357–373.

5 Reinhold Wagnleitner: Coca-Colonisation und Kalter Krieg. Die Kulturmission der USA in Österreich nach dem Zweiten Weltkrieg, Vienna 1991, 307. Moser, Propaganda, 29.

Vertriebsgesellschaft (Austrian Film Distribution and Sales Company). The Soviet occupation authorities protested, demanding not only the return of Austria-Film but also independent Austrian distribution and production.[6]

Whereas during the previous year it had been common to exchange films and weekly newsreels between the zones, the Soviets now tended to place restrictions on Western film productions. In March 1946, the Soviet occupation authorities ended their collaboration with the ISB and placed its film distribution under the Austrian department of Sovexportfilm. In turn, Soviet productions were practically boycotted in the Western zones from 1947 onwards. They could only be screened at closed events of the KPÖ or the Österreichisch-Sowjetische Gesellschaft (Austro-Soviet Society, ÖSG). After long negotiations, in 1947/48 Sovexportfilm managed to secure an agreement on film quotas with the British and the French; the US occupiers refused to come to such an arrangement.[7] Parallel to these developments, the initial cooperation turned into confrontation in film censorship. The Americans in particular originally valued a well-organized system of censorship within their zone, and decided which films were permitted via the ISB film department. After the break with the ISB, the Soviets strengthened their censorship activities. While the Americans, the British, and the French put an end to film censorship in 1948, the Soviets clung to it unreservedly until the late August of 1953.[8] The increasingly evident conflict between East and West impeded and ultimately ended the inter-Allied cooperation, especially in the Austrian media sector.

---

6 Oliver Rathkolb: Die "Wien-Film"-Produktion am Rosenhügel. Österreichische Filmproduktion und Kalter Krieg, in: Hans-Heinz Fabris/Kurt Luger (eds.): Medienkultur in Österreich. Film, Fotografie, Video und Fernsehen in der 2. Republik, Vienna 1988, 117–132, 120. Wolfgang Mueller: Sowjetische Filmpropaganda in Österreich 1945–1955, in: Moser, Besetzte Bilder, 86–118, here: 91f.

7 Wolfgang Mueller: Informationsmedien in der "Besatzungszeit". Tagespresse, Rundfunk, Wochenschau 1945–1955, in: Matthias Karmasin/Christina Oggolder (eds.): Österreichische Mediengeschichte, Vol. 2: Von Massenmedien zu sozialen Medien (1918 bis heute), Wiesbaden 2019, 75–98, 92. Mueller, Filmpropaganda, 92, 95.

8 Elfriede Sieder: Die alliierten Zensurmaßnahmen zwischen 1945–1955. Unter besonderer Berücksichtigung der Medienzensur, doctoral thesis, University of Vienna 1983, 123, 179–181.

FILME AMERIKA	FILME AUS ENGLAND xxxx	FILME AUS FRANKREICH	FILME AUS RUSSLAND
Ich suche meinen Mörder In Originalfassung Mozart, IX.	FILME AUS ENGLAND — FILME AUS ENGLAND — FILME AUS ENGLAND — FILME AUS ENGLAND	FILME AUS FRANKREICH — FILME AUS FRANKREICH — FILME AUS FRANKREICH — FILME AUS FRANKREICH	FILME AUS RUSSLAND — FILME AUS RUSSLAND **Nasreddin in Buchara** Tabor, II.
Mission im Pazifik In Originalfassung Lux-Film-Palast, XVI.	**Ein Herz geht verloren** In Originalfassung Burg, I. Imperial, I.	FILME AUS FRANKREICH — FILME AUS FRANKREICH — FILME AUS FRANKREICH	**Jugend unseres Landes** Mariahilf, VI.
Musikrausch In Originalfassung Apollo, VI.	**Donnernde Hufe** In deutscher Sprache Breitenseer, XIV. Währinger Gürtel, XVIII.	**Der Bucklige** Urania, I. Schwegler, XV. Savoy, XVI.	**Schatzinsel** Wohlmuth, II.
Pazifik-Expreß In Originalfassung Felber, XV.	**Gaslicht und Schatten** In deutscher Sprache Rabenhof, III.	**Herz auf Reisen** Wolfgang, XII.	**Unruhige Wirtschaft** Zentral, X. Kaisermühlen, XXI.
Die Waise von Lowood In Originalfassung Gartenbau, I.	**Heiße Liebe** In deutscher Sprache Rabenhof, III. Bellaria, VII. Schubert, IX. Kagran, XXI.	**Ihr erstes Rendezvous** Lichtbildbühne, XI. Reindorf, XV.	**Mädchen von Charakter** Augarten, II. Zentral, X.
Laura In deutscher Sprache Baumgarten, XIV. Gloria, XVII. Gersthofer, XVIII. Iris, XVIII.	**Die Jahre dazwischen** In deutscher Sprache Metropol, V. Lainz, XIII. Tivoli, XV.	**Die letzte Chance** Schwegler, XV. **Marie-Louise** Meidlinger, XII. Maxim, XV.	**Die namenlose Insel** Nestroy, II. Poppenwimmer, XXI. **An der Grenze** Mittersteig, IV. Edison, X. Kepler, X. Weltbild, XXI.
Louis Pasteur In deutscher Sprache Urania, I. Wienzeile, VI. Schönbrunn, XIV. Universum, XV.	**Madonna der sieben Monde** In deutscher Sprache Kreuz, I. Landstraßer Bürger, III. Mozart, IX. Almanadorfer, XII. Hellweg, XX.	**Der Mann vom Niger** Lichtbildbühne, XI. **Satansboten** Gloriette, XIV.	**In den Wüsten Zentralasiens** Stadion, XXI. **Schild des Tschurgal** Poppenwimmer, XXI.
Rendezvous nach Ladenschluß In deutscher Sprache Radetzky, III. Erika, VII.	**Ungeduld des Herzens** In deutscher Sprache Wieden, IV. Reindorf, XV. Arneth, XVI.	**Versprechen an die Unbekannte** Margaretner Bürger, V. **Mädchenhändler** Kruger, I.	**Zweikampf** Nestroy, II. **Die Lieder des Abaj** Bürger, X.
Der verlorene Engel In deutscher Sprache Margaretner Bürger, V. Maxim, XIV.	**Der letzte Schleier** In deutscher Sprache Kagran, XXI. FILME AUS ENGLAND — FILME AUS ENGLAND	FILME AUS FRANKREICH — FILME AUS FRANKREICH — FILME AUS FRANKREICH — FILME AUS FRANKREICH	**Die steinerne Blume** Mariahilf, VI. **Meine Liebe** Sandleiten, XVI.
Ziegfeld-Girl In deutscher Sprache Alserkino, IX.	FILME AUS ENGLAND — FILME AUS ENGLAND	FILME AUS FRANKREICH — FILME AUS FRANKREICH	FILME AUS RUSSLAND — FILME AUS RUSSLAND

Fig. 1: A list of the Allied film productions screened in Austria in July 1947, compiled by the distribution company British Film Verleih. British Film Verleih to Col. C. Beauclerk, 28 July 1947 (The National Archives, Public Record Office, Foreign Office, 1020/580)

Self-images

An important task of Allied propaganda was position presentation of the Allies' respective societal and political systems, including in competition with the other powers. A high-priority aim of the French occupation authorities was denazification and cultural and ideological detoxification of the population, strengthening of Austria going hand in hand with the intention to weaken Germany.[9] The French considered Austria a "befriended country", and Austrian self-awareness was to be reinforced. The French officials responsible for information and culture noted "a high mental affinity" between the two countries and their populations.[10] Within the French information department, the Section Cinématographique was tasked with the selection and supply of French films. The productions were to raise France's prestige, and hence they looked to films of high technical and artistic value. At the same time, the French sought to meet Austrian tastes;[11] the film department staff came to the conclusion that the local population preferred comedies and operettas along with adventure and "cloak and dagger" films. In contrast, there was little demand for war, Résistance, or sociocritical pictures.[12]

Dubbing was recognized to be a fundamental problem. Usually taking place in Germany for economic reasons, it thereby "injured" Austrians' "linguistic sensibilities". However, from 1948 at the latest, French newsreels specific to Austria were dubbed at the Rosenhügelstudios, with the voice of Radio Wien announcer Hans Kovar. Overall, a representative cross-section of French productions from the years 1935–1955 was offered, especially films directed by Christian-Jaque, Jean Delannoy, Richard Pottier, Jean Boyer, Julien Duvivier, Marc Allégret, Robert Vernay, Henri Decoin, and Georges Lacombe.[13] Cinemas in the French Zone also screened the Austrian edition of the newsreel *Les actualités françaises* (AF) every two weeks. Local cameramen provided regional events from the fields

---

9 Thomas Angerer: Französische Freundschaftspolitik in Österreich nach 1945. Gründe, Grenzen und Gemeinsamkeiten mit Frankreichs Deutschlandpolitik, in: Manfried Rauchensteiner, Robert Kriechbaumer (eds.): Die Gunst des Augenblicks. Neue Forschungen zu Staatsvertrag und Neutralität, Vienna/Cologne/Weimar 2005, 113–138, 135–137. Elisabeth Starlinger: Aspekte französischer Kulturpolitik in Österreich nach dem Zweiten Weltkrieg (1945–1948), Diplomarbeit, University of Vienna 1993, 42f.
10 Cf.: Barbara Porpaczy: Frankreich – Österreich 1945–1960. Kulturpolitik und Identität (Innsbrucker Forschungen zur Zeitgeschichte, Vol. 18), Innsbruck 2002, 123ff. Starlinger, Aspekte, 67–69.
11 Films that offended Austrians' religious sensibilities were to be avoided, as were films showing the House of Habsburg from a French perspective.
12 Le chef du Service de Presse [Meyer] to Chef de la Division Information [Ray], 8 January 1948, MAE/C AUT 244. Cit.: Porpaczy, Kultur- und Propagandapolitik, 143.
13 Porpaczy, Kultur- und Propagandapolitik, 144, 149f. Karin Moser: Les Actualités Françaises – Fragment 2. Die Exotik der französischen Besatzungswochenschau, in: Moser, Besetzte Bilder, 547–561, here: 549.

of politics, culture, and sport.[14] Notably, in 1946 emphasis was still placed on the topic of denazification. A number of reports were devoted to the National Socialist atrocities, and coverage was also given to war crimes trials of Austrian perpetrators.[15] Primarily, however, the newsreels featured events of direct interest to France. A great deal of footage of Africa, India, and Indochina pointed, moreover, to a French colonial era that was drawing to a close. Ultimately, the world of the French newsreels remained alien to Austrian audiences; they were stopped in November 1949.[16]

For the British occupation authorities, the "cultural mission" enforced for their zone was part of security policy. Since Britain – especially in comparison to the USA – increasingly lacked economic and military strength, self-presentation in the culture policy sphere – termed "projection of Britain" – was intended to keep alive the idea that it was a Great Power.[17] Like the French, the British ensured that only their best film productions found access to the Austrian market. However, for several months it proved difficult to offer cinemas any English films at all. It was not until the late November of 1945 that Austria's first post-war screening of a British production took place, with *Rembrandt* (GB 1936, dir.: Alexander Korda). By mid-1947, distribution could be massively ramped up, however; in the late June of 1947, more British productions were screened than those of the other Allies.[18] Films were selected carefully; those that shone a critical light on British society and/or politics were avoided, as were productions that were all too propagandistic in their motivation.[19]

Britain presented itself as a peace-loving, strong, democratic nation striving for global security and prosperity. A British alternative to "capitalism" and "communism" was offered – known as "third-force propaganda". The British socialism propagated guaranteed a higher standard of living and protection against the privilege economy and exploitation while also appealing to Christian values. It identified "average common citizens" (workers and the middle class) as a core target group that should be able to identify with Britain's population and its political and social system.[20] The British and American occupation newsreel

---

14 Österreichische Kino-Zeitung, no. 87, 27 March 1948, n.p.
15 Cf. for instance: *Prozess der SS* (AF 37/46). *Wiederaufbau der zerstörten Synagoge* (AF 50/46), *Was ich in Griechenland sah* (AF 50/46).
16 Österreichische Kino-Zeitung, no. 171, 5 November 1949, n.p.
17 Gabriele Clemens: Die britische Kulturpolitik in Deutschland: Musik, Theater, Film und Literatur, in: Gabriele Clemens (ed.): Kulturpolitik im besetzten Deutschland 1945–1949, Stuttgart 1994, 200–28, 210.
18 Neue Steirische Zeitung, 30. November 1945, n.p. Cit. Beer, Kultur- und Informationspolitik, 128f.
19 Clemens, Kulturpolitik, 213.
20 Gerda Treiber: Großbritanniens Informationspolitik gegenüber Österreich 1945 bis 1955. Publicity und Propaganda sowie deren Instrumente in Printmedien und Rundfunk, dar-

Welt im Film (The World in Film, WIF) showed English citizens (primarily from the working class) faced with struggles similar to those the Austrians wrestled with: they applied to the authorities in the hope of getting better housing and queued for food rations. Austrians were offered work in England, and Austrian children could spend a three-month holiday in Britain.[21] On the whole, the British cultural mission concentrated on presenting Britain in a positive light and avoided attacks on other powers.

The Americans were in a better economic and financial position that any of the other powers and knew how to sell this strength via the media. The European Recovery Program and the progressive development process in industry and technology were central elements of American filmic self-presentation. Specially produced films about the Marshall Plan reported on the financial, organizational, and technical support from the USA but also emphasized that the Europeans could ultimately earn economic success by virtue of their own actions; the Americans "helped them to help themselves" with the intention of strengthening the European peoples' self-confidence. The impact of this assistance was demonstrated primarily in volume and mass. A striking feature of the American "self-propaganda" was the use of superlatives: in California, reported *Welt im Film*, the world's largest plane was being built. The series also presented the world's largest and technically innovative crane and the world's most important calculating machine.[22] American stood, then, for wealth, innovation, and modernity. But it also represented a new attitude towards life; American feature films transported the idea of mass prosperity and consumer and entertainment culture. However, the US occupiers also firmly pursued their own economic interests in the field of film: the Film Section of the ISB blocked an independent Austrian film industry until it had secured American distribution in Austria and Germany and free access to their markets for the Hollywood film industry. In 1949, some 150 of the 277 films imported to Austria were from the USA, representing a market share of over fifty per cent. The Austrian film market had been conquered.[23] On the political level, the United States ultimately portrayed itself as the power best equipped to offer protection against the worldwide "threat of communist rule by

---

gestellt anhand britischer Dokumente, doctoral thesis, University of Vienna 1997, 81f., 88, 100f. Beer, Kultur- und Informationspolitik, 121.

21 *England: Der Tag einer Hausfrau* (WIF 142/48), *Unsere Kinder in London* (WIF 130/47 bzw. 131/47), *Britische Maschinen für Österreich* (WIF 131/47 bzw. 132/47).

22 Cf.: *Die US-Hilfe für Österreich* (WIF 135/48), *Saatgut aus USA* (WIF 146/48), *Das größte Flugzeug der Welt* (WIF 131/47 bzw. 132/47), *Der größte Arbeitskran der Welt* (WIF 142/48), *Wunder der Technik: Das mechanische Rechengenie* (WIF 145/48).

23 Andrea Ellmeier: Von der kulturellen Entnazifizierung Österreichs zum konsumkulturellen Versprechen. Kulturpolitik der USA in Österreich, 1945–1955, in: Moser, Besetzte Bilder, 61–85, here: 73–75. Gertraud Steiner: Die Heimat-Macher. Kino in Österreich 1946–1966, Vienna 1987, 48–51.

violence". Its military strength in the Cold War against the Soviet Union was displayed in pictures of stratospheric missiles and nuclear tests.[24]

Of all the Allies, the Soviet occupation authorities had the worst starting point. Austria was and still is a country with an anti-communist tradition. The excesses of the Red Army during its invasion towards the end of the Second World War and the Soviet dismantling of industrial plants reinforced the negative image many Austrians had of "the Russians". The medium of film had an important role to play in reproducing positive counter-images; the programme included productions by renowned filmmakers such as Sergei Eisenstein, Mark Donskoi, Vsevelod Pudovkin, Vladimir Petrov, or Grigorii Aleksandrov in addition to films from the DEFA studios in East Berlin or from China.[25] The focus was placed on Russian historical and present-day heroic epics, but also on anti-American productions, although such films were shown almost exclusively in the Soviet Zone, often in cinemas confiscated by the Soviets, such as the Tabor-Kino in Leopoldstadt. Additionally, Soviet film festivals were held annually from 1946 onwards, showcasing the achievements of Soviet film production. The Soviet productions were not particularly popular, with the exception of the high-quality animations and films aimed at children and adolescents, particularly fairytales and films of novels, regularly screened at Vienna's Urania cinema as part of the Soviet youth film weeks.[26]

After the Soviet Union had confiscated the Wien-Film production company's studios and with it the production facility on the Rosenhügel hill as German Property, it embarked on filmmaking. From 1950 onwards, a slew of films were made under Soviet auspices: musical and operetta productions (e.g. *Eine Nacht in Venedig* [A Night in Venice], A 1953), biographies of artists (e.g. *Der Komödiant von Wien* [The Comedian of Vienna], A 1954), revues (e.g. *Seesterne* [Lake Stars], A 1952), and films based on literary works (*Herr Puntila und sein Knecht Matti* [Mr Puntila and His Man Matti], A 1955). The monarchist past was not idealized, but rather, critical distance was sought to this chapter of the past. Although some of these productions enjoyed international success, they were boycotted in Austria outside of the Soviet Zone.[27]

---

24 *USA – Versuch mit einer Stratosphärenrakete* (Austria Wochenschau = AW 41/52), *USA – Der Raketentod* (AW 51/54), *USA – Die taktische Atombombe explodiert* (AW 14/55), *USA – Atombombenmanöver der Geschichte* (AW 15/55).
25 Austrian State Archives (Österreichisches Staatsarchiv, henceforth ÖStA), Allgemeines Verwaltungsarchiv, Bundesministerium für Handel und Wirtschaft, Geschäftszahl: V-107/9-39, Zl. 116.494/23a/1949. Österreichische Zeitung, 1 April 1955, n.p.
26 Mueller, Filmpropaganda, 93, 103f., 107, 110–112.
27 Rathkolb, "Wien-Film"-Produktion, 121. Eva Binder: Die Rosenhügelproduktionen, in: Moser: Besetzte Bilder, 475–492.

The Soviet newsreels for Austria were also produced in the Rosenhügelstudios. In 1945, the series *Zeitgeschehen, schnell gesehen* (Contemporary Events, Viewed Quickly) entered cinemas; from 1946 onwards, the newsreels were called *Spiegel der Zeit* (Mirror of Time) and from 1947, finally, *Wir sind dabei* (We Are There). The aim was to make the population of Austria acquainted with the cultural, economic, scientific, and social achievements of the USSR, with the people who benefited from these achievements always at the centre. Class divisions were dissolved, and emphasis was placed on the communal spirit of the Soviet citizen. Film material from Czechoslovakia, Hungary, Yugoslavia, Italy, Romania, and Germany's eastern zone complemented the visual canon. When all the Allied newsreels were disbanded in the course of 1949, an Austrian production in the form of the *Austria Wochenschau* hit cinemas. The Russian controlling authority had demanded, however, that each edition contain a feature provided by Sovexportfilm, unedited.[28]

Conclusion

At the beginning of the control phase, the Allies cooperated closely on the level of film and media. As the Cold War set in, not only a clear demarcation but also the filmic fronts became manifest. Each of the four occupation authorities ultimately pursued their own strategy of positive self-presentation, aiming to build a bridge to the Austrian population. In the sphere of film, however, economic self-interest also became evident. In Austria, the propaganda war between East and West was also clearly decided in favour of the Western Allies in the field of film and newsreel production.

---

28 Vertrags-Niederschrift Austria Wochenschau Ges-m.b.H. und Sovexport-Film, in: ÖStA, Archiv der Republik, Bundesministerium für Energiewirtschaft und Elektrifizierung, Gsch.: 2017-Pr/49. Cf.: Karin Moser, Die sowjetischen Wochenschauproduktionen für Österreich – Fragment 1. Der visualisierte Kampf der "fortschrittlichen Kräfte", in: Moser, Besetzte Bilder, 527–546.

Agnes Meisinger

Ready, Set, Go! Allied Sport and the Revival of Sporting Events in Vienna, 1945–1955

On 13 April 1945, the Red Army had won the Vienna offensive. After liberation by the Allies, the Second World War on Austrian soil came to an end, and with it began the laborious rebuilding of the country, which for ten years stood under Allied control. Vienna lay in ruins, as did most sports grounds, which during the National Socialist period had served as venues for Reich and regional contests or had offered the population on the "home front" diversion from the day-to-day of wartime. Larger facilities were confiscated or occupied by the Allies. For instance, for weeks Russian soldiers used the buildings belonging to the Wiener Eislauf-Verein (Vienna Ice Skating Club) on Heumarkt as accommodation and stables for their horses.[1] The stadia in the Prater and on the Hohe Warte hill, which had been damaged by air raids, were also taken over by the Red Army.[2] However, before sport could regain its relevance for society and become part of everyday life for a municipal population traumatized by the war, new regulations were drawn up for all levels, from leisure through junior to competitive sport. The Constitutional Law of the Provisional Government headed by Karl Renner of 8 May 1945 disbanded all National Socialist organizations and their associated federations, and hence the sporting system, which had also been brought into line with the Nazi regime ("gleichgeschaltet"), also collapsed.

---

1 Agnes Meisinger: 150 Jahre Eiszeit. Die große Geschichte des Wiener Eislauf-Vereins, Vienna/Cologne/Weimar 2017, 138.
2 Bernhard Hachleitner: Das Wiener Praterstadion / Ernst-Happel-Stadion. Bedeutungen, Politik, Architektur und urbanistische Relevanz, doctoral thesis, University of Vienna 2010, 248; Die Geschichte der Naturarena Hohe Warte: Zerstört und Fremdbestimmt, https://www.firstviennafc.at/hohe-warte-geschichte/zerstoert-und-fremdbestimmt.html (1 August 2024).

New Beginnings

On 26 April, a day before the Provisional Government of the three newly formed parties, the Socialist Party of Austria (SPÖ), the Austrian People's Party (ÖVP), and the Communist Party of Austria (KPÖ), was constituted and had announced the establishment of an independent, democratic Republic of Austria, several sportsmen and former sports functionaries met at the office of KPÖ Municipal Councillor for Culture and Public Education Viktor Matejka and founded the Central Office for the Re-establishment of Austrian Sport (Zentralstelle für die Wiedererrichtung des österreichischen Sports, ZÖS). Under the auspices of the KPÖ and with the support of the Soviet military administration, the ZÖS would ring in the rebuilding of Austrian sport. The priority was securing the existing sporting facilities and equipment, followed by founding sporting organizations.[3] Just a little later, the sporting governing bodies were constituted: the Arbeiterbund für Sport und Körperkultur Österreich (ASKÖ; Workers' Union for Sport and Physical Culture Austria), formed with the assistance of political representatives of the SPÖ and amounting to a merger of former workers' sports clubs, and the Österreichische Turn- und Sportunion (UNION; Austrian Gymnastics and Sport Union), supported by the ÖVP, as the successor to the Christlich-deutsche Turnerschaft (Christian German Gymnastics Association).[4] Originally founded as an above-party organization but dominated by the Communists, the ZÖS's jurisdiction remained limited to the Soviet Occupation Zone. After the National Council elections in November 1945, when the KPÖ won just 5.4 per cent of the vote, the ZÖS lost influence before being disbanded in January 1946.[5] It was replaced by the Hauptverband für Körpersport (Main Federation for Physical Sport), the predecessor to the Bundessportorganisation (BSO, Federal Sport Organization) founded in 1949.

The war had left deep wounds in Austrian sport too. Many talented sportspeople had died, and the destruction, re-appropriation, and confiscation of sports grounds meant that a return to regular sport was unimaginable. Despite this difficult starting point, sports events began in Vienna as early as May 1945. For instance, track and field athletes contested the traditional run through Vienna (Quer-durch-Wien-Lauf) and cyclists raced an inner-city criterium between the piles of rubble. Football too was soon played once more on Vienna's desolate sports fields. On 6 May, Wiener Sport-Club and First Vienna FC played

---

3 "Ein Jahr österreichischer Sport", in: Österreichische Zeitung, 13 April 1946, 9; Norbert Adam: 1945–2005. 60 Jahre Sport in Österreich. Eine Erfolgsgeschichte, Vienna 2005, 9–10.
4 Adam, 1945–2005, 10.
5 Gunnar Mertz: Die umstrittene Nachfolge des nationalsozialistischen Deutschen Alpenvereins in Österreich, in: Marcus Böick, Marcel Schmeer (eds.): Im Kreuzfeuer der Kritik. Umstrittene Organisationen im 20. Jahrhundert, Frankfurt am Main/New York 2020, 511–512.

the first post-liberation football match between top-flight teams, Vienna winning 3–2. Two weeks later, the City Hall bulletin reported: "Sporting activities bloom for the Whit holidays."[6]

In June and July 1945, a competition organized by the Soviet military administration was played for the Liberation Cup (Befreiungspokal). The final, held at the Pfarrwiese ground in Hütteldorf and won by First Vienna FC, attracted 17,000 spectators. The Prater Stadium too hosted football matches, with some sectors closed due to bomb damage. Although the stadium was difficult to reach after the destruction to the public transport network, on 6 December more than 50,000[7] watched the first international match in liberated Austria. The newly formed national team won a friendly against France 4–1, with representatives of the American, British, French, and Russian Allied administration in attendance.[8]

From September 1945 onwards, championships returned for many sports. Along with football, crowds were drawn to speedway or boxing. For the population of Vienna, the first post-war winter was characterized by shortages and hunger, but committed members of the Wiener Eislauf-Verein managed to repair their facilities in time to open a small natural ice rink in December 1945. From 1 September, the British occupying forces moved into their zones in Vienna, including the 3rd District, home to the ice skating club. Thanks to the provision of construction material, the club was able to put on a gala for the British troops. Further displays for American and Russian soldiers followed.[9]

The Allies' Influence on Sport in Vienna

With the zones agreement of 1 September 1945, the Western Allied troops took over their sectors in the city, which had previously been under Soviet control. One of the results of this was that two large sports grounds, on the Hohe Warte hill in Döbling and the post office ground (Postsportplatz) in Hernals, on which the Russian army stored heavy equipment, came under the administration of the United States Forces in Austria (USFA). Special regulations placed the Freudenau horse racecourse, located in the Soviet Zone, under British administration.[10]

---

6 Meldungen der Rathauskorrespondenz, 20 May 1945, https://presse.wien.gv.at/historische-rk/1945/-/asset_publisher/BoVbj8qARs8t/content/mai-1945?redirect=%2Fweb%2Fpresse%2Fhistorische-rk%2F1945&inheritRedirect=true (1 June 2024).
7 Neues Österreich, 7 December 1945, 3.
8 Österreich gegen Frankreich 1945 – Anpfiff in Ruinen, https://www.oepb.at/allerlei/oesterreich-gegen-frankreich-1945-anpfiff-in-ruinen.html (1 June 2024).
9 Meisinger, 150 Jahre Eiszeit, 139.
10 Rolf M. Urrisk-Obertyński (ed.): Wien. 2000 Jahre Garnisonsstadt, Vol. 6: Die vier Alliierten 1945–1955, Gnas 2015, 318.

As in Germany, the Allied administration in Austria also sought to demilitarize and democratize society, and this extended to the sporting sphere too. In December 1945, the Allied Council, which controlled the Austrian federal government's lawmaking process, announced in its official *Gazette of the Allied Commission for Austria* a decision forbidding the foundation of associations involved in military training, including sports organizations of a military nature.[11] A closer inspection of this medium reveals that in the period between 1945 and 1955, the Allied powers did not establish joint guidelines for sport in Vienna or Austria. Nevertheless, certain sports, including shooting or flying, initially remained prohibited in parts of Austria.[12] In 1948, for instance, a request by Federal Chancellor Leopold Figl to form the Union Airmen Club was initially rejected by the Allied Commission. The Soviet command argued that the club could be used to prepare for military action.[13]

Requests from children's and youth groups seeking support for the establishment of leisure activities and the procurement of sports equipment were frequently directed to the US military administration in particular.[14] Indeed, many measures in the US Zones throughout Austria were aimed at the country's youth. The programme Austrian Youth Activities (AYA), set up in 1951, sought to democratize its young members via education and by communicating American culture. AYA ran eighty youth centres in the US-controlled areas, offering club rooms, gymnasia, pitches, or swimming baths, many of them in Vienna. The activities mainly included, besides film screenings and talks, leisure and sports events such as boxing or basketball tournaments and summer camps. In its first year, AYA already had around 12,000 active participants.[15]

In the Soviet-occupied sectors, works sport took on an important role. After the confiscation of many Austrian industrial plants, from July 1946 the Soviet Union had at its disposal an enormous industrial complex, including the country's entire oil industry, important iron, steel, and electronics companies, and several trade and mercantile businesses. These companies, most of them based in the east of Austria, came under the umbrella of the USIS corporation (Upravlenie Sovetskim Imushchestvom v Avstrii = Administration of Soviet Property in Austria), which had over 50,000 employees. A specially established cultural department offered the workers a broad leisure programme ranging from trips and theatre visits to dances and reading groups. As balance to daily

---

11 Gazette of the Allied Commission for Austria 1 (1945), Dec. 1945 – Jan. 1946, 34.
12 Paul Nittnaus, Michael Zink: Sport ist unser Leben: 100 Jahre Arbeitersport in Österreich, Vienna 1992, 86.
13 Report of the United States High Commissioner, Civil Affairs Austria, March 1949, No. 41, 41.
14 Report of the United States High Commissioner, Military Government Austria, April 1947, No. 18, 45.
15 Office of the US High Commissioner for Austria, Report on Austria 1951, 37.

Fig. 1: The Vienna Soap Box Derby in Döbling on 29 August 1948, organized by the 1st Battalion of 350th Infantry Regiment of the US Army as part of the Austrian Youth Activities (AYA) (National Archives at College Park, Maryland, NARA 307608)

work, the sports on offer also proved popular. All of these activities were part of the occupation authorities' political work; a main aim was conveying the Soviet ideal image of the proletarian.[16]

Located on Austrian territory alongside the USIA, the Soviet Mineral Oil Administration (Sowjetische Mineralölverwaltung, SMV) also had culture and sports clubs, staging championships for sports such as football, volleyball, table tennis, chess, skittles, or swimming at its own venues. The annual highlight was the Soviet works' sports festival. The number of participants increased year after year following its inception in 1947; in 1953, over 5,000 workers and staff from 113 USIA and SMV companies and a few hundred from private companies took part in fifteen different sports. The contests were held at thirty different sports grounds, most of them in Leopoldstadt, Favoriten, Floridsdorf, and Donaustadt, with the Wiener Athletiksport Club (WAC) ground in the Prater serving as the main venue.[17]

Reporting on the large event, the Communist *Österreichische Volksstimme* emphasized the achievements of the Soviet occupation authorities in promoting

---

16 Michael Kraus: "Kultura". Der Einfluss der sowjetischen Besatzung auf die österreichische Kultur 1945–1955, Diplomarbeit, University of Vienna 2008, 131.
17 Der Erdölarbeiter. Wochenorgan der Arbeiter und Angestellten in der Erdölindustrie, 9 July 1953, 11.

sport in Austria: "The Soviet-administered companies have spent several million schillings on the cultivation of physical sport in the companies. Five new football pitches have been built in Vienna, 13 in Lower Austria. Many private clubs have received support from the companies to enable them to get their sports facilities devastated by the war back up and running and to buy new equipment."[18] The company initiatives triggered a significant growth spurt in Austrian post-war sport, particularly for grassroots and mass sport in Vienna.

In the Austrian National Council, sport did not play a role during the early post-war years; rebuilding and securing daily life were much more pressing issues. To finance sport, in 1948 the Sporttoto – state-organized sports betting – was introduced: fifty per cent of the net proceeds were to be allocated to sports federations, the construction of sports facilities, and the staging of competitions. The Allies also supported the upkeep of sports grounds and gymnasia in their respective sectors, partly out of self-interest. After the re-adoption of the Austrian constitution of 1920, however, sport became the remit of the federal provinces.

Sport among the Allied Forces

Leisure activities to balance out daily work also played an important role among the occupying troops. Each of the four occupation authorities had their own culture department that offered members of the armed forces opportunities for recuperation via cultural, educational, and sporting programmes. Self-administered sports grounds in the respective zones quickly became popular meetings spots for soldiers, and public sports facilities such as swimming baths, including the Schafbergbad and the Jörgerbad, or ice rinks like the Wiener Eislauf-Verein and the Engelmann Arena were reserved at certain times for members of the army.[19]

There were also frequent encounters between Vienna teams and those of the Allied forces. As early as 29 April 1945, just a few days after the liberation of Vienna, a football friendly was played between a Vienna select XI and a Soviet military team at the Helfort ground in Ottakring. After the game, the Soviet

---

18 Österreichische Volksstimme, 4 July 1953, 8, cit. Bernhard Denscher (ed.): Tagebuch der Straße – Wiener Plakate, Publikation zur Ausstellung in der Volkshalle des Wiener Rathauses (29 April–12 July 1981), 328.
19 Ronald Pretsch: Sport in den amerikanischen Streitkräften, in: Hubert Prigl (ed.), "off limits". Amerikanische Besatzungssoldaten in Wien 1945–1955, publication accompanying the exhibition of the same name at the Vienna Municipal and Provincial Library (Stadt- und Landesbibliothek), Vienna 2005, 118–127, here: 121.

commander gave each of the Vienna players two loaves of bread.[20] Regular inter-Allied sports events brought together the soldiers of the four occupying powers. The WAC ground in the Prater served as a central venue, and was used by both the Allies and various Viennese sports clubs until the former withdrew in 1955.

The US forces attached particular importance to sporting culture; along with promoting health and camaraderie, sport was also supposed to offer soldiers opportunities to raise their profiles for promotion. This explains the high number of sporting events organized by the US forces in comparison to the other three occupation authorities, with extensive press coverage too.[21] Immediately after the arrival of the US forces, leisure facilities were created all over the city, intended to enable participation in sports on all levels and to serve as a "connection to the homeland"[22] for members of the armed forces. These included, besides clubs, bars, theatres, and cinemas, several sports, initially run by the Red Cross, and later by the USFA Special Services Vienna. The USFA ran tennis courts, bowling alleys, a golf course, and gymnasia. Women could train at Gym No. 3 at Neubaugasse 36, for example. Members of the armed forces even had the opportunity to take skiing lessons in the Vienna Woods.[23]

The US national sports American football, baseball, and basketball were particularly popular with the soldiers. As an identifying measure, some sports grounds were renamed, being given American names: baseball and softball were played at Viking Field on the Hohe Warte or the Pot O'Gold Field in Roggendorfgasse (Postsportplatz), American football at, inter alia, Belvoir Bowl Field at Alszeile 19 (Sport-Club-Platz).[24] The main sporting attraction for the US military was the USFA Sports Arena in the Messepalast, today's MuseumsQuartier. The building housed a weights room and gymnasia for table tennis, badminton, handball, fistball, and volleyball or boxing. The highlight was the basketball court, which was booked around the clock, including by Viennese teams.

Of the sports largely established by the Allies in Vienna, it was basketball in particular that fascinated the Viennese, especially adolescents. US sport had been known to Austrians since the 1920s, but it had remained a marginal practice, played mainly at the universities and by the military.[25]

---

20 Ludwig Stecewicz: Trotz Hunger waren die Sportnarren da, in: Franz Danimann, Hugo Pepper (ed.): Österreich im April '45. Die ersten Schritte der Zweiten Republik, Vienna/Munich/Zurich 1985, 263–265, here: 264.
21 Urrisk-Obertyński (ed.), Die vier Alliierten, 312.
22 Hubert Prigl: Clubs und Einrichtungen der amerikanischen Besatzungsmacht, in: idem (ed.), "off limits", 42–59, here: 43.
23 Urrisk-Obertyński (ed.), Die vier Alliierten, 316.
24 Ibid., 312.
25 Agnes Meisinger: Wie Basketball nach Österreich kam – eine Spurensuche, in: Manfred Schnurrer, Hanns Vanura: Österreichs Basketball Geschichte(n), Vienna 2019, 9–14, here: 11.

Fig. 2: American footballers on the US team Vienna Vikings at Pot O' Gold Field in der Roggendorfgasse 2, no year, presumably 1949 (estate of Hubert Prigl, Department of Contemporary History, University of Vienna)

In the American occupation zones in Austria, there were several basketball leagues with around seventy soldiers' teams. In the capital, there was the Vienna League, with games played at the USFA Sports Arena and at Gym No. 1 in Lange Gasse.[26] Some games were even broadcast live on Blue Danube Network, the US soldiers' radio station.[27] Two local teams, the Austrian national side and the AYA select team, sometimes took part in the US army championships too.[28]

For Vienna's re- or newly forming basketball clubs, on the other hand, there were hardly any opportunities to train or compete. The sports journalist Norbert Adam wrote of the prevailing conditions, "When in 1948 I first came into contact with this sport, the only useable sports halls were those of the American occupation authorities, which we were available to us Austrians on an hourly basis. [… W]e then found Palais Ferstel in Herrengasse, where we put laborious work into doing up the former officers' casino. The occupying troops had spent some time dwelling in this hall, in the full sense of the word, and it looked like it. Piles of dirt and refuse, every single window smashed, completely destroyed sanitary

---

26 Pretsch, Sport in den amerikanischen Streitkräften, 119.
27 Ibid., 120.
28 Urrisk-Obertyński (ed.), Die vier Alliierten, 313.

facilities – there was plenty of work, performed by members of all clubs with a large portion of idealism. After a good half year, the hall was reusable again."[29]

The court in Palais Ferstel, today's banqueting hall, was henceforth used as a meeting place for Vienna's basketball players. One of the young sportspeople won over by the hype around the game was the later Austrian federal chancellor Franz Vranitzky. He was introduced to it via contact with US soldiers during his schooldays in the 17th District. He attended games in the USFA Sports Arena and was soon training with the US soldiers. Vranitzky, whose basketball skills saw him selected for the national team, even met his future wife in the sports hall in Herrengasse.[30]

While the population of Vienna took great interest in the American soldiers in various sporting contexts, members of the three other Allied powers tended to play sport amongst themselves. Soviet troops used Augarten area in the 2nd District and the park in the grounds of the Theresianum, which was occupied by the Soviet army, in the 4th District, for leisure and sports activities. The grounds at Favoritenstrasse 15 including a large sports field and a swimming pool.[31]

Leisure activities for personnel of the British military authorities, headquartered in Schönbrunn Palace, were run by the NAAFI (Navy, Army and Air Force Institutes). The main spot for sporting activities was the Murrayfield Ground in the Fasangarten (Pheasant Garden) and the Gloriette Lido in the Schlosspark, today's Schönbrunnerbad.[32] The Blue-White Club, which had taken over the facilities of the Hietzinger Tennisvereinigung at Geylinggasse 20, hosted several tournaments in which civilians also competed.[33]

The French soldiers' sport was the remit of France Club de Vienne. One of its venues was the garden of Palais Clam-Gallas in the US-controlled 9th District, where there was also cross-country skiing in winter. The British and French military administrations attached great importance to equestrian sports and fencing. Riding and jumping competitions were held at the Freudenau racecourse and in Schönbrunn's Schlosspark, the proceeds also going to charitable causes.[34] In August 1947, the French military administration staged an international competition, collecting 100,000 schillings for the children of Vienna, with which

---

29 Paul Nittnaus, Michael Zink, Sport ist unser Leben, 89.
30 Alexander Huber, Alexander Strecha, Ex-Kanzler Vranitzky: "Hier wird auch seelischer Missbrauch betrieben", in: Kurier, 24 December 2021, https://kurier.at/sport/ex-kanzler-franz-vranitzky-im-interview-ueber-sport-und-politik-wichtig-ist-die-mannschaftsdisziplin/401850436 (1 July 2024).
31 Urrisk-Obertyński (ed.), Die vier Alliierten, 321.
32 Idid., 149.
33 Ibid., 320.
34 Ibid., 318–319.

the French high commissioner to Austria, General Antoine Béthouart, presented Mayor Theodor Körner in the form of a cheque.³⁵ The fencing salle at Mariahilfer Strasse 71 in the French Zone and the Barracks Or's Club in Schönbrunn in the British Zone provided suitable venues for inter-Allied and international tournaments.³⁶

Cycling, which had been popular in Austria before the National Socialist era, also received new impetus: many races were held in this sport considered typically French, some of them organized by the French military administration, for instance on the Schmelz in the 15th District or in the Prater, and drawing great public interest. Inspired by the Tour de France, in 1947 the two newspapers published by the French occupation authorities, *Welt am Montag* und *Welt am Abend*, organized the long-distance Quer durch Österreich (Across Austria) race over all the zonal boundaries. Commencing on 11 June 1947, the four-stage race covered a total of 791 kilometres from Bregenz to Vienna. Two years later, the first official Österreich-Rundfahrt (Tour of Austria) took place, becoming one of the country's most prestigious cycling events and making a significant contribution to the development of a new national consciousness.³⁷

Sport as a Genre of Entertainment

Post-war sport was also popularized in no small measure by the Allied media and the newly formed Austrian newspapers under Allied supervision. Although the newspapers and radio stations pursued different aims in terms of media policy, many allocated plenty of space to sports reporting.³⁸ An assessment of the "News Productions" of the Rot-Weiss-Rot (Red, White, and Red, RWR) broadcasting group under US control dated January 1949 shows the high proportion of sports reports. Of the total of around seventy-five hours of news broadcast per month, nine were dedicated to sport; only global and local news received more air time.³⁹ Live broadcasts of sporting events were as well received, as were new formats such as boxing and catching championships with international competitors, or events

---

35 Meldungen der Rathauskorrespondenz, 28 August 1947, https://presse.wien.gv.at/historische-rk/1947/-/asset_publisher/wlyuW1CMwd9x/content/august-1947?redirect=%2Fweb%2Fpresse%2Fhistorische-rk%2F1947&inheritRedirect=true (1 July 2024).
36 Urrisk-Obertyński (ed.), Die vier Alliierten, 315.
37 For further details, cf. Bernhard Hachleitner, Matthias Marschik, Rudolf Müllner, Johann Skocek: Etappenziel Österreich. Radsport 1930 bis 1950 – Helden, Raum und Nation (Zeitgeschichte im Kontext, Vol. 21), Göttingen 2024, 103–118.
38 For extensive analysis, cf. Theodor Venus: Sport im Rundfunk: 1945–1964, in: Matthias Marschik, Rudolf Müllner (eds.): "Sind's froh, dass Sie zu Hause geblieben sind". Mediatisierung des Sports in Österreich, Hildesheim 2010, 77–86.
39 Report of the United States High Commissioner, January 1949, No. 39, 74.

with US sports. In August 1953, the Wiener Eislauf-Verein pulled off a coup by booking the American basketball exhibition team Harlem Globetrotters. The two displays, both with capacity crowds of 10,000, were preceded by a free performance for schoolchildren, the Eislauf-Verein venue packed to the rafters. The shows were an experience not only for the Viennese, but also for the US soldiers, hundreds of whom filled into the arena. The basketball stars reinforced the pre-existing enthusiasm for the American sport, especially among children and adolescents, leading to the formation of several new teams.[40]

Conclusion

Although sport was revived relatively quickly in post-war Vienna due to Allied support, on the organizational level the restoration of sporting activities rested in the hands of Austrian organizations and authorities. Whereas in Berlin the Allied Control Council, the supreme occupation authority, issued Directive 23 on the "Limitation and Demilitarization of Sport in Germany" in December 1945, with the aim of restructuring sport in all four occupation zones,[41] there was no such plan for Austria. The decision for Germany was made against the background of the special role sport had played in the country's remilitarization after the First World War. From the Allied perspective, this called for stricter measures after the Second World War concerning the formation of national federations or those representing pre-military sports such as fencing or shooting. In Austria, such a law pertained only to flying gliders. On 22 December 1949, the Allied Council ultimately lifted the ban, which had prohibited any sporting activity by Austrian glider pilots after the Second World War.[42]

A significant factor behind the revival of sport in Vienna was the interaction between sportspeople among the Allied occupying troops and Viennese sports enthusiasts. The sporting activities of the Allies, especially the US Army, attracted great interest from spectators while offering a platform for cultural exchange, lending the local sports scene new impetus and contributing to the re-cultivation of social life in post-war Austria. As in the sphere of art and culture, in sport the decade of occupation displays the beginnings of the construction of a new Austrian identity and the formation of a collective national consciousness. This was also reinforced by the early success of Austrian athletes at international

---

40 Meisinger: 150 Jahre Eiszeit, 148–149.
41 Franz Nitsch: Aus der Geschichte lernen, die Zukunft zu gestalten: Reflexionen zur Nachkriegs-Sportentwicklung anlässlich aktueller Gedenktage, in: SportZeiten 3 (2016), 7–39, here: 10.
42 Die Wiedergeburt des Salzburger Segelfliegens, in: Salzburger Nachrichten, 1 June 2020, https://www.sn.at/kolumne/sport/die-wiedergeburt-des-salzburger-segelfliegens-88330651 (1 July 2024).

competitions, such as the fencer Ellen Müller-Preis's world championship title in 1947, the javelin thrower Herma Bauma's Olympic gold medal in 1948, or third place at the football World Cup in 1954, to name just a few.

Veronika Floch

"Our souls approach, understand, and agree with one another through admiration of the work of art."[1] Allied Cultural Policy and Visual Art in Vienna, 1945–1955

Visual art is an effective medium for conveying narratives, communicating values, and creating connections that shape identities. How did the four victorious powers make use of visual art? What were their aims in the field of cultural policy, which narratives were to be produced, and how did their respective programmes reflect the emerging Cold War?

While there are detailed studies on the fields of literature and architecture,[2] analysis of visual art has been more sporadic.[3] The following examination outlines the Allied cultural programmes with respect to their complex linking of

---

1 Siegfried Weyr: Kunst und Künstler. Malerei eines jungen Landes. US-Gemäldeausstellung in der Kunstakademie eröffnet, in: Wiener Kurier, 5 November 1951, 4, https://anno.onb.ac.at/cgi-content/anno?aid=wku&datum=19511105&seite=4&zoom=33&query=%22amerikanische%2Bmalerei%22&ref=anno-search (30 June 2024).
2 Cf. e.g. Michael Hansel, Michael Rohrwasser (eds.): Kalter Krieg in Österreich. Literatur – Kunst – Kultur (Profile Volume 17), Vienna 2010; Stefan Maurer, Doris Neumann-Rieser, Günther Stocker: Diskurse des Kalten Krieges. Eine andere österreichische Nachkriegsliteratur (Literaturgeschichte in Studien und Quellen, Vol. 29), Vienna 2017; Monika Platzer: Kalter Krieg und Architektur. Beiträge zur Demokratisierung Österreichs nach 1945 (exhibition catalogue, Architekturzentrum Wien), Vienna/Zurich 2019.
3 Cf. Reinhold Wagnleitner: Coca-Colonisation und Kalter Krieg. Die Kulturmission der USA in Österreich nach dem Zweiten Weltkrieg (Österreichische Texte zur Gesellschaftskritik, Vol. 52), Vienna 1991; Christina Hainzl: Abstraktion und Kalter Krieg. Das internationale Programm des Museum of Modern Art New York (1952–1962). Ein Vergleich zwischen Österreich und Italien, doctoral thesis (unpublished), University of Vienna 2004; Barbara Porpaczy: Frankreich – Österreich 1945–1960. Kulturpolitik und Identität (Innsbrucker Forschungen zur Zeitgeschichte, Vol. 18), Innsbruck 2002; Günther Dankl: Von der Form zur Geisteshaltung. Zu Frankreichs Vorbildrolle für die bildende Kunst in Österreich, in: Thomas Angerer, Jacques Le Rider (eds.): "Ein Frühling, dem kein Sommer folgte"? Französisch-österreichische Kulturtransfers seit 1945, Vienna/Cologne/Weimar 1999, 195–204; Günter Bischof, Peter Ruggenthaler: Österreich und der Kalte Krieg. Ein Balanceakt zwischen Ost und West, Vienna 2022, 89–102; Sigrid Matulik: Die Rezeption der internationalen Moderne in der bildenden Kunst in Österreich 1945 bis 1955 und die Bedeutung der alliierten Kulturpolitik, Diplomarbeit, University of Vienna 2005. Veronika Floch's doctoral thesis is devoted to this topic and the sustained impact of the Allied cultural transfer in Vienna after 1955 (completion planned for 2025).

visual art with ideology and provides an overview of the respective premises, aims, and concepts.

"Paris à Vienne":[4] The French Allies' Cultural Policy

France, portraying itself as a friendly country, sought to compensate for its geopolitical and economic losses with a cultural offensive. Austria was to act as a "bridgehead" for France's cultural transmission and political impact in Central and Eastern Europe.[5] The cultural initiatives aimed to rehabilitate art denigrated as "degenerate" by the National Socialists and to underpin France's own cultural self-presentation. A further measure was strengthening an Austrian cultural identity – on the one hand by emphasizing its historical cultural achievements, and on the other hand by developing a young generation of artists which was to be rooted in an international art discourse. The aim was to clearly delineate Austria from Germany while boosting the country's self-confidence as a young democracy.

In Vienna, French cultural policy was closely connected to the figure of Eugène Susini. From 1945 onwards, he headed the Büro für Erziehung und schöne Künste (Office of Education and the Fine Arts), having been installed in the role by the French military government, before running the French Cultural Institute from 1947 onwards. In contrast to Maurice Besset, who headed the French Cultural Institute in Innsbruck and principally exhibited contemporary arts, Susini had a more conservative understanding of art.

Although visual art – unlike music, literature, and theatre – accounted for only 14 per cent of the French cultural initiatives in Vienna, a number of exhibitions could be staged.[6] The first, "Von Ingres bis Cézanne" (From Ingres to Cézanne) was held at the Albertina in the autumn of 1945 and was organized by Susini,[7] showing French graphic art from the nineteenth century to what was then the present day. The use of art to political ends is demonstrated by the opening speech given by Secretary of State Ernst Fischer (Communist Party of Austria, KPÖ), in which he emphasized the commonalities between the two countries and France's role in the historical process of democratization, overlooking Austria's involvement in the crimes of National Socialism.[8]

---

4 The subtitle of the exibition "Salon d'Automne. Paris à Vienne". Kunstgewerbemuseum 1946.
5 On Franco-Austrian cultural transfer, cf. Angerer, Le Rider, Frühling.
6 Cit. Porpaczy, Frankreich, 234.
7 Ibid., 67.
8 G.K.B: Französische Graphik in der Albertina, in: Arbeiter-Zeitung, 24 October 1945, 3f., https://anno.onb.ac.at/cgi-content/anno?aid=aze&datum=19451024&seite=3&zoom=33 (30 June 2024).

The French military government used France's national holiday on 14 July for a series of artistic events, including two large exibitions.⁹ "Französische Phantastik", showcasing four centuries of works, was held at the Albertina, while the Wiener Kunstgewerbemuseum (Vienna Museum of Arts and Crafts)¹⁰ presented "Salon d'Automne. Paris à Vienne". To this end, the French military government financed the partial renovation of the museum, which had been damaged during the war.¹¹ The Salon d'Automne, the "Autumn Salon", was Paris's most important exhibition of contemporary artists, assembling a cross section of recent paintings, sculpture, drawings, arts and crafts, architecture, and ecclesiastical art.¹² Hitherto, the Salon d'Automne exhibition had only ever been held in France; Vienna was the site of its first international tour. This was emphasized in the media as France's generous gesture towards Austria.¹³

The first exhibition within the framework of the renewed cultural convention was staged in 1950, entitled "Klassiker des Kubismus in Frankreich" (Classics of Cubism in France). It was hosted by the Albertina, which had been managed since 1947 by Otto Benesch¹⁴ – a key figure in international cultural exchange. This exhibition was followed by "Meisterwerke aus Frankreichs Museum" (Masterpieces from France's Museums); receiving over 16,000 visitors, it was by far the most successful exhibition at the Albertina since 1945.¹⁵

Another French measure was strengthening Austria's young art scene. Cultural officer Jean Rouvier liaised with the Neue Galerie, Vienna's avant-garde gallery with an international orientation, to put on exhibitions of young artists such as Johannes Behler, Gerhild Diesner, and Paul Flora.¹⁶ Shortly thereafter, the

---

9 Cf. M.: Kunst und Künstler. Das Pariser Colonne-Orchester kommt, in: Kurier, 8 July 1946, 4, https://anno.onb.ac.at/cgi-content/anno?aid=wku&datum=19460708&seite=4&zoom=33 (30 June 2024).
10 Today: MAK– Museum für angewandte Kunst (Museum of Applied Arts).
11 Richard Ernst, Direktor Kunstgewerbemuseum an Stadtrat Viktor Matejka, 17 September 1946, in: Archiv MAK – Museum für angewandte Kunst, Mappe 139/1946, Zl.:753–46.
12 Der "Salon D'Automne" im Wiener Kunstgewerbemuseum, in; Salzburger Nachrichten, 12 July 1946 6, https://anno.onb.ac.at/cgi-content/anno?aid=san&datum=19460712&seite=6&zoom=33 (30 June 2024).
13 Cf. e. g. Mahrer: Der Pariser "Herbst-Salon" in Vienna, in: Österreichische Zeitung, 13 July 1946, 6, https://anno.onb.ac.at/cgi-content/anno?aid=oez&datum=19460713&seite=6&zoom=33 (30 June 2024).
14 Benesch had worked at the Albertina before the Second World War and was forced to emigrate to the USA in 1938. He taught at Princeton and Harvard and had excellent international contacts.
15 Ausstellungen in der Albertina (1945–1951), in: Archiv Albertina, Box 1951. Ausstellungen, Einzelakte, Gesetzte 1950–65, Folder 1137/51Öst. Leistungsschau, Statistik.
16 Vita Künstler to Norbert von Bischoff, 30 July 1946 and Vita Künstler to Jean Rouvier, 25 April 1947, in: Archiv Neue Galerie/Archiv Belvedere, https://digitale-bibliothek.belvedere.at/viewer/image/1439289954935/1/ und https://digitale-bibliothek.belvedere.at/viewer/image/1439799826237/1/LOG_0001/ (30 June 2024).

latter two became members of the Art Club, which was founded in 1947 and was Austria's most important avant-garde movement after the war. Cultural ties between the two countries were also to be deepened by visiting fellowships; recipients included the art historian Renate Rieger[17] and the artist Kurt Moldovan.[18]

The British Council and the British Allies' Cultural Policy

The British found themselves in a similar position to the French: weakened militarily and economically by the war, they sought to compensate for their decline via cultural self-presentation. There were institutional parallels too: to implement this cultural programme, they called on the British Council, which had been founded by the British government in 1934 and opened a branch in Vienna in 1946.[19] The institution's Fine Arts Department curated travelling exhibitions of British artists, and several of these presentations were shown in Vienna. The first, in 1946, was a representative selection of works from the Tate Gallery, held at the Akademie der bildenden Künste (Academy of Fine Arts) and presenting English painting from the first half of the twentieth century – from English impressionism to the recent positions of Henry Moore. Britain's role in the war was thematized with a series of works depicting, for instance, English air raid shelters. For the *Weltpresse* newspaper, published by the British, the exhibition provided a "glimpse into a hitherto hidden world that now suddenly opens up. A wonderful, free, masculine world".[20]

In subsequent exhibitions, Britain presented itself exclusively via contemporary works. It thereby contributed to a re-orientation while reinforcing its own position in the international art discourse. In 1949, the British Council brought together works by Ben Nicholson, Barbara Hepworth, and Graham Sutherland for an exhibition at the Albertina in 1949, entitled "Moderne englische

---

17 Benesch to Susini, 14 May 1949, in: Archiv Albertina, Box 1949. 156/3-1168/49, Folder NC 535-792/49.
18 Benesch to Susini, 30 April 1951, in: Archiv Albertina, Box 1951. Unprotok. Korr. v. Ausst. Rundschreiben, Folder Korr. Frankreich.
19 On the British Allies' cultural policy, cf. Johannes Feichtinger: Zur Kulturpolitik der Besatzungsmacht Großbritannien in Österreich, in: Alfred Ableitinger, Siegfried Beer, Eduard G. Staudinger (eds.): Österreich unter alliierter Besatzung 1945–1955 (Studien zu Politik und Verwaltung, Vol. 63), Vienna/Cologne/Graz 1998, 495–530; Isabella Lehner: Anglo-Austrian Cultural Relations between 1944 and 1955. Influences, Cooperations and Conflicts, Diplomarbeit, University of Vienna 2011.
20 F.T.: Die Tate Gallery in Wien, in: Die Weltpresse, 7 September 1946, 6, https://anno.onb.ac.at/cgi-content/anno?aid=dwp&datum=19460907&seite=6&zoom=33 (30 June 2004).

Graphik und Aquarellkunst" (Modern English Drawings and Watercolours).[21] A comprehensive solo exhibition at the Albertina in 1951, also held in Graz and Linz, honoured the sculptures and drawings of the important British artist Henry Moore.

Between Figurative Art and Abstraction: The American Allies' Cultural Policy

"These works contain America and the American. They get close. They give us an inkling",[22] wrote the *Wiener Kurier* in 1951 on the exhibition "Amerikanische Malerei" (American Painting). The USA, which did not have a long tradition of fine art, had a much tougher task communicated via paintings, sculptures, or drawings what was "America and the American". At the same time, in order to tie Austria to the West, it had to respond to a deep-rooted anti-Americanism and propaganda that portrayed the USA as a state 'without culture'.[23] One of the USA's main strategies was to focus on contemporary art. After 1945, New York developed into a new centre for art, replacing Paris as the axis of contemporary developments.[24] Formally, the new artistic tendencies were characterized by an abstraction that combined with positions in the Western art world to form an international, artistic language that "connected peoples". In the competition between the political systems, abstract expressionism, understood as an expression of freedom and individuality, was consciously deployed as the antithesis of Soviet Socialist Realism.

The main institutions supporting the American art programmes in Vienna were the United States Information Service (USIS)[25] and the New York Museum of Modern Art (MoMA).[26] One of the aims of the USIS was to promote cultural

---

21 Vorwort, in: Moderne englische Graphik und Aquarelle Kunst (Ausstellungskatalog Albertina), Vienna 1948, 3.
22 Siegfried Weyr: Kunst und Künstler. Malerei eines jungen Landes. US-Gemäldeausstellung in der Kunstakademie eröffnet, in: Wiener Kurier, 5 November 1951, 4, https://anno.onb.ac.at/cgi-content/anno?aid=wku&datum=19511105&seite=4&zoom=33 (30 June 2024).
23 On the circumstances of US cultural initiatives, cf. Christian H. Stifter: Zwischen geistiger Erneuerung und Restauration. US-amerikanische Planungen zur Entnazifizierung und demokratischen Neuorientierung österreichischer Wissenschaft 1941–1955, Vienna/Cologne/Weimar 2014, 562–593.
24 Cf. Serge Gibault: Wie New York die Idee der modernen Kunst gestohlen hat. Abstrakter Expressionismus, Freiheit und Kalter Krieg, Dresden/Basel 1997.
25 The United States Information Agency (USIA) from 1953 onwards.
26 On cultural policy under US occupation, cf. Oliver Rathkolb: Die Entwicklung der US-Besatzungskulturpolitik zum Instrument des Kalten Krieges, in: Friedrich Stadtler (ed.): Kontinuität und Bruch 1938-1945-1955. Beiträge zur österreichischen Kultur- und Wissenschaftsgeschichte, Vienna/Munich 1988, 35–50.

Fig. 1: Taking in the exhibition "Peintres naïfs – Amerikanische Volksmalerei von 1670 bis heute" (Peintres naïfs – American Folk Painting from 1670 to Today), Vienna Museum of Applied Art (Museum für angewandte Kunst), 1954 (ANL/Vienna, US 12.529/1)

activities for propaganda purposes, while MoMA played a significant role in transatlantic cultural transfer via its exhibitions circulating globally.[27] MoMA's first cooperation in Austria was with the Albertina in 1949. The exhibition "Amerikanische Aquarelle" (Amercian Watercolours) offered an overview of the development of American painting since the eighteenth century. There was also an Austrian connection represented by MoMA's director, the Austrian-born René d'Harnoncourt.[28] In 1951, "Frühe und zeitgenössische Malerei der USA" (Early and Contemporary Painting in the USA) was on display at the Academy of Fine Arts, mostly showing contemporary works by artists such as Edward Hopper, Georgia O'Keeffe, and Mark Rothko.[29] The historical works exhibited were fewer in number, but certainly representative, for instance the portrait of

---

27 Cf. Christina Hainzl: American Painting: The New York Museum of Modern Art's International Program in Austria, in: Günter Bischof/Anton Pelinka (ed.): The Americanization/Westernization of Austria (Contemporary Austrian Studies, Vol. 12), Cologne/New Brunswick, NJ/London 2004, 139–152.
28 René d'Harnoncourt, born in Vienna in 1901, emigrated to the USA in 1933. He worked for MoMA from 1944 onwards, as director from 1949.
29 Cf. Siegfried Weyr: Kunst und Künstler.

first US president George Washington. The USA also presented itself via pure abstract works in the exhibition "Internationale Graphik" (International Graphic Art),[30] organized at the Secession by Gustav K. Beck[31] in 1952. All the works featured were loaned by MoMA. Under the auspices of the US Embassy's Public Affairs Division,[32] among other organizations, an extensive show of contemporary 'Western' works presented the representatives of the Austrian Art Club in an international context, works by Wander Bertoni, Maria Bilger-Bilja, and Josef Mikl featured alongside those of Marc Chagall, Henry Moore, or Lyonel Feininger.[33]

As well as propagating abstraction, at least two exhibitions used a realistic, folk visual language. These were planned and organized by the New York-based gallery owner Otto Kallir[34] in collaboration with the US State Department or the USIA respectively. The first exhibition was dedicated to then ninety-year-old American Anna Mary Robertson, known as Grandma Moses, a self-taught artist whose figurative painting was characterized by idyllic rural scenes. The media noted that Grandma Moses's America showed "[…] not the gigantic and mighty continent of a state of 150 million, but a tiny excerpt so often forgotten this side of the Atlantic: America as a homeland, a homeland of the 'little man' […]".[35] The second exhibition put on by Kallir took up similar narratives. "Peintres naïfs – Amerikanische Volksmalerei von 1670 bis heute" (Peintres naïfs – American Folk Painting from 1670 to Today) was held at the Museum of Applied Arts in 1954.[36]

---

30 The exhibition was also shown in Salzburg, Linz, and Graz. For Munich and Berlin, it was taken over by the Foreign Office of the United States. Cf. Gustav K. Beck to Porter Mc Gray, MoMA, 3 November 1952, in: The Museum of Modern Art Archives, New York (in future: MoMA Archives, NY), International Council and International Program Records (IC/IP), I.A.9.
31 Gustav K. Beck was the founder of the Austrian section of the international Art Club and, from 1952 onwards, director of the Galerie Kunst der Gegenwart (Gallery of Present-Day Art) in Salzburg. He played a central role in the establishment of the young Austrian avant-garde.
32 Information leaflet, U.S. Representation: Internationale Graphik, 1952, Secession Gallery, in: MoMA Archives, NY, IC/IP, I.A.6.
33 Heute Eröffnung der Graphikschau. Ausstellung moderner Kunst in der Secession, in: Wiener Kurier, 18 October 1952, 4, https://anno.onb.ac.at/cgi-content/anno?aid=wku&datum=19521018&seite=4&zoom=33 (30 June 2024).
34 Otto Kallir was born in Vienna in 1894 and founded the Neue Galerie in 1923 as a central site for the avant-garde. In 1938, he emigrated to New York and opened Galerie St. Etienne, which he managed until his death in 1978.
35 Grandma Moses, in: Salzburger Nachrichten, 29 July 1950, 10, https://anno.onb.ac.at/cgi-content/anno?aid=san&datum=19500729&seite=10&zoom=33 (30 June 2024).
36 Jean Lipman: Über die volkstümliche Richtung in der Kunst Amerikas, in: Peintres naïfs – Amerikanische Volksmalerei von 1670 bis heute (exhibition catalogue, Museum of Applied Arts), Vienna 1954, 10.

"Soviet art is realistic art."[37] The Soviet Allies' Cultural Policy

At the start of the Cold War, at the latest, there emerged a canon of Western art, characterized by abstraction which ignored the Soviet Union or from which the latter explicitly demarcated itself. Between the wars, the communist state was still propagating the avant-garde, which was banned after Stalin came to power, however. It was replaced by the Socialist Realist style. In this context, visual art did not play as important a role for the Soviet Allies; they relied primarily on theatre, music, or literature, which they mainly employed in the Austrian–Soviet Friendship Weeks, held annually from 1949 onwards.[38] As Wolfgang Mueller writes, the Soviet Union's aim was "[…]'anti-fascist-democratic' re-education, promoting the Soviet Union, promoting socialism, and counter-propaganda".[39]

The biggest display of Soviet art was the "Ausstellung Sowjetischer Malerei" (Exhibition of Soviet Art), which took place at the Kunstgewerbemuseum in 1947.[40] Featuring the works of the four contemporary artists Aleksandr and Sergei Gerasimov, Aleksandr Deineka, and Arkadii Plastov, this exhibition was devoted to presenting the lifework of the Soviet people. The aim was to show the booming Soviet Union and its political and economic achievements. According to the catalogue, the exhibition displayed "[t]he nature of the new man, his life and his works, the nature of the homeland in all its wonderful diversity, the most important events in the life of the country […]". At the same time, a position was adopted towards Western art: "The painters in the Soviet Union do not produce abstract works, removed from life and hermetically sealed."

The intensification of the East–West conflict also led to polemic reports in the Soviet daily newspaper *Österreichische Zeitung* (ÖZ). On abstraction, it wrote: "Of course, in this abstract desert all social consciousness, all portrayal of reality, and all adoption of a critical stance towards it are hopelessly lost."[41]

---

37 Einführung, in: Ausstellung Sowjetischer Malerei (Ausstellungskatalog Kunstgewerbemuseum), Vienna 1947, 15.
38 Cf. Michael Kraus: "Kultura". Der Einfluss der sowjetischen Besatzung auf die österreichische Kultur 1945–1955, Diplomarbeit, University of Vienna 2008, 138–140.
39 Wolfgang Mueller: "Die Kanonen schießen nicht … Aber der Kampf geht weiter". Die Propaganda der sowjetischen Besatzungsmacht in Österreich im Kalten Krieg, in: Stefan Karner, Barbara Stelzl-Marx (eds.): Die Rote Armee in Österreich. Sowjetische Besatzung 1945–1955, 344.
40 Ibid., 356.
41 ek: "Triste Abstraktionen" – die amerikanische Kunst von heute, in: Österreichische Zeitung, 22 October 1952, S. 6, https://anno.onb.ac.at/cgi-content/anno?aid=oez&datum=19521022&seite=6&zoom=33 (30 June 2024).

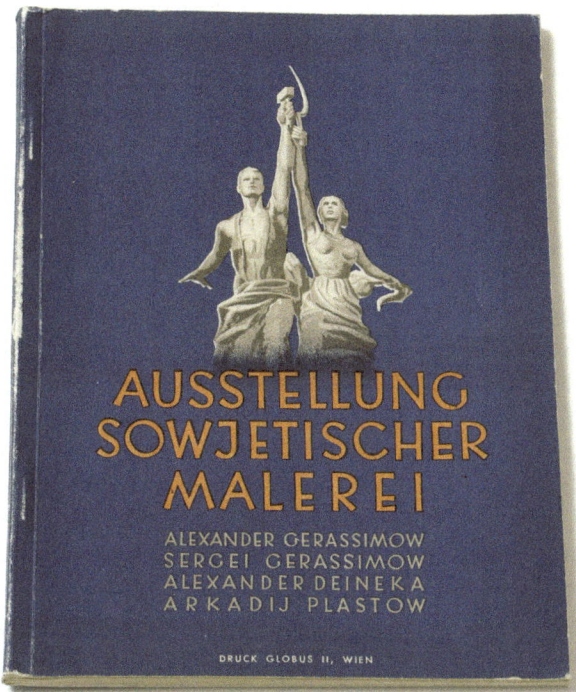

Fig. 2: Cover of the catalogue *Ausstellung Sowjetischer Maler* (Exhibition of Soviet Painters) at the Kunstgewerbemuseum (Museum of Arts and Crafts), 1947 (photo: TimTom, from the private collection of Veronika Floch)

The Art Club and Cold War Tensions

In 1947, the Austrian section of the international Art Club was formed in Vienna. It would go on to determine the development of the post-war avant-gardes in Austria.[42] The Art Club is a prime example of how the Western Allies promoted the young Austrian art scene and used it for their own cultural self-presentation. The Art Club's big annual exhibition at the Secession in 1950 was co-funded by the USIS and brought together Art Club exponents and international positions.[43] For the artist Arnulf Neuwirth, the presentation "opened a window on the world

---

[42] Cf. Christian Bauerm, Brigitte Borchardt-Birbaumer (eds.): Aufbrüche. Künstlerinnen des Art Club (exhibition catalogue, Landesgalerie Niederösterreich), Krems/Cologne 2021; Wolfgang Denk (ed.): Mythos Art Club. Der Aufbruch nach 1945 (Ausstellungskatalog Kunsthalle Krems) Krems 2003; Otto Breicha (ed.): Der Art Club in Österreich. Zeugen und Zeugnisse eines Aufbruchs (Ausstellungskatalog Museum des 20. Jahrhunderts), Vienna 1981.

[43] Mitteilungen des Art Club, 15 November 1950, no. 4, 1.

through which we could see how in all Western countries abstract art is breaking through with increasing intensity. The art of the United States has a large part in this process. [...]."⁴⁴ In 1951, cooperation between the Art Club, MoMA, and the USIS introduced Viennese audiences to the work of Alexander Calder, one of the most important American artists of the times. The exhibition was held at the Neue Galerie and showed sculptures intended to "deepen understanding of modern art of the West but also to help our country's artists striving for expression to expand their horizon".⁴⁵

The Art Club's reception made the cultural competition between the two systems visible. While reports in media published by the Western Allies were mostly positive, the ÖZ featured several articles opposing the USA, the Art Club artists, and abstraction: the Art Club was "[....] a soul-catching headquarters of the American 'culture missionaries' [....]",⁴⁶ and its artists were "Americanized smearer-awayers" ("Amerikanisierte Drauflosschmierer").⁴⁷ It continued, "why should they painstakingly study nature and the model when of course it is easier to create 'portraits' with the eyes on the nose and the head hanging on the heel [...]. The young Austrian artists have no cause to adapt to the subversive art that flows over from the other side of the ocean in a filthy stream."⁴⁸

The Western Allies' cultural transfer proved more sustained – also due to Austria's integration into the West – and can be illustrated, finally, in the example of Werner Hofmann, one of the most influential cultural managers of the postwar era.⁴⁹ As a young art historian, in the early 1950s Hofmann worked as an assistant to Otto Benesch at the Albertina and was also able to participate in the Harvard Summer School at Schloss Leopoldskron in Salzburg, partly due to his recommendation by Jean Rouvier. A scholarship funded by the French enabled him to spend time in Paris, and, working at the Secession, he played a large role in hosting the large MoMA travelling exhibition "Kunst aus USA" (Art from USA)

---

44 Arnulf Neuwirth: Alexander Calder. Eine Rede, in: Mitteilungen des Art Club, n. d., no. 7, 1.
45 Ibid., 2.
46 j.: Kunst unterm Straßenniveau. Ein Besuch im Art-Club, in: Österreichische Zeitung, 15 January 1952, 5, https://anno.onb.ac.at/cgi-content/anno?aid=oez&datum=19520115&seite=5&zoom=33 (30 June 2024).
47 Herm.: Ein Kritzler schämt sich nicht, in: Österreichische Zeitung, 24 January 1953, 6, https://anno.onb.ac.at/cgi-content/anno?aid=oez&datum=19530124&query=%22art+club%22&ref=anno-search&seite=6 (30 June 2024).
48 W. Menschikow: Auf welch' ein Erbe die österreichischen Modernisten verzichten!, in: Österreichische Zeitung, 29 November 1953, 5, https://anno.onb.ac.at/cgi-content/anno?aid=oez&datum=19531129&seite=5&zoom=33&query=%22C3%B6sterreichische%2Bzeitung%22%2B%22w%C3%BCrthle%22&ref=anno-search (30 June 2024).
49 Cf. Veronika Floch: Reflecting the American Cultural Canon: Vienna's Museum of the Twentieth Century in the Context of Westernization Discourses, in: Waldemar Zacharasiewicz, Siegfried Beer (eds.): Cultural Politics, Transfer, and Propaganda. Mediated Narratives and Images in Austrian-American Relations, Vienna 2021.

in 1956. Hofmann used his time teaching in New York to become familiar with the orientation of MoMA's content. Equipped with a travel grant organized by René d'Harnoncourt, he then visited several American museums. It was MoMA, no less, which he chose as his model as the founding director of Vienna's Museum des 20. Jahrhunderts (Museum of the 20th Century)[50] in 1958.

---

50 Today: mumok–Museum moderner Kunst Stiftung Ludwig Wien (Museum of Modern Art Ludwig Foundation Vienna).

in 1936, [illegible] his time teaching in New York [illegible] with the [illegible] of MoMA's [illegible]. Equipped with a travel grant organized by [illegible] Rockefeller Foundation, [illegible] he visited several American museums. It was MoMA, however, which he chose as his model as the founding director of Vienna's Museum des 20. Jahrhunderts (Museum of the 20th Century) in 1958.

[illegible]

Monika Knofler

Art as a Weapon – on the Allies' Exhibitions Policy

All four occupying powers agreed that Austria could look back on a long and rich cultural and artistic history. The Soviet authorities placed a focus on opera, theatre, concert, and cinema, which in their zones had already reopened in the late April of 1945. In the subsequent years, the Western Allies held around forty art exhibitions, beginning with the "Masterpieces from the Picture Gallery of the Museum of Art History", a selection of paintings US forces had secured in the Emperor Franz Josef mine at Lauffen, near Bad Ischl, on 13 May and had secretly transported to Vienna. This exhibition for propaganda purposes was opened on 19 December 1945 in the presence of the supreme commanders of the American and French troops, the generals Mark W. Clark (1896–1984) and Émile Antoine Béthouart (1889–1982), Federal Chancellor Leopold Figl (1902–1965), and the director of the State Art Collections, Alfred Stix 1882–1957), in the former imperial apartments in the Hofburg.

On the initiative and with financial support of the Soviet occupation authorities and in collaboration with the Vienna city councillor for art, Viktor Matejka (1901–1993), the Austrian Federal Association of Former Persecuted Anti-fascists held a large anti-fascist exhibition at the Künstlerhaus from 14 September to 26 December 1946. Entitled "Niemals vergessen!" (Never Forget!), it was attended by some 260,000 peoples and was also taken to Linz and Innsbruck in 1947.[1]

The exhibitions organized by the Western Allies from December 1945 onwards, primarily showing contemporary art, were held at the Academy of Fine Arts Vienna (Academy), the Graphic Art Collection of the Albertina (Albertina), the State Arts and Crafts Museum (from 1947: Austrian Museum of Applied Art), and the Secession. Further venues were the City Hall, the foyer of the Konzerthaus, the Künstlerhaus, the Zedlitzhalle, Palais Lobkowitz (used by the Institut

---

[1] Viktor Matejka, Lev C. Friedlaender (eds.): Niemals Vergessen! Antifaschistische Ausstellung. Ein Buch der Anklage, Mahnung und Verpflichtung, Gemeinde Wien, Kultur und Volksbild, Vienna 1946.

Fig. 1: General Mark W. Clark with Marie Émile Béthouart and Federal Chancellor Leopold Figl at the opening of the exhibition "Masterpieces from the Picture Gallery of the Museum of Art History" in the Hofburg, 1946 (ANL/Vienna, 134.895 B)

Français), the Italian Cultural Institute, the studio Atelier am Modenapark, Galerie Würthle, and the Neue Galerie.[2] These activities were of great importance particularly for artists exploring contemporary currents, since they had previously been isolated from all relevant information. Exhibitions held by the Swiss foundation Pro Helvetia, the Italian Cultural Institute, and the Art Club were also important sources of information.

It began with the French Cultural Institutes in Vienna and Innsbruck, which cited the fundamental aims of French cultural policy, defined with following catchwords: "désannexion" (the total structural, economic, political, and mental disentanglement of the new and independent Austria from Germany), "democratisation", and "dénazification".[3] The last was to be achieved via "désintoxication", cultural and intellectual detoxification. The stated aim was the dissemination of French cultural achievements, "especially with respect to a potential further expansion into the states of Eastern Europe power shut off from

---

[2] Gabriela Nagler: Der Weg zur Abstraktion in Österreich 1945 bis 1950, doctoral thesis, University of Vienna 1989, 137–145.
[3] Klaus Eisterer: Die französische Besatzung in Tirol 1945–1955, in: Tirol – Frankreich 1946–1960. Spurensicherung einer Begegnung, Innsbruck 1991, 115.

France's direct influence by the Communists' seizure of power".[4] With reference to Austria's cultural past prior to 1914, High Commissioner Béthouart and the head of the Cultural Institute in Vienna, Eugène Susini (1900–1982), who had previously held the post from 1925 to 1939, supported the development of Austria's own identity and position in the Danube region. The first post-war exhibition was opened as early as 20 October 1945, at the Albertina: "Von Ingres bis Cezanne. Französische Graphik" (From Ingres to Cezanne. French Graphic Art). As a response, the exhibition "Moderne französische Graphik" (Modern French Graphic Art) was held at the Academy from 11 December 1945 to 13 January 1946. The accompanying catalogue, entitled *Exposition d'Œuvres de la Gravure Française Contemporaine*, lists a total of sixty-three artists, including Pierre Bonnard, Raoul Dufy, André Lhote, Jean Lurçat, Henri Matisse, Pablo Picasso, and Georges Rouault.[5] The Albertina followed in May 1946 with "Französische Phantastik", an overview of Mannerism.[6]

The large-scale exhibitions of contemporary art began with the Museum of Applied Art's "'Paris à Vienne' – 250 Artistes du Salon'd'Automne" from 11 July from 31 August 1946, which showed approximately six hundred works of the last Salon d'Automne in Paris, attracting some 35,000 visitors.[7] In February 1947, the museum provided an overview of French painting from the previous eighty years with the exhibition "Meister der modernen französischen Malerei (Classiques de la Peinture Française moderne)", showing works by artists such as Georges Braque, Paul Cezanne, Marc Chagall, Edgar Degas, Maurice Denis, Paul Gauguin, Marie Laurencin, Ferdinand Leger, Jean Lurçat, Aristide Maillol, Eduard Manet, Berthe Morisot, Claude Pissaro, Odilon Redon, Auguste Renoir, Henri Rousseau, Paul Signac, Henri de Toulouse-Lautrec, Maurice Utrillo, Suzanne Valadon, and Éduard Vuillard, as well as those already named above.[8]

The first and only extensive exhibition by the Soviets took place on the Stubenring from 20 February to 22 March 1947. "Sowjetische Malerei" (Soviet Painting) showed ninety works by the most important exponents of Socialist Realism, Alexander and Sergei Gerasimov, Alexander Deineka, and Arkadii Plastov. This show was organized by the Committee for Artistic Affairs of the Council of Ministers of the Soviet Union and by the All-Union Society for Cultural Relations with Foreign Countries, introducing the official art doctrine

---

4 Günther Dankl: "… über das Chaos des Augenblicks hinausführende Denkanstöße …" (Maurice Besset). Zur Rezeption der französischen Kunst in Österreich von 1945 bis 1966, in: Kunst in Österreich 1945–1995, Vienna 1996, 68.
5 The University Archives of the Academy of Fine Arts Vienna (Universitätsarchiv der Akademie der bildenden Künste Wien, henceforth UAAbKW), VA 1945, Zl. 1075.
6 Austrian National Library (Österreichische Nationalbibliothek, henceforth ÖNB) 596856-B.
7 UBAbKW, shelf mark 17.417-E.
8 UBAbKW, shelf mark 17.384-E.

countering Expressionism, Surrealism, and abstraction. The introduction to the catalogue,[9] by an anonymous author, stresses that Soviet painting was devoted entirely to the nature of the New Man. "The painters in the Soviet Union do not produce any abstract works that are remote from life and self-enclosed. The Soviet masters' creative searching is ineluctably connected to reality [...]."[10] From the very outset, then, a polarity was evident between the contemporary art propagated by the Western Allies, especially the United States, particularly abstraction, and Socialist Realism, which was reminiscent of National Socialist art doctrine. From 1950 onwards, the exhibitions held at the Soviet Information Centre in the Porr-Haus[11] were mostly political in nature.[12]

The French Cultural Institute in Vienna could not open until 10 November 1947 due to renovation work at Palais Lobkowitz. It hosted the exhibition "Französische Maler um 1900 und die Schule von Paul Gauguin" (French Painters around 1900 and the Paul Gaugin School) in October and November 1949 and "August Rodin. Zeichnungen. Aquarelle (August Rodin. Drawings. Watercolours)[13] in the November and the December. In 1951, the Institut Français moved to Palais Clam-Gallas in Währinger Strasse.[14] In June and July 1952, it put on its last contemporary exhibition, "Handzeichnungen französischer Bildhauer des 20. Jahrhunderts" (Drawings by Twentieth-Century French Sculptors).[15]

After an agreement was reached with the French occupation authorities to hold reciprocal large art exhibitions, in March 1950 the Albertina hosted an exhibition of the classic representatives of Cubism, "Picasso, Braque, Juan Gris und Leger", and in the autumn of 1950 "Meisterwerke aus Frankreichs Museen. Zeichnungen französischer Künstler vom Ausgang des Mittelalters bis Cezanne" (Masterpieces from France's Museums. Drawings by French Artists from the Early Middle Ages to Cezanne)[16] was shown, followed by pages from the estate of March Chagall in February and March 1953.[17]

---

9 Wien Kunstgewerbemuseum (ed.): Aleksandr Mikhailović Gerasimov, Sergei V, Gerasimov, Arkadii A. Plastov, Aleksandr Aleksandrović Deineka, Komitet po Delam Iskusstv, Katalog zur Ausstellung sowjetischer Malerei Ölgemälde, Aquarelle, Vienna 1947, 15; UBAbKW, shelf mark 17.386-E.
10 Sowjetische Malerei, 15.
11 In Vienna's 4th District, at Treitlstrasse 3 and Operngasse 9.
12 Michael Kraus: "Kultura". Der Einfluß der sowjetischen Besatzung auf die österreichische Kultur 1945–1955, Vienna 2008, 269.
13 UBAbKW, shelf mark 18.565.
14 In Vienna's 9th District, at Währinger Strasse 30.
15 Nagler, Abstraktion, 142.
16 UBAbKW, shelf mark 15.468-E/6.
17 UBAbKW, shelf mark 15.468-E/11.

On 8 July 1946, General Béthouart and director Marcel Decombis (1916–2003) marked the opening of the Institut Français in Innsbruck with the exhibition "Chefs d'œuvre du Musée d'art Moderne de Paris (Meisterwerke der französischen Malerei der Gegenwart)" (Masterpieces of Contemporary French Painting). The Institut Français would prove influential both within and beyond the art scene in the Tyrol. In 1947, the art historian Maurice Besset (1921–2008) took over as director; in the years that followed, together with the art historian Lilly von Sauter (1913–1972), he shaped its programme with a focus on Fauvism, Cubism, and Art Informel. From the outset, this programme departed from Vienna's demands for an "educational" and "propagandist" line. The aim was to "lead the discussion about modern art out of the cul-de-sac of the then spiteful, barren controversy about the well-worn 'respect for the idea of humanity'".[18] Above all, they should give the visitors an opportunity for direct encounter with the works of classic French Modernism and contemporary art.

Until 1948, Britain was militarily and economically the leading occupying power and in charge of post-war planning.[19] Art and culture were the remit of the British Council, which was subordinate to the political division of the British section of the Allied Council (ACA/BE). In November 1945, the British Council rented twelve rooms at the headquarters of the Anglo-Austrian Bank on the Freyung.[20] It considered the most important requirements to be books, music, and a reading room. The first director of the British Council was the historian Charles Richard Hiscocks (1907–1998), who remained in the post from February 1946 to October 1949. In support of the "re-education policy", the focus was placed on English language learning, instruction on British art and science, and the presentation of British institutions. Unlike the United States and France, the British Council made no attempt to have a direct influence on the visual arts.

A summary of the British Council's policy is provided by its annual report from 1946: "The Council's main task in Austria can be summarised as the satisfying of the cultural needs, so far as British interests are concerned of a country which in the past has always considered itself one of the cultural leaders of Europe."[21]

In March 1946, some 5.5 tonnes of books were shipped to Austria, 20,000 of which were on display in the new reading room at Kärtner Strasse 15-30 in

---

18 Dankl, Chaos 69-71.
19 Siegfried Beer: Die Besatzungsmacht Großbritannien in Österreich 1945-1949, in: Alfred Ableitinger, Siegfried Beer, Eduard G. Staudinger (ed.), Österreich unter Alliierter Besatzung 1945-1955, Vienna/Cologne/Graz 1998 (Studien zu Politik und Verwaltung 63), 47.
20 Johannes Feichtinger: "Zur Kulturpolitik der Besatzungsmacht Großbritannien in Österreich", in: Ableitinger, Siegfried Beer, Eduard G. Staudinger, Österreich, 505–506.
21 Isabella Lehner: Anglo-Austrian Cultural Relations between 1944 and 1955. Influences, Cooperation and Conflicts, Diplomarbeit, University of Vienna 2011, 40.

the first exhibition on "Bücher aus England" (Books from England) from 15 to 30 March 1950. This exhibition had a large influence on Austrian architecture, especially city planning, since Britain was considered the pioneer of a modern welfare state, and was the subject of extensive discussion in the architecture magazine *Der Aufbau*, published by the City of Vienna.[22] Further exhibitions of books took place in Klagenfurt from 22 February to 1 March 1947 and in Graz from 22 February to 1 March, and thereafter at branches in Innsbruck and Linz.[23]

In 1946, the Albertina put on the exhibition "Meister der englischen Graphik" (Masters of English Graphic Art), and from 7 September to 2 October 1946 the Academy hosted "Moderne britische Bilder aus der Tate Gallery" (Modern British Pictures from the Tate Gallery),[24] curated by the Tate's director, John Rothenstein (1901–1992), with the motto "Projecting Britain abroad", with works by artists such as Henry Moore, Paul Nash, Lucien Pissaro, Edward Wadsworth, and Christopher Wood. In March and April 1948, the Albertina collaborated with the British Council to show "Moderne englische Graphik und Aquarellkunst" (Modern English Graphic and Watercolour Art), including works by Lucian Freud, Ben Nicholson, and Graham Sutherland.[25] The Academy followed from 20 October to 10 November 1948 with an exhibition organized by the Victoria and Albert Museum in London entitled "Das englische Bühnenbild" (The English Stage Set).[26] At the Neue Galerie, the exhibition "Alexander Calder" took place from 10 May to 15 June 1951. In contrast, the Academy ran an exhibition of watercolours from the British Museum's William Turner collection, from 22 November to 30 December.[27] At the same time, the Albertina showed "Henry Moore. Zeichnungen – Kleinplastik – Graphik" (Henry Moore. Drawings – Figurines – Graphic Art).[28] These were followed by two exhibitions in 1953, "Buchkunst und Gebrauchsgraphik aus England" (Book Art and Commercial Art from England)[29] at the Museum of Applied Art in the March, and "Lithographien zeitgenössischer britischer Künstler" (Lithographs by Contemporary British Artists) at the Albertina in the June.[30] The British Council's last exhibition, "Graham Sutherland. Gouachen, Aquarelle und Zeichnungen" (Graham Su-

---

22 Monika Platzer: Kalter Krieg und Architektur: Beiträge zur Demokratisierung Österreichs nach 1945, Vienna 2019, 65.
23 Feichtinger, Kulturpolitik, 521.
24 Ibid., 515–517.
25 UBAbKW, shelf mark 17.534-E.
26 UBAbKW, shelf mark 17.603-E.
27 UBAbKW, shelf mark 18.571-E.
28 UBAbKW, shelf mark 15.468-E/8.
29 Nagler, Abstraktion, 141.
30 Ibid., 139.

therland. Gouaches, Watercolours, and Drawings)[31] took place at the Academy, from 1 February to 6 March.

For the Americans, the priority was to convey the image of a culturally advanced country with profound values. Unlike the other occupation authorities, which held exhibitions from as early as December 1945, the Americans did not enter the fray until the autumn of 1949, with the exhibition "Amerikanische Meister des Aquarells" (American Watercolour Masters) at the Albertina, whose director, Otto Benesch (1896–1964), had lived in Cambridge, Massachusetts from 1940 to 1947, working at the Fogg Art Museum at Harvard University. He had an excellent knowledge of American art, and hence he received support from the New York Field Office, Department of the Army and the US Information Service in Austria. The jury was virtually a who's who of the American twentieth-century art scene: the director of the Museum of Modern Art (MoMA) in New York, the Austrian René d'Harnoncourt (1901–1968); MoMA curator Dorothy Miller (1904–2003), the curator of the Brooklyn Museum; I. H. Bauer, the deputy director of the Whitney Museum, Lloyd Goodrich (1897–1987); the director of the Detroit Institute of Art, E. P. Richardson (1902–1985); and the director of the Music and Art Section of the New York Field Office, Harrison Kerr (1897–1978). The letter sent to all museums and private collections in the USA received an overwhelming response; besides MoMA, the most important American museums lent works, such as the Metropolitan Museum of Art, the Whitney Museum of American Art, the Fogg Art Museum in Cambridge, the Detroit Art Institute of Arts, the art museums of Cleveland, Newark, Syracuse, and Worcester, the St. Louis City Art Museum, the Philipps Gallery in Washington, D.C., the Atkins Museum of Fine Arts in Kansas, the Columbus Gallery of Fine Arts in Ohio, and the Frank K. M. Rehn Galleries in New York. The catalogue texts were written by Otto Benesch and Lloyd Goodrich.[32] A total of fifty-nine works were exhibited, by artists including Thomas Eakins, Charles Burchfield, Charles Demuth, Lyonel Feininger, Morris Graves, Winslow Homer, Edward Hopper, and Maurice Predergast.

It would be two years until the next exhibition, "Amerikanische Malerei – Werden und Gegenwart" (American Painting – Becoming and the Present", at the Academy from 3 to 18 November 1951.[33] It was curated by the director of the National Gallery of Art in Washington, D.C. in collaboration with a committee of fifteen and was financed by the American Federation of Arts and the Oberlaender Trust. The first part of the exhibition showed the development of American painting in the eighteenth and nineteenth centuries. Most of the

---

31 UBAbKW, shelf mark 20.358.
32 UBAbKW, shelf mark 15.468-E/3.
33 UBAbKW, shelf mark 18.556-E.

twentieth-century artists were representatives of a traditional-realist school, with the exception of Edward Hopper. There were also abstract works by Wilhelm A. Baziotes, Stuart Davis, Lee Gatch, John Marin, Robert Motherwell, Georgia O'Keeffe, Irene Rice Pereira, Jackson Pollock, Mark Rothko, and Mark Tobey.

For post-war architecture, the "Amerikanische Wohnbauausstellung" (American Housing Exhibition) at the Messepalast in 1950 and the exhibition "Architektur der USA seit 1947" (Architecture of the USA since 1947) at the Museum of Applied Art in 1952 were of great importance. The same year, the exhibition "Internationale Grafik" (International Graphic Art), financed by MoMA, was held in the gallery Kunst der Gegenwart (Art of the Present), opened in Salzburg by the founders of the International Art Club, Kurt Beck (1902–1983) and Slavi Soucek (1898–1980). The exhibition was subsequently shown in Linz.[34] In September 1954, Galerie Würthle in Vienna showed the farewell exhibition of the work of the head of the Pictorial Section of the American Information Service (USIS) in Austria, Yoichi R. Okamoto (1915–1985), part of whose estate is held today by the picture archive of the Austrian National Library. One of the most successful exhibitions, drawing almost 10,500 visitors, was "Peintres naïfs – Amerikanische Volksmalerei von 1670 bis heute" (Peintres naïfs – American Folk Painting from 1670 to Today) at the Austrian Museum of Applied Art in collaboration with USIS, the Smithsonian Institute, and Otto Kallir's Gallery St. Etienne, from 28 October to 21 November 1954.[35]

Coverage of artistic activities was largely provided by the daily newspapers that were under the patronage of the individual occupation authorities, such as the Americans' *Wiener Kurier*, the Russians' *Österreichische Zeitung*, the British's *Weltpresse*, and the French's *Welt am Abend*. The content displayed the corresponding political orientations. The *Wiener Kurier*, the *Neuer Kurier* from 1955 onwards, featured reports by Fritz Novotny (1903–1983), Siegfried Weyr (1890–1963), and Alfred Schmeller (1920–1990). The cultural editor of the *Wiener Zeitung* was Hans Ankwicz-Kleehoven (1883–1962). Cultural magazines of note were *Die Schönen Künste* (1946–1948), *Die Zeit*, for which Arthur Roessler (1877–1955) and Fritz Karpfen (1897–1952) wrote, *Der Turm, Surrealistische Publikation*, edited by Max Hölzer (1915–1984) and Edgar Jené (1904–1984), *Plan, Woge*, and *Austria International*, for which Jorg Lampe and Werner Hofmann wrote.[36] The many reviews and articles on contemporary art were "often extremely polemical and emotional [...], with the effect that they contribute little to

---

34 Christina Hainzel: American Painting: The New York Museum of Modern Art's International Program in Austria, in: Günter Bischof, Anton Pelinka: The Amercanization / Westernization of Austria, Contemporary Austrian Studies, Cologne/New Brunswick (USA)/London 2004, 147.
35 Hainzel, American Painting, 146; UBAbKW, shelf mark 30.994-E.
36 Nagler, Abstraktion, 30–37.

explaining the situation or to differentiation" and should "be seen more as artistically composed self-reviews and self-historicizations than as substantiated examinations of contemporary art".³⁷

Fig. 2: The exhibition "Moderne Kunst aus USA" (Modern Art from the USA) at Vienna's Secession; unpacking a painting by Jackson Pollock, 2 May 1956 (ANL/Vienna, US 12.927/3)

---

37 Dankl, Chaos, 198.

Monika Platzer

Architecture in Four Acts, 1945–1955

After liberation by the Allies, each of the four occupation authorities established their own varied cultural programme. Hence Britain, France, the USA, and the Soviet Union all used architecture exhibitions as a means of cultural, ideological, economic, and technological transfer. The architecture on display and the accompanying discourses became instruments of an "education programme" for a new world and societal order reflecting the global competition of the Cold War.[1] Besides the Allies' respective specific political interests, their measures for exerting cultural influence were aimed at different target groups, revealing the frictions between local reactionary forces and the values imported by the occupiers.

Britain

The increasing decline in Britain's economic and military significance shifted the spotlight to the country's self-presentation or propaganda, which the British themselves referred to as "projection of Britain".[2] Competing for supremacy with the other victorious powers, the British increasingly relied on a modern, dynamic image of their country with the ambition of actively helping to shape the future of the post-war order.[3] One of the first architecture exhibitions the Allies put on Vienna was initiated by the British in 1947. The exhibition on urban construction entitled "England im Aufbau" ("Replanning Britain"), exhibited at the Austrian Museum of Applied Arts from 11 October to 15 November 1947, was staged by the

---

1 Cf. Monika Platzer, Architekturzentrum Wien (ed.), Kalter Krieg und Architektur: Beiträge zur Demokratisierung Österreichs nach 1945, Zurich 2019 [*Cold War* and Architecture: The Competing Forces that Reshaped Austria after 1945, Zurich 2020].
2 Gabriele Clemens, Die britische Kulturpolitik in Deutschland: Musik, Theater, Film und Literatur, in: eadem (ed.), Kulturpolitik im besetzten Deutschland 1945–1949 (Historische Mitteilungen, Beiheft, 10), Stuttgart 1994, 210.
3 Ibid., 217.

British Council and the Royal Institute of British Architects[4] and presented the New Towns Act of 1946 enabling the construction of new urban spaces. Stevenage in Hertfordshire was first of a total of fifteen New Towns built up to 1955 under this law intended to put an end to the uncontrolled growth of cities. Reporting on the tendencies in the construction of New Towns in England pervades the specialist publication of the Vienna Stadtbauamt (City Construction Office), *Der Aufbau.*[5]

During the war, the Special Operations Executive (SOE) headed by Labour minister Hugh Dalton made contact with leading exiled Austrian Social Democrats in London, including Oscar Pollak and Franz Novy. British cooperation with the Austrians was based on the idea of establishing a left-wing counterweight to the Communists in an independent Austria after the war.[6] In 1945, Novy returned to Austria and was appointed city councillor for building matters in 1946. In this function, he was responsible for rebuilding Vienna, and in 1949 he introduced a paradigm shift for the city: "From the social[/communal] housing of the interwar period to the social city planning of the free welfare state of the future."[7] His statement shows the Social Democrats' process of demarcation and transformation from the social construction of communal housing influenced by Austromarxism in Red Vienna towards a national welfare state with clear ties to the West. After 1945, city planning focused on creating new large-scale housing and industrial areas outside the urban core, with the aim of democratizing the population. The New Towns Act and the County of London Plan were named as examples.[8]

Conforming to Austria's integration into the West as part of the post-war order and the SPÖ's ideological ties with the British Labour Party, Vienna's Social Democrats came to see the British way of a democratic welfare state as an alternative to authoritarian National Socialism, totalitarian communism, and laissez-faire capitalism. This enabled the architects to make the transnational urban model of the garden city and the structuring principle of the neighbour-

---

4 British Council / Royal Institute of British Architects, England im Aufbau. Eine britische Städtebauausstellung, [Vienna] 1947.
5 Eduard Sekler: Stevenage, Eine neue Stadt, in: Der Aufbau, No. 1/2: 2, January/February 1947, 17–20. Eduard Sekler: Besuch in Welwyn Garden City, in: Der Aufbau, No. 5/6: 2, May/June 1947, 61–63, 81.
6 Peter Pirker: Subversion deutscher Herrschaft. Der britische Kriegsgeheimdienst SOE und Österreich (Zeitgeschichte im Kontext, Vol. 6), Göttingen 2012, 33.
7 Franz Novy: 25 Jahre sozialer Wohnungsbau in Wien, in: Der Aufbau,1,4, January 1949, 4. The term "Sozialer Städtebau" (social urban development) was used by Johann Gundacker as early as 1947. Cf: Stadtbaudirektor Dipl.-Ing. Gundacker: Nachkriegsaufgaben des Wiener Stadtbauamtes, in: Österreichische Rundschau, No. 5/6: 2, 1947, 135.
8 A. Zimmermann: Das Beispiel London, in: Österreichische Rundschau, No. 5/6: 2, 1947, 136–137.

hood as a social space, which had also belonged to the repertoire of urban planning under the Third Reich, the "new" post-ideological model of social urban development without it being associated with the original ideologically motivated aspects.[9]

France

Like Britain, France used cultural policy to compensate for its loss of political and economic influence in Central and Eastern Europe. An economically and intellectually independent Austria was to become a stepping stone allowing France to regain its position in the world and supporting French interests.[10] With its two cultural institutes in Innsbruck and Vienna, French cultural policy positioned itself as a kind of "intellectual intermediate power between the new 'materialist system' of the mercantile 'Anglo-Saxon' bloc and Soviet 'utilitarianism'".[11]

The first French exhibition of architecture and urban development was held at the Kunstgewerbemuseum in Vienna from 10 to 30 May 1948, on the initiative of the high commissioner of the French Republic. In the foreword to the catalogue, General Marie Émile Antoine Béthouart points to the sphere of operations of French architects and urban developers, which had never been as extensive in the country's history. In most destroyed cities, there were already "new dwellings built in accordance with the most modern methods", and "French architecture [has] lost nothing of its traditional genius".[12] The exhibition presented André Lurçat's plans for Maubeuge, a steel town near the Belgian border, as well as Le Corbusier's unrealized plans for Saint-Dié (1944–1946) and La Rochelle-La Pallice (1945). Le Corbusier opened the exhibition with a talk on the "Synthesis of the Arts", which was printed in the magazine *Der Aufbau* in 1948.[13] Le Corbusier

---

9 Under National Socialism, many plans for housing estates for the German "Volksgemeinschaft" were based on the garden city model. Winfried Nerdinger calls the garden city movement one of the most enduring and adaptive architectural utopias of the twentieth century. Cf: Winfried Nerdinger, Architekturutopie und Realität des Bauens zwischen Weimarer Republik und Drittem Reich, in: Wolfgang Hardtwig: Utopie und politische Herrschaft im Europa der Zwischenkriegszeit (Schriften des Historischen Kollegs, Kolloquien, 56), Munich 2003, 269–286, here: 286.
10 Barbara Porpaczy: Frankreich – Österreich 1945–1960. Kulturpolitik und Identität (Innsbrucker Forschungen zur Zeitgeschichte, Vol. 18), Innsbruck 2002, 56.
11 Elisabeth Starlinger: Aspekte französischer Kulturpolitik in Österreich nach dem Zweiten Weltkrieg (1945–1948), Diplomarbeit, University of Vienna 1993, 36.
12 Marie Émile Antoine Béthouart: Vorwort, in: Staatliches Kunstgewerbemuseum in Wien, Französische Ausstellung Architektur und Städtebau (exihibition catalogue, Staatliches Kunstgewerbemuseum in Wien, 10 to 30 May 1948), Vienna 1948, n.p.
13 Le Corbusier: Synthese der höheren Kunstform, talk given on 11 May 1948, in: Der Aufbau, No. 12: 3, December 1948, 290–292.

was critical of official plans for Vienna. There was no desire for radical interventions in the city's existing urban structure, and Le Corbusier's blueprints for a vertical city were at odds with the ideals of Vienna's urban developers. At the universities, any engagement with his oeuvre was frowned upon. Friedrich Achleitner speaks of a "ban" imposed by Holzmeister's assistant Eugen Wachberger, who remarked when he saw anyone with a Le Corbusier book, "Why don't you just join the Communist Party?"[14]

In the free avant-garde scene that emerged in connection with the Austrian national group of CIAM[15] from 1947 onwards and became a catalyst for the internationalization of Austrian architecture, the talks by the French architects Le Corbusier, André Lurçat, and Marcel Lods found great resonance.[16] The sustained impact of these talks became evident years later, as demonstrated by a section dedicated to the principles of urban development at the CIAM-Austria conference in Vienna in 1951, which gave rise to the publication of a special edition of the Athens Charter in German.[17]

USA

The merits of the Marshall Plan with its European Recovery Program[18] (ERP) for the socioeconomic rebuilding of Austria are well documented.[19] Its use in the construction of social housing and the ideological background to this financing are barely known, however. Under US leadership of the Economic Cooperation Administration (ECA – succeeded by the Mutual Security Agency, MSA, in 1951), some fifteen residential estates emerged in the Federal Republic of Germany up to 1953, built with ERP funding. With the increasing clash of political systems during the Cold War, the American model of home ownership became a bulwark against the communist model of collective housing.

---

14 Architekturzentrum Wien: Sonja Pisarik und Ute Waditschatka im Gespräch mit Friedrich Achleitner am 18.3.2009, typescript.
15 The Congrès Internationaux d'Architecture Moderne (CIAM) was an international organization formed by the leading Modernist architects from 1928 onwards.
16 For instance, Oswald Haerdtl, Erich Boltenstern, Eugen Wörle, Karl Schwanzer, Eugen Wachberger, Max Fellerer, Carl Auböck, Roland Rainer, Friedrich Zotter, Johannes Spalt, Friedrich Kurrent, and Wilhelm Holzbauer.
17 Österreichische Gruppe der internationalen Congresse für Neues Bauen: Charta von Athen C.I.A.M. Vienna 1951, special edition.
18 Countries receiving funds of the ERP were Belgium, Denmark, France, Britain, Greece, Iceland, Italy, Luxembourg, the Netherlands, Norway, Austria, Sweden, Switzerland, and Turkey.
19 Günter Bischof, Anton Pelinka, Dieter Stiefel (eds.): The Marshall Plan in Austria (Contemporary Austrian Studies, 8), New Brunswick, NJ, et al. 2000; Helmut Lackner / Technisches Museum Wien: Österreich baut auf. Wieder-Aufbau & Marshall-Plan (exhibition catalogue, Vienna Museum of Technology and Science, 17 March–2 October 2005), Vienna 2005, 39.

Similar efforts can be observed in Austria: in 1951/52, five million schillings in ERP funding were made available for building society homes (*Bausparheime*).[20] Up to 1958, the government received from the ECA mission an initial injection of 9.3 million schillings for building private homes,[21] and the Americans launched a showcase project in the form of the Veitingergasse model estate (1952-1954), designed by Carl Auböck and Roland Rainer. The project was aimed at families in Vienna who did not wish to live in "subsidized housing" but rather wanted to take responsibility for their own home. The houses were offered at very favourable conditions: the owner had to pay 15 per cent of the entire price up front, while the rest was financed by a building society loan within the framework of the ERP housing subsidies, for a period of twenty-nine years and at an interest rate of 5.25 per cent.

As well as encouraging people to buy their own homes, the plan was to introduce the production and export of affordable serial houses. The Americans thought that creating a market for pre-fabricated houses would pave the way to Austria's independence and that the "Trade Secrets House", developed by the National Association of House Builders in 1952, would stimulate the Austrian pre-fab industry. The aim was to industrially prefabricate at least half, if not two thirds, as standard components (including windows, doors, and walls) in the factory.

The model housing exhibition was opened on 9 October 1954 and received around 40,000 visitors. The novel pre-fab house and the creation of homes for ownership were rejected by consumers and the Vienna city administration, and thus ended the Americans' educational housing experiment. In their own country, the Veitingergasse project was considered an outstanding example of transatlantic knowledge transfer, as demonstrated by the editorial on the "world's most advanced, all-modular, all-component houses".[22]

---

20 Kurzberichte vom Wiederaufbau, in: Der Aufbau, No. 2: 7, February 1952, 93.
21 Franz Tinhof (ed.): Zehn Jahre ERP in Österreich 1948-1958. Wirtschaftshilfe im Dienste der Völkerverständigung, Vienna 1958, 82.
22 The Industrial Revolution in Housing, Progress Report 5, in: House and Home, July 1960, n.p.

USSR

Fig. 1: In 1952, the Soviet authorities built the Pavilion of the Union of Soviet and Socialist Republics for Vienna's Autumn Trade Fair. Curated by Viktor S. Andreev and Wilhelm Schütte (consultant), Vienna Trade Fair, 1952 (ANL/Vienna, US 10.406/14)

Unlike the Americans, the Soviets did not start to set up information centres until 1950. On 16 September 1950, the first Sowjetisches Informationszentrum (SIZ) was opened in the Porr-Haus. Communicating the achievements of Soviet culture, architecture, and knowledge was part of the Soviet strategic agenda from the outset. The exhibition "200 Millionen bauen die Natur um. Die Großbauten des Friedens in der Sowjetunion" (200 Million Transform Nature. The Great Projects of Peace in the Soviet Union) took place from 8 November to mid-December 1952, at the height of the Korea crisis. The exhibition was intended to counter the assertions of Western propaganda that the USSR was primarily engaging in armament. Hence the peace-loving construction achievements were foregrounded. In an exhibition hall bearing the title "Fundamente der Zukunft" (Foundations of the Future), the spotlight was shone on technological masterpieces such as the world's largest hydroelectric plant on the Volga[23] at Kuibyshev (today's Samara) and Stalingrad (today's Volgograd), the Main Turkmen Canal,[24] and the Volga–Don Canal, opened on 27 July 1952. Besides the "message of peace", the strategic aim involved showing the productivity of the Soviet people hand in hand with the efficiency of the systematic economic development on the basis of the Five-year Plan.[25]

The instrumentalization of exhibitions for socio-political aims was part of the Allies' repertoire. An open-air exhibition on Moscow University at the Friedensbrücke in the Brigittenau was to convey to the Viennese that the workers could study in the Soviet Union as a country where education was not the privilege of the few.[26] The "Palace of Knowledge" was built under the direction of Lev Rudnev from 1949 to 1953.[27] The university became a symbol of equal opportunities in education for all social sections of the population. This was legitimized by reproducing visitors' responses verbatim: "What? That's a university? Looks more like a huge palace." "Franzl, look. This is how workers study in Russia. Interesting, isn't it?"[28]

Soviet hopes that such cultural policy efforts would sway Austria towards people's democracy were not fulfilled. Compared to the dominant Western integration of Austria, the Soviets' cultural propaganda work with its dogmatic orientation remained a niche product.

Postscript

After the establishment of Austrian sovereignty and neutrality in 1955, the global contest of the Cold War played out in Vienna. Before the summit between John F. Kennedy and Nikita Khrushchev in 1961, direct confrontation between East and West took place at the Vienna Fair in the autumn of 1957. The USA commis-

---

23 No fewer than nine new hydroelectric power stations were built on the Volga, Europe's longest river (3,534 kilometres).
24 The canal, some 1,445 km in length, runs between the River Amu Darya (near Kerki) and the Caspian Sea via the Karakum Desert and the northern edge of the Kopet-Dag mountain range on the border with Iran. The Soviet Union began construction in 1954 in order to meet the growing demand for water for the cotton and rice plantations it had forced on the region. The canal was the largest in the Soviet Union.
25 G. O.: Großer Erfolg der Ausstellung "200 Millionen bauen die Natur um", in: Österreichische Zeitung, 25 November 1952, 7.
26 Die Moskauer Universität – in der Brigittenau, in: Die Brücke Österreich-Sowjetunion, No. 10, 1954, n.p.; Land ohne Bildungsprivileg, Interview mit Landesschulinspektor Albert Scharf, in: Die Brücke Österreich-Sowjetunion, No. 5, 1950, n.p.
27 Ein Palast des Wissens, in: Die Brücke Österreich-Sowjetunion, No. 8, 1953, n.p.
28 Die Moskauer Universität – in der Brigittenau, in: Die Brücke Österreich-Sowjetunion, No. 10, 1954, n.p.

sioned Walter Dorwin Teague to build an American pavilion right next to the Pavilion of the Union of Soviet and Socialist Republics planned by Viktor Andreev for 1952.[29]

It was the architectural clash of two systems: the US construction, reduced to the essential structural elements of steel, aluminium, redwood, plastic, and fibre materials, confronts a representative building born of the formal repertoire of Socialist Realism, crowned with a red star.

Fig. 2: Direct confrontation between East and West took place at the Autumn Trade Fair in 1957, over the American pavilion, 1957 (ANL/Vienna, US 12.986/58)

Architecture became the communication channel of the political conflict in the Cold War, something understood both by those who commissioned the structure and their audience: "The trim-lined, modern U.S. building contrasted favorably with its neighbor, the older style structure of typical Russian Baroque architecture. The local press availed itself of the opportunity to make frequent comparison, such as: 'modern Architecture against Stalin-Baroque' and 'two worlds at the Vienna Fair' – the colorful steel pavilion of the Americans with its clear

---

29 Die USA im eigenen Pavillon, in: Amtsblatt der Stadt Wien, No. 73, 11 September 1957, 11–12.

modern architecture, and in the background the Stakhanov[30] mosque of Russians."[31]

---

30 The faceworker Aleksei Grigor'evich Stakhanov produced 102 tonnes of coal in single shift in a mine in the Donbas on 31 August 1935. Assisted by seven colleagues, he thus surpassed the required norm thirteen-fold. It can be assumed, however, that the amount of coal he actually mined was below the levels claimed. Divided amongst him and his colleagues, the norm was still surpassed by 75 per cent. Subsequently, the trade unions and the CPSU organized the Stakhanov movement to increase productivity in the Soviet Union by making him an exemplary worker.
31 Third Semi-Annual Report, President's Special International Program, July 1, 1957, December 31, 1957, 41–43.

Markus Stumpf

"Books are undoubtedly not furniture." The Library as a Battleground: Reorientation through Denazification and Book Donations

When the National Socialist dictatorship came to an end in 1945, the re-established Austria and the Allies were confronted with the problem of rebuilding the democratic and peaceful foundations from scratch. To this end, the "penetration and flooding with National Socialist writings"[1] and the resultant gaps in holdings had to be eliminated, libraries thus becoming part of the battleground in the sphere of education and cultural policy.

That consideration was given the role of libraries as essential institutions for disseminating information, culture, and memory in the plans for the internal mobilization of the US population (Education for Victory) and the plans for the re-education of the enemy states in European post-war society is illustrated by the example of the USA. For instance, before the USA entered the war in October 1941, the director of the Library of Congress (LOC) in Washington D.C., Archibald MacLeish (1892–1982), had already been appointed head of the Office for Facts and Figures, a department of the Pentagon directly below the president. The role of this organization was to consider the question of the population's moral attitude and the use of propaganda measures in cultural foreign policy. MacLeish envisaged an appropriate US educational cultural propaganda response to the threat of the Axis powers to be expanding cultural relations by depicting US culture as something worth striving for. After the US entered the war, in 1942 the department was transferred to Office of War, itself directly below the president and tasked with producing war propaganda. MacLeish became the Office of War's deputy director ultimately representing the USA during the founding of UNESCO and working on the preamble to the UNESCO constitution.[2]

---

[1] Dieter Stiefel: Entnazifizierung in Österreich. Vienna/Munich/Zurich 1981, 238.
[2] Cf. Christian H. Stifter: Zwischen geistiger Erneuerung und Restauration. US-amerikanische Planungen zur Entnazifizierung und demokratischer Neuorientierung österreichischer Wissenschaft 1941–1955, Vienna/Cologne/Weimar 2014, 110–111.

For the Allies, the "political purging of societal and economic life of all National Socialist and fascist influence" represented "an unconditional prerequisite for the further democratic development in Europe, as had already been established at the Yalta Conference in February 1945".[3] Besides demilitarization, denazification was the precondition for a democratic restructuring of society and for rebuilding the entire culture and education system, including libraries. Even if one cannot speak of a dedicated Allied library policy – with the exception of the USA – it can be said to have played a role in denazification, propagandistic information policy, and restitution. In post-war Austria, the political positions of the individual actors, such as the Allied, the Allied Council, the National Council, the Austrian government, the Federal Council, parties, etc., were negotiated in parallel processes. These political stances must also be considered in the context of the Cold War.[4]

Denazification

Denazification included purging personnel (dismissals, employment bans), pruning laws of National Socialist content or racial discrimination (for instance, removing reference to the "Führer and Reich Chancellor"), returning stolen and seized property (restitution), but also purging holdings of National Socialist writings and literature. A peculiarity of denazification is also the "positive" influencing of library holdings and thus information policy by donating books.

Self-cleansing and Attempts to Expand Holdings by Nazi Libraries

In April 1945, both the population and the authorities removed National Socialist literature "spontaneously and without orders from above"[5] in an act of (self-) cleansing. Member of the National Council Anton Frisch (1889–1963, ÖVP) reported in parliament in March 1946: "With the collapse of National Socialism, our people has itself instinctively conducted this purge of literature. Pictures and

---

3 Brigitte Bailer: Gegen nationalsozialistische Wiederbetätigung und Holocaustleugnung. Das NS-Verbotsgesetz 1947 bis heute, in: Mathias Lichtenwagner, Ilse Reiter-Zatloukal (eds.): "… um alle nazistische Tätigkeit und Propaganda in Österreich zu verhindern". NS-Wiederbetätigung im Spiegel von Verbotsgesetz und Verwaltungsstrafrecht (Veröffentlichungen der Forschungsstelle Nachkriegsjustiz 6), Graz 2018, 13–26, here: 13.
4 Cf. Gerhard Renner: Entnazifizierung der Literatur, in: Sebastian Meissl, Klaus-Dieter Mulley, Oliver Rathkolb (eds.): Verdrängte Schuld, verfehlte Sühne. Entnazifizierung in Österreich 1945–1955, Vienna 1986, 202–229.
5 Stiefel, Entnazifizierung, 238.

inscriptions have disappeared at once. As just as much a matter of course, these books disappeared from bookshop windows, and the Nazis, too, prudently hid their books. [...] Without first waiting for a demand from above, the lower authorities from the libraries and statute books have all removed these works by themselves."[6]

As early as 19 May 1945, it was reported that fourteen of Vienna's Municipal Libraries (Städtische Büchereien) had been able to reopen, since holdings comprising over 20,000 works had already been checked for National Socialist content.[7] However, the cleansing of libraries of literature was initially undertaken in line with act of 8 May 1945 banning such works, but without any special legal basis. In addition to removing National Socialist works, an important goal of the libraries was to refill the gap in their holdings that had developed under National Socialism and due to losses in the course of the war (as a result of bombing and the looting of storage facilities).

Hence donations of books were requested – "aesthetic, particularly Austrian literature, as well as works of world literature".[8] As early as April 1945, the Office for Culture (Amt für Kultur) put up placards asking the Viennese to report private libraries in empty homes of National Socialists who had fled, so that the books could be collected and made available to the wider public.[9] The basis for these appeals was a broad interpretation of the Allies' decision to leave the furniture and fittings of National Socialists who had fled to the authorities in the respective territories; in Vienna, this was established by an agreement between the Municipal Libraries and the Asset Protection Office (Vermögenssicherungsamt) on 5 July 1945.[10] Immediately, scholarly libraries also laid claim to these holdings resulting from the "securing of unattended assets".

---

6 11. Sitzung des Nationalrates der Republik Österreich, V. G.P., 20. März 1946, Stenographisches Protokoll, 141.
7 Spendet Bücher für die Städtischen Büchereien! In: Neues Oesterreich, 19 May 1945, 3.
8 Neues Oesterreich, 10 May 1945, 4.
9 Cf. Heimo Gruber: Bücher aus dem Schutt. Die Wiener Städtischen Büchereien 1945–1950, Vienna 1987, 12.
10 Cf. Gruber, Bücher, 23–24.

Nazi Libraries for Vienna University Library

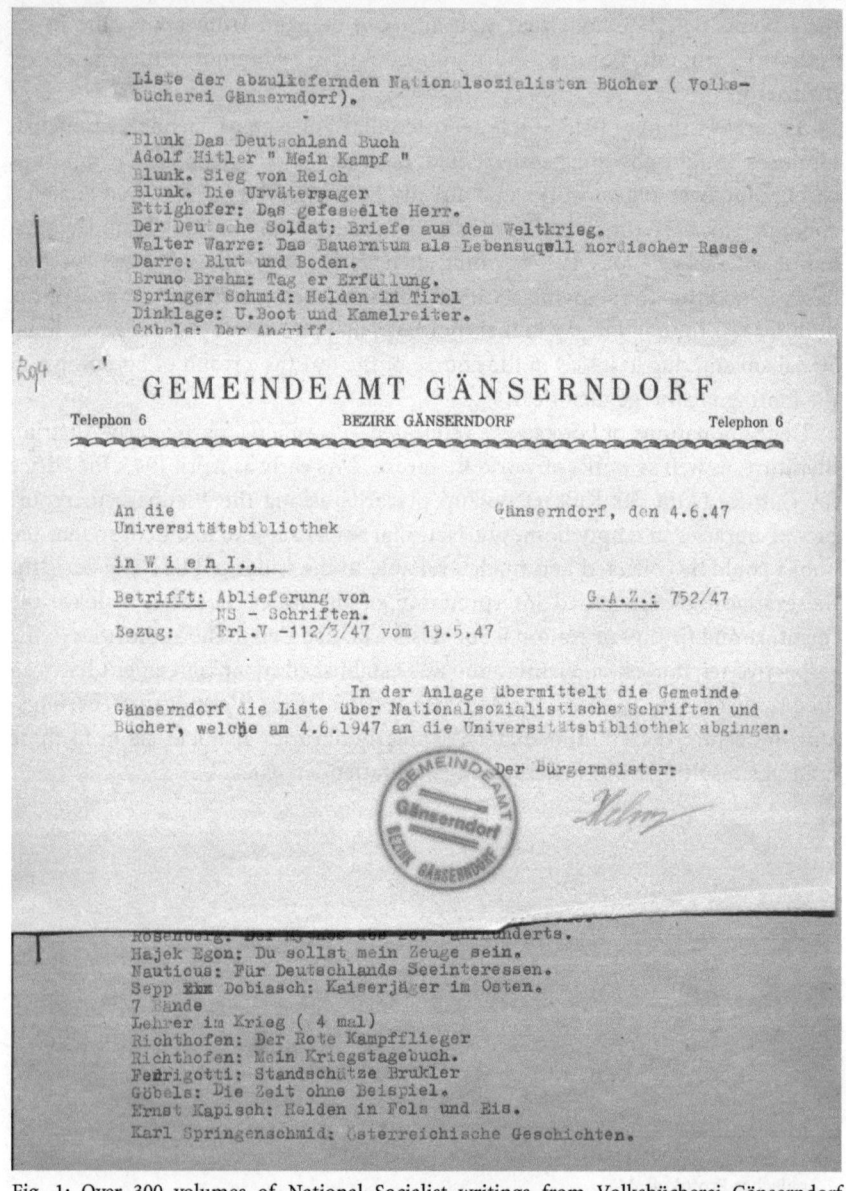

Fig. 1: Over 300 volumes of National Socialist writings from Volksbücherei Gänserndorf (Gänsendorf Public Library) being delivered to Vienna University Library, 1947 (University Archive, University of Vienna, UB SO 7, folder: Belege 1946–1947, Gemeinde Gänserndorf)

Driven by the large losses suffered by Vienna University Library,[11] re-installed director Johann Gans (1886–1956) approached the district chairman of Währing, Alois Püringer (KPÖ), as early as June 1945.[12] He also requested "friendly consideration" for Vienna University Library by the chief of police for the 18th District "in the distribution of the books secured there".[13] His intervention proved immediately successful; from 10 July 1945, the first large batches of books came in, from what was eventually a total of twenty private libraries seized in the 18th District.[14]

A little later, Gans also got in touch with the communes' administration (Gemeindeverwaltung) in Vienna: "Among the private libraries confiscated by Gemeindeverwaltung, especially those of university teachers, there are works, if not entire collections, with purely scholarly content and textbooks. […] I now request you […] to task the relevant authority [with ensuring] that scholarly works, textbooks, and possibly series of such journals are handed over to the University Library in order to promote teaching here insofar as it is possible."[15]

In particular, Gans intervened in order to receive the libraries of the musicologist Robert Lach (1874–1958) and the historian Heinrich Srbik (1878–1951), ultimately in vain. Both had been members of the antisemitic group of professors known as the "Bärenhöhle" ("Bears' Cave") as well as the NSDAP.[16] In the case of Srbik, he lost out to the Academy of Sciences; he was forced to recognize that "a resolution by the academic senate exists according to which the successor to the professor in question is responsible for the bequeathed library of his prede-

---

11 On the loss of holdings and the denazification of personnel at Vienna University Library, cf. Christina Köstner-Pemsel, Markus Stumpf: Ein Spiegelbild machtpolitischer Umbrüche – Die Universitätsbibliothek Wien, in: Karl Anton Fröschl et al. (eds.): Reflexive Innensichten aus der Universität. Disziplinengeschichten zwischen Wissenschaft, Gesellschaft und Politik, Göttingen 2015, 513–528.
12 Vienna University Archive (VUA), UB SO.4.5, Folder: Listen der übernommenen Privatbibliotheken von Nationalsozialisten 1945–1951, letter from Johann Gans to Mayor Püringer, 12 June 1945.
13 VUA, UB SO.4.2, Folder: Sichergestellte Privatbibliotheken von Nationalsozialisten, Listen A–M übergeben 1950, Letter from Johann Gans to Chief of Police Bernhard, 7 July 1945.
14 VUA, UB SO.4.5, Folder: Listen der übernommenen Privatbibliotheken von Nationalsozialisten 1945–1951. The figures apply only to Vienna University Library, not the faculty and departmental libraries, which then operated separately.
15 VUA, UB SO.4.2, Folder: Sichergestellte Privatbibliotheken von Nationalsozialisten, Listen A–M übergeben 1950, Schreiben Johann Gans an die Gemeindeverwaltung Wien, Verwaltungsgruppe XI – Kultur und Volksbildung, zuhanden des Herrn Obermagistratsrates Dr. Krauss, 27 July 1945.
16 Cf. Klaus Taschwer: Geheimsache Bärenhöhle. Wie eine antisemitische Professorenclique nach 1918 an der Universität Wien jüdische Forscherinnen und Forscher vertrieb, in: Regina Fritz, Grzegorz Rossoliński-Liebe, Jana Starek (eds.): Alma Mater Antisemitica. Akademisches Milieu, Juden und Antisemitismus an den Universitäten Europas zwischen 1918 und 1939, Vienna 2016, 221–242.

cessor".[17] He responded with an angry letter to the Asset Protection Office: "If the University Library is to take over a collection of books, this can only happen on the basis of clear ownership with the right to unlimited control over the books. [… A]fter all, each of these allocations involves time, effort, and money that are all in vain if the University Library is to be used only as a depository."[18]

In March 1946, during a meeting with the scholarly libraries at the Federal Ministry for the Securing of Assets, the Municipal Libraries' efforts to secure books were praised by the director general of the Austrian National Library, Josef Bick (1880–1952), and the director of Vienna University Library, but they wished to transfer ultimate inspection and decision making on the use of books to a board of interested parties. It was established that around 200,000 books had been secured hitherto, around 50–60,000 of which could be used by the Municipal Libraries. "Scholarly works, unique items, and such like are intended for the public libraries, the Viennensia found for the City Library [Stadtbibliothek]. National Socialist thought will of course be removed."[19]

It was emphasized that "the Commune of Vienna has not confiscated, but merely secured" the works and that this had been done by various bodies, and hence "during the deliveries during the first months the owners of the books secured can hardly be established any more. In future their securing would be conducted by municipal organs, and inspection and allocation, hitherto undertaken by specialist officials of the Commune Administration, will take place with the consent of a committee; however, importance will be attached to ensuring that allocations also take into consideration the City Library, the municipal collections, and the City Archive."[20]

Hence a board for the inspection and allocation of secured books was formed on 3 April 1946. It comprised single representatives of the National Library, the Administrative Library of the Federal Chancellor's Office, Vienna University Library, Vienna University of Technology Library, Vienna City Library, and Vienna's Municipal Libraries.[21] It was soon disbanded, however; for the Federal

---

17 VUA, UB SO.4.5, Folder: Listen der übernommenen Privatbibliotheken von Nationalsozialisten 1945–1951, Letter from Johann Gans to the State Office for Public Enlightenment, for Education and Upbringing, and for Cultural Affairs (Staatsamt für Volksaufklärung, für Unterricht u. Erziehung u. f. Kultusangelegenheiten), 13 August 1945.
18 Ibid.
19 VUA, UB SO.4.3, correspondence concerning the destruction of National Socialist books, 1945–1949, result of the discussion at the Federal Ministry for the Securing of Assets and Economic Planning, 21 March 1946, regarding the securing of holdings of National Socialist books for the Vienna City Administration (Magistrat).
20 Ibid.
21 Cf. Heimo Gruber: Die Wiener Städtischen Büchereien 1945 bis 1949, in: Friedrich Stadler (ed.): Kontinuität und Bruch 1938-1945-1955. Beiträge zur österreichischen Kultur- und Wissenschaftsgeschichte, Vienna/Munich 1988, 93–132, here: 107–108.

Ministry of Education in 1948, the National Socialist Act of 1947 meant that "only furniture ('which is usually part of a home's furnishing') [has been] transferred from confiscated homes to property of the relevant regional authority. Books are undoubtedly not furniture. Hence there are no concerns on behalf of the Commune of Vienna about returning to the owners the books handed over to the University Library from confiscated homes, unless the owner has been sentenced by the People's Court to forfeiture of assets or such proceedings are pending. Inquiries in this matter will need to be conducted in each individual case."[22]

Ultimately, the efforts to secure the private libraries did indeed prove to be a laborious "free security measure"[23] for returning actual or alleged National Socialists; in the following years, the holdings had to be returned to the original owners – if they could be identified. To this end, the University Library even displayed the relevant books in the reading room[24] – a practice those who had had their books stolen under National Socialism, or their descendants, would surely have wanted for their own holdings too.[25]

Purging Literature[26]

While it ultimately proved a mistake to enlarge holdings by acquiring Nazi libraries, an official denazification and acquisition of literature took place. In 1945, all libraries and bookshops had been instructed by the Ministry of Education and the provincial governments "to keep a lock on National Socialist literature and all writings hostile to reconciliation between nations and promoting racial hatred".[27] At the suggestion of the Soviets, in October 1945 the Allied Council engaged in the removal of fascist literature in Austria, and in late 1945 the Allies produced a Directive on the Denazification of Literature, which the Allied Council ratified on 10 January 1946, proscribing the extensive removal

---

22 VUA, UB SO.4.3, Folder: correspondence on the destruction of National Socialist books, 1945–1949. Letter from the Ministry of Education to the directorate of Vienna University Library, 5 September 1948.
23 Cf. Gruber: Büchereien, 106.
24 VUA, UB SO.4.5, Folder: Listen der übernommenen Privatbibliotheken von Nationalsozialisten 1945–1951, letter from Johann Gans to the laywer Dr. Rudolf Granichstaedten-Czerva, 28 October 1950.
25 For findings and publications pertaining to research on restitution and provenance at Vienna University Library, cf. the website https://bibliothek.univie.ac.at/provenienzforschung.html (19 August 2024).
26 For an extensive discussion of the chapter, cf. Markus Stumpf: Sinnvoll, angemessen und gerecht? Digitale Wiederveröffentlichung von NS-Schrifttum durch Bibliotheken, in: Markus Stumpf, Hans Petschar, Oliver Rathkolb (eds.): Nationalsozialismus digital, Göttingen 2021, 225–266.
27 Stiefel, Entnazifizierung, 239.

and destruction of fascist printed materials and pictorial works of any kind and in all territories.[28] The Allied Council also demanded that a Central Commission be deployed by the Ministry of Education and similar commissions by the Landeshauptmannschaften (offices of the provincial governors) and the Commune of Vienna to examine and monitor all rules for its implementation,[29] although two copies of each edition of works to be removed could be left at the National Library and the University Library. Responsibility for the regular collection of these holdings and use of this literature lay with the education minister.[30]

For instance, the *Liste der gesperrten Autoren und Bücher* (List of Banned Authors and Books) published by the Ministry of Education for the book trade and libraries in January 1946 and compiled on the basis of the earlier lists[31] stated, "Since it is impossible to name and summarize in lists the entire collection of fascist, National Socialist writing of the past 25 years, all books and writings the content of which clearly pursues National Socialist or fascist ideology are barred from print, sales, and lending. This ban applies of course to all printed works the authors of which are renowned fascist leaders or war criminals, such as Hitler, Goebbels, Rosenberg, Mussolini, etc., as well as [works whose] titles indicate the forbidden content, for example themes pertaining to the glorification of war[,] positive militarism, the racial question, or such like."[32]

The "Autorensperrliste" (Banned Authors List), which even included less well-known works but cited as the basis for the bans the *Nationalsozialistische Bibliographie. Monatshefte der Parteiamtlichen Prüfungskommission zum Schutz des NS-Schrifttums* (National Socialist Bibliography. The Party Office Monitoring Commission's Monthly for the Protection of National Socialist Literature) from 1936 to 1944, was initially in force up to 1 September 1946, but it was then extended indefinitely in October 1946.[33] The main intention of the Allies and post-war policy in Austria in dealing with National Socialist works was to avoid their abuse for propaganda purposes.[34]

---

28 Ibid., 239–240.
29 Cf. Ministerratsprotokoll Nr. 3, 14.01.1946, in: Protokolle des Ministerrats der Zweiten Republik. Kabinett Leopold Figl I: 20. Dezember 1945 bis 8. November 1949, Vol. 1: 20. Dezember 1945 bis 9. April 1946, Vienna: 2004, 43–65, here: 46.
30 Cf. Stiefel, Entnazifizierung, 240.
31 By the summer of 1945, a list of 2,200 works to be banned had been compiled. A list of 600 titles followed in the late August. The inspecting commission convening at the Office for Culture and People's Education (Amt für Kultur und Volksbildung) comprised representatives of the City Library, the Union of Democratic Writers and Journalists, and the State Office for Education.
32 Liste der gesperrten Autoren und Bücher. Maßgeblich für Buchhandel und Büchereien. Hrsg. vom Bundesministerium für Unterricht. Jänner 1946, 3.
33 Cf. Murray G. Hall, Christina Köstner: ... Allerlei für die Nationalbibliothek zu ergattern. Eine österreichische Institution in der NS-Zeit, Vienna/Cologne/Weimar 2006, 471.
34 Cf. Bundesministerium für Unterricht: Liste, 3.

The Austrian federal government complied with the Allied mission and presented the National Council with a Federal Constitutional Act on the Destruction of Printed and Pictorial Works with National Socialist Content or of a Character Hostile to One of the Allies (Bundesverfassungsgesetz betreffend die Vernichtung von Druck- und Bildwerken nationalsozialistischen Gehalts oder eines den alliierten Mächten feindlichen Charakters). After discussion by the parties represented in the National Council, the latter adopted the Purging of Literature Act (Literaturreinigungsgesetz) on 20 March 1946.[35] This essentially corresponded to the Allies' demands; for instance, the owners of private libraries were also obliged to surrender works, the Ministry of Education set up a Central Commission, and all the Landeshauptmannschaften established commissions of their own. Hiding a work that had to be handed in was punishable by a prison sentence of at least six months. It was also established that for "scholarly purposes two copies of every work subject to mandatory surrender (§ 1) [are to] be retained in special departments at the Austrian National Library and at those university libraries that require such works to fulfil the scope of their functions."[36]

However, the National Council had passed the Purging of Literature Act with two amendments the Allied Council had rejected.[37] On the one hand, delivery was extended to further "scholarly institutions" such as federal province libraries and Vienna Municipal Library (Städtische Bibliothek Wien). On the other hand, natural and legal persons were permitted to keep such forbidden books in their private libraries where it was in the interests of their public duties, subject to approval by the Education Ministry and the Ministry of the Interior (parliamentary privilege).[38]

In December 1946, the National Council also passed an amendment extending the "sphere of printed works subject to mandatory surrender by including those containing agitation to hatred or persecution of a community on the basis of religion, origin, or nationality, especially Jews". This amendment was not initially forwarded to the Allied Council, however, since it had yet to approve the law itself.[39]

Further, in the spring of 1946, the Purging of Literature Act, then still in development, had been used by the Federal Ministry of Education to combat

---

35 Cf. Stiefel, Entnazifizierung, 240–242.
36 Regierungsvorlage, 109 der Beilagen zu den stenographischen Protokollen des Nationalrates (V. Gesetzgebungsperiode).
37 According to the First Allied Control Agreement of 4 July 1945, laws made by the Austrian National Council had to be ratified unanimously by the Allied Council.
38 Cf. Regierungsvorlage, 109 der Beilagen; cf. Also Stiefel, Entnazifizierung, 243–244.
39 656 der Beilagen zu den stenographischen Protokollen des Nationalrates (V. Gesetzgebungsperiode).

National Socialist literature.[40] While it was initially responsibly for creating the list of authors and literature to be banned, pursuant to the 1947 Ban Act (Verbotsgesetz), it was ultimately tasked with the groundwork for registering the National Socialists and with listing "composers of printed materials of any kind or of film scripts declared forbidden works by the commission formed by the Federal Ministry of Education due to their National Socialist content".[41] Within the framework of the Ban Act,[42] it convened twenty times between 1948 and 1949; ultimately, thirteen authors with one or several works were placed on the list of writers to be banned. Some twenty-nine other writers with one or several works were listed for withdrawal.[43] When the Purging of Literature Act failed to emerge – ultimately, it was discussed six times by the National Council and thrice by the Allied Council (in April 1946, December 1946, and April 1948)[44] – the Central Commission was disbanded.

New regulations were also created for the use and surrender of the National Socialist holdings. Following the instructions of the Ministry of Education of February 1946, at Vienna University Library, for instance, "forbidden literature" could only be "granted to those persons who need this literature strictly for scholarly purposes".[45] In fact, however, after Austria retained its sovereignty in November 1955, it was not possible either to find a legal basis for maintaining the ban on literature with National Socialist content or to speak of violation of the National Socialism Act if the scholarly libraries also made literature with National Socialist content available to users. The indexing of the works declared forbidden by the Central Commission due to their National Socialist content came to an end only with the amnesty on National Socialists of 1957, since when the Federal Constitutional Law entered into force, pursuant to Article 1 Section 1 Paragraph 1, listing pursuant to the 1947 Ban Act no longer took place. It was only then that the libraries were informed that the *Liste der gesperrten Autoren und Bücher* (List of Banned Authors and Books) had been annulled.[46]

---

40 Cf. Ministerratsprotokoll Nr. 11, 05.03.1946, in: Protokolle des Ministerrats der Zweiten Republik. Kabinett Leopold Figl I: 20. Dezember 1945 bis 8. November 1949, Vol. 1: 20 Dezember 1945 bis 9. April 1946, Vienna 2004, 293–315, 304.
41 Verbotsgesetz 1947, Article II, §4. (1) d.
42 Cf. 64. Verordnung über die Durchführung des Verbotsgesetzes 1947, Section V, §45 "Besondere Bestimmungen über Kommissionen".
43 Cf. Claudia Wagner: Die Zentralkommission zur Bekämpfung der NS-Literatur. Literaturreinigung auf Österreichisch. Diplomarbeit, University of Vienna 2005, 92.
44 Cf. 43. Sitzung des Bundesrates der Republik Österreich, Stenographisches Protokoll, 24 May 1949, 741–744.
45 VUL, UB L. 17, Laufer an Beamte und Aufseher, 12 February 1946.
46 VUA, UB Eingangsprotokoll, letter by the Federal Ministry of Education: "Aufhebung der Liste der gesperrten Autoren und Bücher", Z. 96.034-1/55, 22 December 1956.

The Expansion of Holdings via the Centralization of National Socialist Literature and Book Donations: The Example of the Vienna University Library

In April 1946, the libraries were instructed to centralize the banned National Socialist holdings in Austria at the National Library, the university libraries, and the libraries of other higher education institutions. A further decree by the Federal Ministry of Education in July 1946 stipulated that the entire National Socialist holdings were to be removed from all public, educational institution, and school libraries. Vienna Municipal Libraries, for instance, transferred all their National Socialist literature to the National Libraries, and all Lower Austrian libraries sent theirs to Vienna University Library.[47]

In order to pull from circulation all the other National Socialist holdings at the institute and faculty libraries that were then not part of the respective university libraries, in the May the Federal Ministry of Education instructed all university rector's offices to send their several copies to the National Library and the university libraries of Vienna, Graz, and Innsbruck and the Studienbibliothek Salzburg (Salzburg Study Library), which then had to destroy them.[48] Against the backdrop of the paper shortage in the post-war years, in 1947 the printed works with National Socialist ideas withdrawn from Vienna University Library were sent to paper mills for pulping. Overall, several heavily guarded transports of over eighteen tonnes of National Socialist printed materials were delivered and pulped. In 1949, over eleven more tonnes were delivered.[49]

Vienna University Library retained two copies of each item of National Socialist printed materials for Swiss libraries (the Zentralbibliothek Zürich and the Landesbibliothek Bern), however.[50] Indeed, as early as December 1945 Secretary of State Ernst Fischer of the State Office for Public Enlightenment (Staatsamt für Volksaufklärung) had sent a letter to the library directors indicating that these books "are mainly intended" to be "submitted in a process of exchange with large scholarly libraries abroad […] for other works of literature. In this way, the possibility exists to complete to some extent the Austrian libraries that have been

---

47 Cf. Gruber: Büchereien, 115; VUA, UB SO.7 Listen der im Jahre 1946 abgelieferten NS Bücher (1946–1947).
48 Cf. Markus Stumpf: "Aus einer liquidierten jüdischen Buchhandlung". Provenienzforschung an der Universitätsbibliothek Wien – Kontinuitäten und Brüche, in: Gerhard Renner, Wendelin Schmidt-Dengler, Christian Gastgeber (eds.): Buch- und Provenienzforschung. Festschrift für Murray G. Hall zum 60. Geburtstag, Vienna 2009, 171–186.
49 VUA, UB SO.4.3, Folder: Korrespondenz betreffend die Vernichtung von NS Bücher 1945–1949.
50 Ibid., letter from Johann Gans to the Federal Ministry of Education, 25 April 1947.

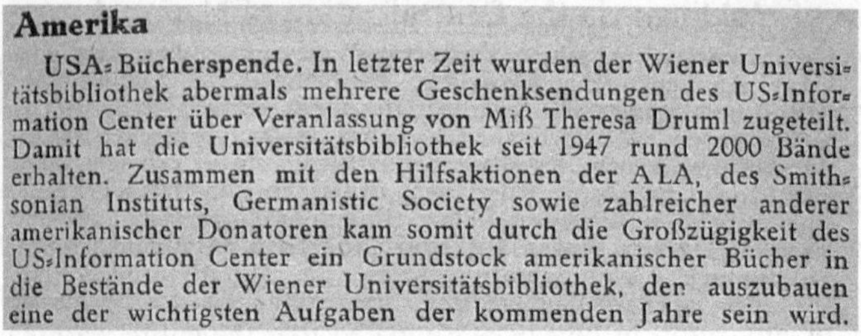

> **Amerika**
>
> **USA-Bücherspende.** In letzter Zeit wurden der Wiener Universitätsbibliothek abermals mehrere Geschenksendungen des US-Information Center über Veranlassung von Miß Theresa Druml zugeteilt. Damit hat die Universitätsbibliothek seit 1947 rund 2000 Bände erhalten. Zusammen mit den Hilfsaktionen der ALA, des Smithsonian Instituts, Germanistic Society sowie zahlreicher anderer amerikanischer Donatoren kam somit durch die Großzügigkeit des US-Information Center ein Grundstock amerikanischer Bücher in die Bestände der Wiener Universitätsbibliothek, den auszubauen eine der wichtigsten Aufgaben der kommenden Jahre sein wird.

Fig. 2: Books donated to Vienna University Library by the US Information Center. Source: *Anzeiger für den Buch-, Kunst- und Musikalienhandel*, 15 June 1949, no. 12, 105 (ANNO, ANL/ Vienna)

badly affected by war damage."[51] Overall, Vienna University Library put aside 1,445 bound volumes and 559 brochures;[52] their value in Swiss francs was to be used for the antiquarian acquisition of lost books. The Allies were sceptical,[53] however, and it would be 1955/56 before this transaction could take place due to "difficulties with the occupying powers" after Vienna University Library had already received books with a value of 28,000 Swiss francs and other Austrian public libraries had been donated 22,000 Swiss francs' worth of books.[54]

Apart from the Swiss book donations, it was mainly the Allies, however, that provided gifts to build up the library holdings, the Americans in particular coming to the fore during the years of occupation. They themselves were very interested in information and printed materials from Europe, and had been since 1939 and the losses of acquisitions en route over the Atlantic due to the war. In 1942, this gave rise to the acquisition project European Mission, launched by the Library of Congress in cooperation with other US research libraries, in order to acquire holdings from Europe. Hence in 1946, the United States Occupying Military Government also maintained its own library missions in the American Zones in order to ensure as many German-language printed works as possible were available in the USA.[55] In Vienna, the Library of Congress Mission was located at the Allianz headquarters in Frankhplatz and was also in contact with

---

51 Ibid., letter from the Office for Public Enlightenment, for Education and Upbringing, and for Cultural Affairs to the directorates of the Austrian National Library, the university libraries of Vienna, Graz, and Innsbruck, and the study libraries in Linz, Salzburg, and Klagenfurt, 7 December 1945.
52 Ibid., letter from Johann Gans to the Ministry of Education, 25 April 1947.
53 Cf. Military Government Austria (ed.): Report of the United States High Commissioner, April 1947, No. 18, 23.
54 VUA, UB A.75 Kurrentakten 1955, Folder BmfU, letter from Vienna University Library to the Ministry of Education, 15 November 1955. On the figures, cf. for instance the announcements in *Österreichische Volksstimme* (9 March 1946, 3) and the *Anzeiger für den Buch-, Kunst-und Musikalienhandel* (15 September 1947, no. 18, 5).
55 https://guides.loc.gov/european-mission/ (19 August 2024).

the director of Vienna University Library, who attempted to persuade the head of the Vienna mission, Henry Birnbaum (1917–1999), to leave to his institution American books from the army libraries – in vain.[56]

However, the Americans were also interested in filling gaps in the library holdings, including at Vienna University Library. In August 1946, *Wiener Kurier* had already reported, "As the headquarters as the American Forces in Austria announces, the Smithsonian Institute and the Rockefeller Foundation has [sic] sent two extensive packages of scholarly and sociological works published in the United States during the war as a donation for the Austrian universities and libraries."[57] According to newspaper reports, Vienna University Library received 2,000 further volumes between 1947 and 1949 via the US Information Service.[58] The Allies would donate many more books before they left.[59]

---

56 VUA, UB A.66 Kurrentakten 1946, Folder 2, letter from Henry Birnbaum to Johann Gans, 21 August 1946.
57 Oesterreich erhält amerikanische Bücherspende, in: Wiener Kurier, 9 August 1946, 3.
58 Anzeiger für den Buch-, Kunst- und Musikalienhandel, 15 June 1949, no. 12, 105.
59 Cf. Bücherspende für die Universität, in: Wiener Kurier, 23 April 1954, 3.

Günther Stocker

The Allies and Austrian Literature

Denazification

The history of Austrian literature during the first decade after the war is characterized to a large degree by political tensions, actors, and discourses.[1] After liberation from National Socialism, it seemed important to denazify a literary industry that had been brought into line with National Socialist ideology ("Gleichschaltung") between 1938 and 1945 in order to re-organize a democratic and enlightened public sphere. The Allies went about this mission with different areas of emphasis and shifting levels of commitment. For instance, "public libraries, lending libraries, and bookshops" were to be cleansed of "existing National Socialist, fascist, and militaristic works and writing of literary content by National Socialist authors".[2] To this end, checks of holdings were undertaken on the basis of a provisional "list of banned authors and books" comprising "just over 1,600 authors, with a total ban on 195 of them",[3] revised and published by the Ministry of Education in January 1946. To implement this policy, the Austrian parliament, under Allied pressure, was supposed to devise a "Literaturreinigungsgesetz" (Literature Cleansing Act). This "was probably the most-discussed denazification measure, but the effort, especially on the part of the Allies, was not commensurate with its success",[4] since the Allies repeatedly objected to the government's bills. In the early 1950s, the Western Allies then no longer considered such a law necessary, regarding prior Austrian efforts to weed out and

---

1 Cf. the extensive study by Stefan Maurer, Doris Neumann-Rieser, Günther Stocker: Diskurse des Kalten Krieges. Eine andere österreichische Nachkriegsliteratur, Vienna/Cologne/Weimar 2017.
2 Murray G. Hall, Christina Köstner: ... allerlei für die Nationalbibliothek zu ergattern ... Eine österreichische Institution in der NS-Zeit, Vienna/Cologne/Weimar 2006, 468.
3 Ibid., 469.
4 Gerhard Renner: Entnazifizierung der Literatur, in: Sebastian Meissl, Klaus-Dieter Mulley, Oliver Rathkolb (eds.): Verdrängte Schuld, verfehlte Sühne. Entnazifizierung in Österreich 1945–1955, Vienna 1986, 202–229, here: 211.

pulp such works as sufficient. Another factor was that consensus in the Allied Council also disappeared in view of Cold War tensions.[5]

In principle, Austrian writers who had incriminated themselves as National Socialists were banned by the 1947 Ban Act (Verbotsgesetz). Such categorization could involve both penitence and a ban on their publication. To this end, the Ministry of Education set up a Central Commission for Combating National Socialist Literature (Zentralkommission zur Bekämpfung nationalsozialistischer Literatur), which pronounced only six bans by August 1948, however – an extremely low number if we consider only the seventy-one authors who had enthusiastically welcomed the end of an independent Austria in the *Bekenntnisbuch österreichischer Dichter* (Austrian Poets' Book of Commitment) in 1938. In 1949, the Central Commission was closed as a "toothless, ineffective instrument" "without having achieved anything of note".[6] This is demonstrated not only by the large readership that persisted for former National Socialist writers such as Bruno Brehm or Mirko Jelusich, but also by the fact that the Grand Austrian State Prize for Literature went to incriminated authors such as Max Mell (1954), Franz Nabl (1956), or Franz Karl Ginzkey (1957). In the assessment of the author and director Ernst Lothar, who had returned from exile and was commissioned by the US Information Service Branch (ISB) to denazify the Austrian theatre and music business from 1945 to late 1947, "hardly any task was performed as inadequately as this one, by all involved, including myself. The aims were: the elimination of those involved in the disgraceful regime or those actively in agreement with it, as punishment for them, as a warning to others, and as the foundation for clean rebuilding. What was achieved: a schematic, inconsistent revenge, persistently riddled with exceptions, that undermined faith in the propriety, informedness, or foresight of the cleansers."[7]

Remigrants Recalled by the Allies

From the Allied perspective, Austrian writers returning from exile had a special role to play in the "clean rebuilding" (see above) of the literary industry. However, they often came as citizens of their country of exile and in Allied uniform, which did not make their task any easier.[8] Ernst Lothar, for instance, bore the title Theatre and Music Officer of the United State Forces Austria (USFA), working for

---

5 Cf. ibid., 219.
6 Hall, Köstner, Nationalbibliothek, 468.
7 Ernst Lothar: Das Wunder des Überlebens, Vienna 2020, 258.
8 Cf. Oliver Rathkolb: Ernst Lothar – Rückkehr in eine konstruierte Vergangenheit. Kulturpolitik in Österreich nach 1945, in: Jörg Thunecke (ed.): Echo des Exils. Das Werk emigrierter österreichischer Schriftsteller nach 1945, Wuppertal 2006, 279–295, here: 281.

the ISB. He had three main tasks: "Denazification, rebuilding cultural life in the US Zone in Austria, and Spreading American theatrical and musical works",[9] which he attempted to fulfil from 1946 to the end of his commission in the late December of 1947, with varying degrees of success.

The dramatist *Franz Theodor Csokor* returned from exile in Italy in April 1946 "with a Polish passport and in a British liaison officer's uniform",[10] having served with the combined Allied forces in the peninsula.[11] Since an author with an "entirely anti-fascist stance"[12] was sought for the re-establishment of an Austrian P.E.N. Club centre, the widely-known Csokor seemed the ideal founding president. In the first post-war decade, the P.E.N. Club played an important role in the re-organization of the Austrian literary industry and especially in fostering young authors. A principle of its re-establishment was striving for "total independence from the Austrian government and the Allied occupation authorities".[13] It could not extricate itself from the heated, often denunciatory debates of the Cold War, however. For instance, for years, the author and critic Hans Weigel, who had returned to Austria from exile in Switzerland in the summer of 1945, waged a media campaign against the P.E.N. board, accusing it of having been infiltrated by communists, and against Csokor, whom he accused of not distancing himself clearly enough from communism. In the early 1950s, Weigel became involved with the media of the US occupation authorities: he organized literary evenings at the ISB's Kosmos-Theater, wrote regular pieces for the US Zone's newspaper *Wiener Kurier*, and devised several formats for the American-occupied broadcaster Radio Rot-Weiss-Rot.[14]

The second protagonist of the cultural Cold War in Austria, Friedrich Torberg, did not return to Vienna until April 1951. A US citizen, in 1952/53 he was responsible for relations between Austrian cultural life and the US authorities, under the unwieldy title "consultant to the officer of public affairs" of the Foreign Service, Cultural Division.[15] Torberg agitated in articles, talks, open letters, and intrigues against anyone who he thought did not distance themselves from communism clearly enough. Such efforts were lent particular potency from 1954 to 1966 by his editorship of the journal *FORVM. Österreichische Monatsblätter*

---

9 Ibid., 288.
10 Klaus Amann: P.E.N. Politik. Emigration. Nationalsozialismus. Ein österreichischer Schriftstellerclub, Vienna/Cologne/Graz 1984, 81.
11 Cf. Siglinde Bolbecher, Konstantin Kaiser: Lexikon der österreichischen Exilliteratur, Vienna/Munich 2000, 146.
12 Letter by Robert Neumann to Walter Hollitscher, 23 January 1946, in: Robert Neumann: Mit eigener Feder. Aufsätze, Briefe, Nachlassmaterialien, Innsbruck/Vienna/Bozen 2013, 605.
13 Ibid., 605.
14 Cf. Wolfgang Straub: Die Netzwerke des Hans Weigel, Vienna 2016, 216.
15 Cf. David Axmann: Chronik Friedrich Torberg, in: Marcel Atze, Marcus G. Patka (eds.): Die "Gefahren der Vielseitigkeit". Friedrich Torberg 1908–1979, Vienna 2008, 222–239, here: 232.

für kulturelle Freiheit (Austrian Monthly Pages for Cultural Freedom), which was financed officially by the Congress for Cultural Freedom, but covertly by the CIA.[16]

Exiles with a firm political agenda tended to be the most likely and the earliest to return after the Second World War. This holds especially for Communists like Ernst Fischer and Hugo Huppert. The journalist, author, and politician Fischer returned to Vienna from exile in the Soviet Union as early as 1945. He subsequently became a member of the provisional government under Karl Renner, the Central Committee of the Communist Party of Austria (KPÖ), and the board of the Austrian P.E.N. Club. As editor of the journal *Österreichisches Tagebuch*, as the author of essays and propaganda pieces, and with his political network, Fischer was an influential figure in left-wing Austrian cultural life. The poet and translator Hugo Huppert also arrived in Vienna in 1945, as a Soviet cultural officer, and described himself as "naturally and actually [...] the earliest Austrian emigrant writer to return home [...] a combative patriot of this country, who had, moreover, participated as an active combatant in the liberation of Austria and particularly of Vienna from the fascist yoke".[17] He soon received what he described as "absolute recognition" from "all people and institutions with whom I had had something to do 'hereabouts'"[18] and worked in various institutions: "[S]oon Franz Theodor Czokor [sic], who had returned from other travels and exiles, invited me to collaborate with and join the resurgent Austrian PEN Club."[19] In 1949, still a Soviet citizen, he was ordered to return to the USSR, and did not return to Austria until 1956.[20]

In summary, it can be established that for remigrant writers, the Allies' cultural policy agenda could be an instrument that was both helpful and useful for their political aims and provided some of them with a source of income, at least temporarily. However, the influence remigrants had on the Austrian literary industry after 1945 should not be overestimated; on the whole, the personal continuities from the Austrofascist and National Socialist eras outweighed the propagated new beginning.[21]

---

16 Cf. Anne-Marie Corbin: "Das FORVM ist mein Kind". Friedrich Torberg als Herausgeber einer publizistischen Speerspitze des Kalten Krieges, in: Marcel Atze, Marcus G. Patka (eds.): Die "Gefahren der Vielseitigkeit". Friedrich Torberg 1908–1979, Vienna 2008, 201–221.
17 Hugo Huppert: Einmal Moskau und zurück. Stationen meines Lebens. Autobiographie, Vienna 1987, 393.
18 Ibid., 393.
19 Ibid., 378f.
20 Cf. Bolbecher, Kaiser, Lexikon der österreichischen Exilliteratur, 328.
21 Cf. Karl Müller: Zäsuren ohne Folgen. Das lange Leben der literarischen Antimoderne Österreichs seit den 30er Jahren, Salzburg 1990.

Cultural and Literary Magazines

The occupation authorities also featured as players in the Austrian literary industry on the institutional level, for instance by founding and publishing cultural and literary journals.[22] In doing so, they essentially pursued two aims: firstly, Austria was to be introduced to modern international literature after its phase of *Gleichschaltung* (enforcement of National Socialist norms) and censorship. Each of the Allies focused on their own authors, and their selection was often linked to political goals, from democratization and human rights to processing National Socialist crimes or propagating their own societal systems. And secondly, the Allies' journals also provided opportunities for publishing contemporary Austrian literature.

An example is the journal *Die Brücke* (The Bridge), founded in Vienna in 1945 by the Gesellschaft zur Pflege der kulturellen und wirtschaftlichen Beziehungen zur Sowjetunion (Society for the Cultivation of Cultural and Economic Relations with the Soviet Union). It regularly published literary pieces until 1949. On the one hand, it focused on presenting Russian authors such as Maksim Gor'kii, Vladimir Maiakovskii (in Huppert's translation), or Leo Tolstoi. But it also included classic works of world and Austrian literature by writers such as Ernst Fischer, Gerhard Fritsch, Karl Kraus, and Peter Rosegger. Particularly ambitious plans for cultural journals came from France, which supported the publications *Europäische Rundschau* and *Wort und Tat* with the aim of making Austrians acquainted with French literature as well as publishing domestic contemporary authors. Published by the French Press Service from 1946 to 1949, *Europäische Rundschau* featured texts by Ilse Aichinger, Otto Basil, Franz Theodor Csokor, and Hans Weigel. The monthly journal *Wort und Tat* was published in Innsbruck from 1946 to 1948 and was edited by Lilly Sauter in collaboration with the French Cultural Institute. It presented not only modern French but also contemporary Austrian literature.[23] With few exceptions, all of these journals were short-lived, however.

---

22 Cf. Holger Englerth, Tanja Gausterer, Volker Kaukoreit: Österreichs Literaturzeitschriften 1945–1990 im Überblick. Eine Einleitung, in: Österreichische Nationalbibliothek (ed.): Literaturzeitschriften in Österreich 1945–1990, https://www.onb.ac.at/oe-literaturzeitschriften/Einleitung.pdf (28 May 2024).
23 Lilly Sauter (ed.): Junge österreichische Lyrik, in: Wort und Tat 6 (1947), 83–94.

Publishing Houses

The institutional players also include publishing houses founded, run, or financed by the Allies. They enjoyed an immense economic competitive advantage, since the Allies were in a position to determine the distribution of that rare commodity, paper.[24] A particularly interesting publisher was the Communist Globus-Verlag, the party press of the KPÖ: it sought to provide access both to Austrian literature past and present and to the works of Soviet writers. A brochure marking the publishing house's ten-year anniversary states that some "104 works by Austrian authors with a total run of 1,094,000 copies" were printed between 1945 and 1955.[25] It published classics such as Ferdinand Raimund or Marie von Ebner-Eschenbach, anti-fascist authors, such as the first post-war edition of Jura Soyfer, but also "authors of the day"[26] such as Mira Lobe and Karl Bruckner. "In line with the KPÖ's Austrian patriotism, [...] the publishing house's programme concentrated on literary identity politics."[27] Its political hallmark stood in the way of its economic success, however, since its books were largely boycotted by the book trade and it became increasingly unattractive for Austrian authors in the predominantly anti-communist atmosphere of the Second Republic.[28]

Propagating One's Own Literature

An important aim of all of these activities was propagating the culture or literature of the occupying powers – in the theatre via politically approved plays, for instance.[29] To this end, twelve US Information Centers (US ICs) were set up between 1945 and 1955, referred to as "Amerika-Häuser" (Houses of America) from the late 1940s onwards.[30] They functioned as lending libraries, cinemas, reading rooms, and concert venues and met with high demand for German translations of American literature.[31] The Soviet counterweights to this were not

---

24 Cf. Christoph Kepplinger-Prinz, Elisabeth Prinz: Kampf ums Papier. Literarische Produktionsmittel in Österreich um 1950, in: Journal of Austrian Studies 48 (2015) 3, 41–64.
25 Globus Verlag (ed.): 10 Jahre Globus Verlag, Jubiläumsschrift, Vienna 1955, 3.
26 Ibid., 9.
27 Sebastian Kugler: "So kann kein Verlag existieren". Der Globus-Konzern zwischen Konkurrenz und Kommunismus, in: Jacques Lajarrige, Alfred Prédhumeau (eds.): Österreich – DDR. Literarische Beziehungen in Zeiten des Kalten Krieges, Berlin (in print).
28 Cf. ibid.
29 Rathkolb, Ernst Lothar, 290.
30 Cf. Reinhold Wagnleiter: Coca-Colonisation und Kalter Krieg. Die Kulturmission der USA in Österreich nach dem Zweiten Weltkrieg, Vienna 1991, 160f.
31 Cf. ibid., 176.

only performances of communist propaganda plays at the Neues Theater an der Scala but also the Sowjetische Informationszentren (Soviet Information Centers, SIZ). These were established in the Soviet Occupation Zone from September 1950 onwards and had halls for theatre, talks, and cinema, as well as lending libraries. They also served as venues for amateur dramatic ensembles, which mainly performed political pieces.[32]

Opportunities for Austrian Authors

The cultural activities organized by the occupation authorities also presented opportunities for Austrian authors to make appearances and earn money, which was of particular importance during the years of post-war economic crisis. For instance, Hans Weigel put on "Österreichische Abende" (Austrian Evenings) with literary readings and music by contemporary composers at the Kosmos-Theater, which was managed by the remigrant Ernst Haeusserman. Actors from the Burgtheater and the Theater in der Josefstadt read texts by authors such as H. C. Artmann, Ingeborg Bachmann, Reinhard Federmann, Marlen Haushofer, Ernst Jandl, and Friederike Mayröcker. As a cultural officer for the US occupation authorities, Haeusserman was also head of programming at the radio broadcaster Rot-Weiss-Rot, where Ingeborg Bachmann worked in the newly created Script Department from September 1951 to July 1953, writing the very successful entertainment series *Die Radiofamilie* in conjunction with Jörg Mauthe and Peter Weiser, in addition to translating and copy editing.[33]

While the US media sought to fulfil their ideological mission primarily via entertainment, the Soviets relied more heavily – and less successfully – on explicitly political formats. This also applied to the *Russische Stunde* (Russian Hour),[34] broadcast twice a week by the Radio Wien station within the framework of RAVAG from June 1945 onwards. The programme presented works by Russian writers and consequently also offered Austrian, mostly communist, authors such as Friedl Hofbauer, Hugo Huppert, Susanne Wantoch, or Arthur West the

---

32 Cf. Wolfgang Mueller: "Leuchtturm des Sozialismus" oder "Zentrum der Freundschaft"? Das Sowjetische Informationszentrum im Wiener Porr-Haus, in: Wiener Geschichtsblätter 55 (2000) 4, 261–285.
33 Cf. Ingeborg Bachmann: Die Radiofamilie, Berlin 2011.
34 Cf. Wolfgang Mueller: Eine "scharfe Waffe" im Kalten Krieg? Die sowjetische Rundfunkpolitik in Österreich 1945–1955. Wiederaufbau, Zensur, Radio Moskau und Russische Stunde, in: Anita Mayer-Hirzberger, Cornelia Szabó-Knotik (eds.): Zur Russischen Stunde der RAVAG (1945–55). Ein Kapitel österreichischer Rundfunkgeschichte, Vienna 2023, 11–46, here: 16.

opportunity to earn money with broadcast manuscripts or dramatizations for radio, until the series came to an end with the State Treaty.[35]

Fig. 1: Kosmostheater, "Österreichischer Abend" (Austrian Evening) with Robert Lindner, 1954 (Vienna City Library, NL Hans Weigel)

The Cold War and Anti-communism

On the whole, then, the occupation authorities' engagement in the Austrian literary industry not only pursued the aim of promoting good-quality literature and democratizing a society that had just been freed from twelve years of fascist rule, but also served their own political interests, particularly in the case of the USA and the USSR. Ideologically acceptable literature was promoted, while that

---

35 Cf. ibid., 43.

assumed to be on the other side was impeded or blocked. In the slipstream, as it were, of the new confrontation between the blocs, former National Socialist authors and cultural functionaries could then be reintegrated, while "artists who had worked in the Neues Theater an der Scala, stigmatized as communist, for the Soviet film industry, or for RAVAG's *Russische Stunde*"[36] were ostracized. Hans Weigel, for instance, quite consciously selected only authors he considered "entirely clean with regard to potential membership of the C. P."[37] for *Stimmen der Gegenwart*, a publication which became the most important collection of texts by young Austrian writers. The author and historian Hermann Schreiber recalls that even attempting to make contact with communist intellectuals like Ernst Fischer resulted in "public denunciation in a Weigel column the next week".[38]

Finally, it is difficult to reduce the consequences of the Allies' activities in the field of literature between 1945 and 1955 to a single common denominator. They smoothed the path for a handful of remigrants to return to Austria and to the literary industry, their media offered writers a chance to earn money with their texts in a period of crisis marked by limited opportunities, and they provided a readership that had been cut off from modern literature for years access to international novels, plays, and poems, some of which went on to serve as inspiration to Austrian writers. Of greater and more sustained impact, however, was the antagonism of the Cold War embodied by the former Allies the USA and the USSR, which in their dichotomous constellation demanded commitment to one side or the other; after 1955 at the latest, only an anti-communist, pro-Western stance gave Austrian writers access to opportunities to publish, a readership, and recognition. In Ingeborg Bachmann's story *Unter Mördern und Irren* (*Among Murderers and Madmen*, 1961), the first-person narrator remarks of this situation: "Back then, after 1945, I also thought the world had separated, forever, into good and evil, but the world is already separating again, and again in a different way."[39]

---

36 Oliver Rathkolb: Die paradoxe Republik. Österreich 1945 bis 2010, Innsbruck/Vienna 2011, 25.
37 Hans Weigel: Bemerkungen. Konvolut "Materialien zu Stimmen der Gegenwart", Nachlass Hans Weigel, in: Wienbibliothek im Rathaus, cited in Straub, Weigel, 243. A notable exception is Karl Wiesinger, who was a member of the KPÖ from 1945 onwards but whose literature Weigel considered not explicitly communist; Wiesinger could thus publish a story in *Stimmen der Gegenwart* in 1952. Cf. Straub, Weigel, 255.
38 Hermann Schreiber: Über Reinhard Federmann (1923–76), in: Literatur und Kritik (1993) 273/274, 99–104, here: 103.
39 Ingeborg Bachmann: Unter Mördern und Irren, in: idem: Werke. Vol II: Erzählungen, ed. by Christine Koschel, Inge von Weidenbaum, Clemens Münster, Munich/Zurich 1978, 159–186, here: 174.

Peter Roessler

Dramatic Outlooks. The Allies' Dramas on Vienna Stages

Dramas from the Allied states offered dramatic outlooks on the unknown. They may have seemed alien while also connecting with the audience's experiences – of both everyday life and the theatre. Whereas the choice of plays was also linked to the requirements of the Allies' respective cultural policies,[1] their selection, performance, and impact could follow their own rules.

Reversion and Propaganda: Russian Drama

Russian drama was primarily presented in the form of older works, such as Aleksandr Griboedov's *Verstand schafft Leiden* (*Gore ot uma*; *Woe from Wit*, 1946) at the Burgtheater in the Ronacher (Bth) and Maksim Gor'kii's *Jegor Bulytschow und die anderen* (*Egor Bulychov e drugie*; *Egor Bulychev and Others*, 1949) at the Akademietheater (Ath) or the Soviet playwright Nikolai Volkov's dramatization of Leo Tolstoi's novel *Anna Karenina* (1948), each of them directed by Adolf Rott. Rott, who had also directed propaganda pieces for the National Socialist regime, quickly adapted to the new times, including by bowing to the Soviet occupation authorities. It was certainly possible to act differently in this context, however: Paul Kalbeck, who had fled to Switzerland and had returned from exile to Vienna as a guest director only twice after 1945, staged Anton Chekhov's *Der Kirschgarten* (*Vishnëvyi sad*; *The Cherry Orchard*) at the Theater in der Josefstadt (ThiJ) in 1948.

The scenario during the nascent Cold War already gave rise to the events surrounding the propaganda piece *Die Russische Frage* (*Russkii vopros*; *The Russian Question*) by Konstantin Simonov,[2] broadcast as a radio play in 1947 as

---

1 Cf. Oliver Rathkolb: Planspiele im Kalten Krieg. Sondierungen zur Kultur und Theaterpolitik der Alliierten, in: Hilde Haider-Pregler, Peter Roessler (eds.): Zeit der Befreiung. Wiener Theater nach 1945, Vienna 1998, 40–64.
2 Cf. ibid., 46.

part of the RAVAG station's *Russische Stunde* (Russian Hour). The version planned for the Volkstheater (Vth) was not performed, partly due to differences within the theatre itself, but mainly following objections by the US cultural officer Ernst Lothar. It was not performed until March 1948, after the play's director, Günther Haenel, had moved to the newly opened Neues Theater an der Scala; the theatre was located in the Russian Zone and was supported by the Communists. The Scala, which received considerable support from theatre people who had joined the Zurich Schauspielhaus ensemble during exile and represented a broad repertoire primarily comprising older dramas, also put on pieces by Ostrovskii, Gogol', Chekhov, Gor'kii, and a dramatization of Tolstoi's *War and Piece*.

Staging older pieces corresponded to the Soviet occupation authorities' efforts to rely on 'haute culture' when reopening the theatres. But there were exceptions that were closer to the present, albeit not in terms of their material. In 1945, Günther Haenel at the Volkstheater directed Anatolii Lunacharskii's tragicomedy *Der befreite Don Quichote* (*Osvobozhdennyi Don-Kikhot*; Unbound Don Quixote, 1925), set, like its literary model, in the seventeenth century. This choice met with criticism from head of the American theatre department in Vienna Henry Alter.[3] Incidentally, Lunacharskii, who died in 1933, had been dismissed as people's commissioner for art and education by Stalin and demoted to less influential posts. In 1948, the comedic fairytale for adults *Der Schatten* (*Ten'*; The Shadow) by Evegnii Shvarts was performed at the Burgtheater. The director was again Adolf Rott. Set in a fantasy world, the piece, written in 1940, examines power, threats, and repression – and in Vienna the predictable allusions to Soviet conditions could now refer to the National Socialist dictatorship without having to address the subject directly.

Modernity and Human Existence: French Drama

French drama was associated with the notion of entertainment but also with modernity. Besides nineteenth-century comedies – by authors such as Eugène Labiche – plays by Jean Giraudoux and Jean Anouilh were shown. Some of Giraudoux's pieces, with their fairytale quality said to be related to the rediscovered Surrealism,[4] offered an irrealization expressed in the melancholy poeticization of reality via an adapted legendary figure, in *Undine*, but also through the satirical exposure of society, in *Die Irre von Chaillot* (*La Foulle de Chaillot*, The Madwoman of Challot), in which a morally heightened, courageously crafty

---

3 Cf. Rathkolb, Planspiele, 54f.
4 Cf. Otto Basil's discussion of *Die Irren von Chaillot*: Neues Österreich, 23 April 1948, 2.

female figure counters ruthless societal machinations (Ath, 1947 and 1948 respectively).

Jean Anouilh was considered one of the "France's representative young dramatists",[5] but his play *Passagier ohne Gepäck* (*Le Voyageur en baggage*, *Traveller without Luggage*) had already been seen at the Volkstheater in 1937 – with Hans Jaray and Sybille Binder directed by Heinrich Schnitzler, all three of whom were forced to escape into exile later. In 1946, Anouilh's *Antigone* was performed at the Volkstheater, directed by Günther Haenel – a piece that would become a modern "classic" in the years that followed. "Timeless"[6] was the buzzword, meaning the transposition of Classical models onto the present with which topicality could be both created and retracted. An unusual element was the epic figures of the speaker narrating and passing comment like an author. Another unfamiliar feature was the largely empty stage, delineated only by black curtains,[7] but the placelessness corresponded with experiences of the post-war reality. The dramatist drew attention to the figure of Antigone, who embodies both humanity and rebellion against state power. The ruler Kreon oscillates between dictates and reason, reflecting the audience's readiness to justify hegemony, manifested after 1945 as the idea of pragmatism. By all accounts, in his portrayal of Kreon, the actor Wolfgang Heinz, who had been a member of the Zurich Schauspielhaus in exile, counteracted this complicity.[8]

The horrors of the century were expressed more sharply in the existentialist works of Albert Camus staged at the Volkstheater from the early 1950s onwards. Repression and resistance are the focus in *Die Gerechten* (*Les Justes*, *The Just Assassins*, Vth, 1951), conveyed via the historical subject matter of the anarchist assassinations in tsarist Russia, and in *Der Belagerungszustand* (*L'État de siège*, *The State of Siege*, Vth, 1953) via an allegorical plot based on experiences during the occupation of France. Along with the question of submission and adaptation, the piece also considers the decision to act culminating in self-sacrifice. With these plays, staged by Gustav Manker and an exception to the repertoire, recent events were transformed into existential generalization.

The subject of repression is also addressed in *Die Fliegen* (*Les Mouches*, *The Flies*) by Jean-Paul Sartre, a tragedy written and premiered in occupied France in 1943 and performed at the Kammerspiele in 1948. The Electra–Orestes plot is used to discuss dictatorship, collaboration, and the Résistance; darkly con-

---

[5] See for instance the announcement of *Das Mädchen Therese* in the *Wiener Kurier*, 15 February 1946, 4, which also referred to the performance of *Passagier ohne Gepäck* in 1937, however. Cf. also Wiener Kurier, 25 March 1946, 4.
[6] As in the introductory note to an excerpt printed the *Wiener Kurier* presenting a scene between Kreon and Antingone. Wiener Kurier, 4 May 1946, 10.
[7] Cf. Welt-Illustrierte der Österreichischen Zeitung (1946) 2, n.p. [14].
[8] Cf. for instance Arbeiter-Zeitung, 25 September 1946, 3.

versational but always dramatically moved by Satre's existentialism, the play centres on foreignness and freedom to act. Director Kurt Wessels, however, stressed in an interview that he was primarily concerned with the drama; the philosopher of existentialism was only of secondary interest to him.[9]

Existentialism was a popular catchword, but also suspicious; Sartre was soon suspected of communist leanings, and it was no coincidence that his plays were mostly played on smaller stages. In 1950, the Theater der Courage (ThdC), headed by the Viennese theatre manager Stella Kadmon, who had returned from exile in Palestine, Stella Kadmon, put on Sartre's *Die ehrbare Dirne* (*La Putain respecteuse*, *The Respectful Prostitute*), an effective problem piece against racism in the USA, and in 1951 the Kleines Theater im Konzert Haus staged *Bei geschlossenen Türen* (*Huis clos*, *No Exit*). In 1952, Sartre refused to allow *Die schmutzigen Hände* (*Les mains sales*, *Dirty Hands*) to be performed at the Theater am Parkring, having already blocked it in other countries. In the play, a youth from a bourgeois background joins the Communist Party before ultimately being liquidated by it. Sartre, who planned to participate in the Peace Conference in Vienna the same year, anticipated the work would be instrumentalized in the Cold War for anti-communist purposes.[10]

Entertainment and Demasking: British Drama

Plays from Britain tended to be seen as a unified genre, especially when the dialogue took on the form of conversation. This mode of speaking, be it in pieces from England, France, or Vienna, was popular in Viennese theatre, as were the actors who excelled at it, along with the salon as a stage set. But more than a few of the well-structured British dramas offered an unsparing look behind the façade of marriage and family life and revealed the deceit of bourgeois normality: J. B. Priestley's *Die Conways und die Zeit* (*Time and the Conways*, ThiJ, 1945) shows the collapse of a family over a long period of time. Other works by Priestley were performed too: *Gefährliche Wahrheit*, *Sie kamen zu einer Stadt* (*Dangerous Corner*, *They Came to a City*; both at the Vth, in 1946 and 1947 respectively) and *Ein Inspektor kommt* (*An Inspector Calls*), which became his most famous play and whose title already indicates that something is to be revealed (ThdC, 1953).

Contemporary dichotomies included the question whether a play was to be categorized more as 'optimistic' or 'pessimistic'. Rejection of 'pessimism' could still – or once again – go hand in hand with rejection of criticism, but primarily, an optimist function was now ascribed to art. Certainly, for *Die Conways und die*

---

9 Die Weltpresse, 7 April 1948, 6.
10 Cf. Salzburger Nachrichten, 19 November 1952, 4.

Dramatic Outlooks. The Allies' Dramas on Vienna Stages 191

Fig. 1: Hans Holt and Grete Zimmer in *Die Conways und die Zeit* (*Time and the Conways*) by J. B. Priestley, directed by Rudolf Steinboeck, Theater in der Josefstadt, 1945. Source: *Die Bühne*, no. 7, July 1946, 14 (ANNO, ANL/Vienna)

Zeit the magazine *Die Bühne* (The Stage) went to some lengths to free the play from the label of 'pessimism'.[11] In such works, however, the future was indeed shown to be anything but an uninterrupted progression towards a better world. Priestley broke the continuum of time by following a first act full of enthusiasm about the future with a second act set twenty years later showing the future catastrophe, only to return to the optimistic mood of the first act in the third. The article in *Die Bühne* (The Stage), which pointed out, incidentally, that director Rudolf Steinboeck had toned down the more drastic elements of the original, proclaimed, "It is to the Theater in der Josefstadt's great credit that is has staged a worthy German-language premiere of this substantial piece after seven culturally dreadfully thin years."[12]

J. B. Priestley himself, however, stood for more than this; he was a political author and a socialist, and had taken a firm stand against the National Socialist regime during the Second World War; his speeches in this vein on BBC radio had also been listened to secretly in Vienna. In October 1946, he visited Vienna as a guest of the Austro-British Society, where he delivered a speech in the Großer Konzerthaussaal; one of the subjects he addressed in it was a socialist future for

---

11 Die Wiener Bühne (1945), No. 8, 22.
12 Ibid., 21.

the English state.¹³ Education Minister Felix Hurdes (ÖVP) and Mayor Theodor Körner (SPÖ) were among those who gave welcoming speeches, and this event can be considered typical of the relative openness that prevailed in the early postwar years.

Sensation and tension were repeatedly linked with the question of human behaviour in the modern English crime play. *Gaslicht (Gas Light)* by Patrick Hamilton (Ath, 1946) dealt with the brutal actions of a husband who once committed a murder and now seeks to drive his wife insane. It was directed by Adolf Rott, who was also generally interested in creating effects. Theatre critics wanted such a work to be kept out of the Burgtheater; Hans Weigel, who had returned from exile in Switzerland in 1945, ridiculed the choice of play in his review in *Neues Österreich* and considered its inclusion in the repertoire as symptomatic of a crisis at the Burgtheater.¹⁴

Regarding the phenomenon of the delayed reception of international drama as a consequence of the National Socialist regime, it is interesting that *Time and the Conways* and *Gas Light* were from 1937 and 1938 respectively. For Vienna, however, they were as new as Terence Rattigan's *The Winslow Boy* (*Der Winslow Boy*, ThiJ, 1948), in which a cadet is wrongly accused of theft and is defended by a lawyer with humanist values. An environment that must have been unusual thus presented the utterly familiar themes of defamation and existence as an outsider.

The Psyche and Disillusionment: Drama from the USA

American dramas too, of great importance for Vienna theatre in general, were again interpreted as one entity. This perspective assumed a closed American milieu, which often gave rise to rejection, however. Anti-Americanism was entrenched among some theatre critics, who assumed that plays from the USA had a ruinous effect, sometimes even warning that they endangered the country's youth. This was voiced by, for instance, the writer and critic Friedrich Schreyvogl, a former illegal member of the NSDAP.¹⁵

---

13 Cf. Wiener Zeitung, 18 October 1946, 5.
14 Cf. Neues Österreich, 3 December 1946, 2, (shelf mark H.W.).
15 On the premiere of the Tennesee Williams's play *Endstation Sehnsucht* at the Akademietheater in 1951, directed by Berthold Viertel, cf. Hilde Haider-Pregler: "Daß ich in den letzten fünf Jahren für das Wiener Burgtheater lebe und sterbe ...". Zu Berthold Viertels Tätigkeit am Burgtheater, in: Siglinde Bolbecher, Konstantin Kaiser, Peter Roessler (eds.): Traum von der Realität. Berthold Viertel (Zwischenwelt Jahrbuch 5), Vienna 1998, 239f.

An entirely free selection of plays from the USA was not possible, since approval was required from the US War Department's Reorientation Branch,[16] which was instructed to block plays that showed a negative image of conditions in the USA. For instance, the relevant authorities in Washington banned performances of Arthur Miller's *All My Sons*, a tragedy about guilt and crime driven by capitalist profit-seeking. Ernst Lothar, who had returned to Austria from American exile in 1946 and now worked for the US Information Services Branch as a theatre and music officer, had attempted to push it through, without success.[17]

But the American dramas that were permitted certainly didn't show the bourgeois or petty bourgeois milieu as an ideal world either. Adaptation to new conditions could play a role here too: Lothar Müthel, manager of the Burgtheater under the National Socialist regime, a member of the NSDAP, and director of the antisemitic staging of Shakespeare's *Der Kaufmann von Venedig* (*The Merchant of Venice*, 1943), was already staging Robert Ardrey's *Leuchtfeuer* (*Thunder Rock*) at the Akademietheater as early as September 1945. The story of a disillusioned journalist who has retired to a lighthouse, where he regains hope, could be understood from a variety of perspectives, not least as an apology for withdrawal from society.

There was a different background to the staging of Eugine O'Neills *Trauer kleidet Elektra* (*Mourning Becomes Electra*) at the Akademietheater in 1946. Karl Eidlitz, who had returned from exile in Switzerland, was appointed director, but Ernst Lothar already had a hand in the production, as he often did. This was not the official position, however, since he was still culture officer, which nevertheless enabled him to determine casting for the lead roles.[18] The writer and director Ernst Lothar was familiar with drama from the USA, not only in his role allocating and issuing permits for American plays as theatre and music officer, but also, and primarily, from his time in exile.

Plays by O'Neill had already been performed in Vienna prior to 1938,[19] his works were internationally renowned, and the Nobel Prize he received in 1936 testifies to his recognition The *Wiener Kurier* called him the "man who created

---

16 On this topic, cf.: Oliver Rathkolb: Politische Propaganda der amerikanischen Besatzungsmacht in Österreich 1945–1950. Ein Beitrag zur Geschichte des Kalten Krieges in der Presse-, Kultur- und Rundfunkpolitik, doctoral thesis, University of Vienna 1981.
17 Cf. Rathkolb, Planspiele, 58. For biographical details, cf. Oliver Rathkolb: Ernst Lothar – Rückkehr in eine rekonstruierte Vergangenheit: Kulturpolitik in Österreich nach 1945, in: Jörg Thunecke (ed.): Echo des Exils. Das Werk emigrierter österreichischer Schriftsteller nach 1945, Wuppertal 2006, 279–295; Dagmar Heissler: Ernst Lothar. Schriftsteller, Kritiker, Theaterschaffender, Vienna/Cologne/Weimar 2016.
18 Cf. ibid., 57; Heissler, Ernst Lothar, 250–252.
19 In 1924, *Anna Christie*, directed by Paul Kalbeck, premiered at the ThiJ.

America's modern drama".[20] In post-war Vienna, he seemed new, but his plays weren't; *Verwirrung der Jugend* (*Ah, Wilderness*), directed by Günther Haenel at the Volkstheater in 1947, was written in 1932, and the screen version had been screened in Vienna in 1936.

O'Neill had written *Mourning Becomes Electra* between 1929 and 1931, and the dramatic trilogy had premiered at the Akademietheater in February 1938, directed by Josef Gielen, although it had run only until 7 March. Based on Aeschylus's *Oresteia* and with a timeless dimension, the work depicts murder in an American family between ineluctable fate and guilt. Reminiscent of elements of Freud's theories and drawing dramatically on Ibsen or Strindberg, the plot, centred on murder, revenge, and incest, destroys the idea of the family as a safe space.

Other unusual offerings were Thornton Wilder's plays *Die kleine Stadt* (*Our Town*) and *Wir sind noch einmal davongekommen* (*The Skin of Our Teeth*) at the Theater in der Josefstadt (1946 and 1947 respectively). These works introduced to Vienna an epic theatre that was, however, a long way from the concepts of Bertolt Brecht, whose *Der gute Mensch von Sezuan* and *Mutter Courage und ihre Kinder* had been both played and misunderstood in the Josefstadt in1946 – before the "Brecht boycott" during the Cold War, then. *Die kleine Stadt*, directed by Hans Thimig, is about the seemingly idyllic life of two families; however, a games master – the epitome of epic narration – is present throughout the plot, which is organized as an open series of scenes. There is not a hint of contemporary history, but in the third act at the latest the carefree nature of everyday family life is seriously called into question. When the games master brings the deceased protagonist back to life at her own request, she experiences relations between people as lacking vitality; in life, they are already dead.

The epic is intensified in *Wir sind noch einmal davongekommen*, a revue-like series of three acts with an announcer and figures who step out of their roles, set in the present yet also in historical chaos, with dinosaurs and mammoths. The director was no stranger to revues and parodies from his early days on the ABC cabaret stage in the 1930s. A family by the name of Antrobus experiences and survives the catastrophes of the Ice Age, the Flood, and war. The natural disaster is equated with the war, and after every disaster people nevertheless carry on, usually as if nothing had happened. The father was played by Attila Hörbiger, who was allowed to perform again in Vienna following a 'denazification process'. In Vienna in 1947, the tragicomic work from 1942 could seem like exculpation from responsibility.

An unusual dramaturgy was also served up with Arthur Miller's *Tod des Handlungsreisenden* (Death of a Salesman, ThiJ, 1950), since the imaginings of

---

20 Wiener Kurier, 15 October 1948, 4.

Fig. 2: The staging of *Wir sind noch einmal davongekommen* (*The Skin of Our Teeth*) by Tennessee Williams, directed by Rudolf Steinboeck; from left to right: Aglaja Schmid, Adrienne Gessner, Attila Hörbiger, Hortense Raky, Theater in der Josefstadt, 1947. Source: *Welt-Illustrierte*, supplement to the *Österreichische Zeitung*, no. 13, 30 March 1947, n.p. (ANNO, ANL/Vienna)

the protagonist Willy Loman are embedded in the plot; he converses with people who have died and repeatedly delves into situations from his past, which increasingly dominate his daily life. The topic of the small representative who after years of hard work breaks down in the face of reality was relatable not only to life in the USA. Two theatre people who had returned from exile in America had taken on the epochal play: Ernst Lothar as director and the dramatists Ferdinand Bruckner as translator. The cast included Adrienne Gessner as Loman's wife Linda, who had also returned from exile in the USA, which she had got through with her husband, Ernst Lothar.

Returning from American exile and staging dramas from the USA were combined in a special way by the writer and director Berthold Viertel, who had taken up the offer to direct at the Burgtheater, where his brother-in-law, Josef Gielen, had taken over as manager after returning from exile in Argentina.[21] The plays Viertel directed were Tennessee Williams' *Die Glasmenagerie* (*The Glass Menagerie*, 1949) and *Endstation Sehnsucht* (*A Streetcar Named Desire*, 1951) –

---

21 Cf. Peter Roessler: Doppelkonfrontation: Berthold Viertels Rückkehr nach Wien, in: Thunecke, Echo des Exils, 344–361. On the chronology of his life, cf. Katharina Prager: Berthold Viertel. Eine Biografie der Wiener Moderne, Vienna/Cologne/Weimar 2018, 7–16.

translated into German by Viertel himself – along with *Frankie und die Hochzeit* by Carson McCullers (*The Member of the Wedding*, 1950), all of them at the Akademietheater. Although he was greatly respected and received a lot of recognition, he also came under attack, including in the communist publications, in displays of typical anti-Americanism, a prime example being a headline like "Perversities from the USA"[22] in relation to *Frankie und die Hochzeit*.

The left-wing Berthold Viertel defended the play against this invective,[23] but his practical work was unfurled beyond such attacks. For him, it went without saying that the respective American milieus had to be staged, and it was this that allowed the human and social constellations to be understood universally. Hence Viertel also strove to achieve this in the other dramas he staged, including *Major Barbara* by George Bernhard Shaw (Ath, 1949), *Die Cocktailparty* by T.S. Eliot (Ath, The Cocktail Party, 1951), Shakespeare tragedies (Bth), and Anton Chekhov's *Die Möwe* (*The Seagull*, Ath, 1952). It was not a case of presentations of dramatic nationalities, then, but very different works which all had something to say to audiences of the day.

---

22 Cf. Österreichische Zeitung, 26 November 1950, 7.
23 Cf. Berthold Viertel: Frankie und die Kritik, in: Konstantin Kaiser, Peter Roessler (eds.), in collaboration with Siglinde Bolbecher: Die Überwindung des Übermenschen: Exilschriften, Vienna 1989, 295–298.

Michael Kraus

Vienna State Opera in Occupied Post-War Austria, 1945–1955

One might call it a paradoxical coincidence: around 3:30 p.m. on 30 April 1945, Adolf Hitler shot himself in his bunker in Berlin. Just a few minutes later, the curtain was raised for a Burgtheater performance of Grillparzer's *Sappho* in Vienna's Ronacher theatre. The Second World War was not officially over; in some parts of Austria there was still fighting. But the starting gun had thus been fired for a new Austrian cultural life. Just a day later, on 1 May 1945, Vienna State Opera followed with a performance of Mozart's *Hochzeit des Figaro* (*The Marriage of Figaro*) at the Volksoper (at this point still known as "Opernhaus der Stadt Wien").

Fig. 1: The bomb-damaged Vienna State Opera, 1945 (Wien Museum, inv. no. 195143/76)

Today, this rapid revival of Vienna's cultural life after the war represents one of the founding myths of the Second Republic. It is frequently overlooked that this was more a question of dire necessity than calculated cultural policy. The overall situation was catastrophic; the city was bombed out, the population was starving of hunger, and the Red Army did not have sufficient resources to supply it with the bare necessities. Hence the people were given *circenses* instead of *panem* to at least lighten the desolate mood a little.

The Soviet occupation administration's efforts to get Viennese cultural life underway again immediately after liberation stands in peculiar contrast to the acts of violence towards the civilian population committed in those days by the soldiers of Red Army. But the Soviet military leadership realized that the cultural sphere would have an important role to play in the reconstruction of a denazified Austria. Viennese cultural life was to return to "how it was up to 1938",[1] promised Major Miron Levitas, responsible for cultural agendas, during his first meeting with artists on 21 April 1945. He thereby clearly distanced himself from National Socialist fascism, but not from Austrofascism. His statement nevertheless made it clear that the intention was not to "sovietize" Austrian cultural life. Many of those present who had made careers for themselves in the "Ständestaat" (corporate state) were delighted by what they heard, hoping for power and influence in the new Austria.

There was a good deal of respect for Austrian culture in the Soviet Union, particularly concerning music. Mozart, Beethoven, and especially Johann Strauss enjoyed immense popularity in the USSR. Vienna State Opera, whose opera house had been largely destroyed by an American bombing raid on 13 March 1945, was placed under special protection by the Soviet military leadership from the outset. In the first days after the war, the State Opera singer Alfred Jerger, who had taken over as head of the house following manager Karl Böhm's flight from Vienna, attempted, together with director Oscar Fritz Schuh, conductor Josef Krips, and local singers, to get performances up and running at the Volksoper, which had gone unscathed.[2] In subsequent years, Krips, who, being half-Jewish, had only just managed to survive the National Socialist period in Vienna, became the guiding light of the State Opera ensemble that was formed anew after the war.

Secretary of State for Cultural Affairs Ernst Fischer (Communist Party of Austria; KPÖ) appointed the composer Franz Salmhofer manager of Vienna State Opera from 1 August 1945. Salmhofer possessed no previous experience in management, but he did have a remarkable ability to adapt to all ruling political systems. While he had been rather close to the Social Democrats in the First

---

1 Neues Österreich, 24 April 1945.
2 The Volksoper was owned by the City of Vienna, which gave it to the state free of charge. (Cf. Oliver Rathkolb: Die Paradoxe Republik, Vienna 2005, 320.)

Republic, prior to 1938 he had been a protégé of the corporate state. His application to join the NSDAP had been rejected due his having a Jewish wife, and hence after the war he was considered not to have incriminated himself politically.[3] After the war, he sought to get close to the Soviet occupiers. Salmhofer's pragmatic opportunism would certainly prove a blessing for the State Opera during its re-launch. He was quickly able to renovate the Theater an der Wien, which had stood empty and neglected since 1938, so that it could be reopened for Beethoven's *Fidelio* on 6 October 1945. In the midst of the general desolation, the State Opera thus owned two venues that could now offer parallel performances. At the time, no one could know that this interregnum would last ten years.

The programme during the first months after the war was characterized by improvisation and a strong will to survive. The house initially played light comic operas and operettas, under the toughest conditions, including throughout the entire summer in 1945. More demanding works were added to the repertoire only gradually. The State Opera did not receive any state subventions in those days; for the only time in its history, it had to live off its revenue alone.

In October 1945, the Soviet military leadership donated a million roubles (approximately two million schillings) and hundreds of tonnes of building materials for the restoration of the State Opera, although this was a distant goal at this stage.[4] This generous gesture shortly before the first National Assembly elections after the war, on 25 November 1945, was also intended to boost the KPÖ's campaign. That the Communists only gained 5 per cent of the vote came as a bitter disappointment to the Soviets. An immediate consequence of the election was the loss of the State Secretariat for Popular Enlightenment, Instruction, Education, and Cultural Affairs, whose agendas were subsumed by an education minister from the ranks of the People's Party (ÖVP), Felix Hurdes. In turn, this also led to the ouster of Matthäus Flitsch, hitherto administrative manager of the State Opera. Flitsch was the house's only firm anti-fascist. He was removed from the post by Egon Hilbert, who had been appointed head of the Federal Theatre Administration (Bundestheaterverwaltung) in early 1946. In subsequent years, Hilbert would become a dominant figure at the State Opera.[5] Although he was close to ÖVP circles, Hilbert was primarily a power-crazed quality fanatic and opera enthusiast who brazenly interfered in the State Opera's agendas, feeling secure in the knowledge that he had the backing of Minister Hurdes and Federal

---

3 On Franz Salmofer, cf. Christian Thomas Tengel: Franz Salmhofer: Komponist und Kapellmeister, Chronik 1900–1945, Vienna 1988 (Diplomarbeit).
4 Cf. Stefan Karner, Barbara Stelzl-Marx, Alexander Tschubarjanr: Die Rote Armee in Österreich. Sowjetische Besatzung 1945–1955 (Dokumente), Graz/Vienna/Munich 2005, 245. The sum is roughly the equivalent of 9.7 million euros today.
5 Cf. Oliver Rathkolb: Austriakischer Kulturexport, in: Gert Kerschbaumer, Karl Müller: Begnadet für das Schöne. Der rot-weiß-rote Kulturkampf gegen die Moderne, Vienna 1992, 67.

Chancellor Figl, with whom he had spent years in captivity in Dachau Concentration Camp. At the same time, Hilbert, also a member of the managerial board of the Salzburg Festival, was well connected to the American occupying forces, having occasionally worked for their Information Services Branch as an informer.

After the Western Allies entered Vienna in October 1945, the Soviets' almost sole rule over the city came to an end. The Western Allies possessed much larger financial resources than the Soviets, who had suffered significantly higher losses during the war. Ideological dogmas of the immediate post-war period slowly reversed as the Cold War set in. While the Americans had initially striven for a strict no-fraternization policy and the denazification of the Austrian population, these aims faded into the background in favour of rigorous anti-communism. Meanwhile, the Soviets increasingly used anti-fascism as a weapon against the capitalist West.

The Cold War made Austrian cultural life under occupation an arena for propaganda between the opposing ideologies. Musical theatre with its classical opera canon was only marginally suitable for this, however. Nevertheless, the tensions could not be overlooked in this sphere either. Allied to this was the fact that the new democratic Austria was itself still searching for its identity; the cultural heritage of the Habsburg Monarchy and especially that of the former imperial city of Vienna were perhaps the most important ideational asset for drawing international attention to the country. Pronounced harking back to the past made it difficult for new, progressive currents in Austria to establish themselves. Examination of the present was not pleasant; especially not the recent past, which was largely avoided by pointing to the Allies' Moscow Declaration, according to which Austria was the first victim of Hitler's Germany.

At any rate, Franz Salmhofer's idea of musical modernism in Austria mainly related to his own works adhering to the conservative style, which he regularly included in the State Opera's repertoire (the operas *Das Werbekleid* [The Jingle] and *Iwan Tarassenko*, as well as the ballets *Österreichische Bauernhochzeit* [Austrian Farmer's Wedding] and *Der Taugenichts in Wien* [The Good-for-nothing in Vienna]). As manager, he made sure that potential competitors could not pose a threat to him. He was unable to prevent Hilbert having *Dantons Tod* (Danton's Death) by the young composer Gottfried von Einem transferred from the Salzburg Festival in 1947, the first opera performance to garner international attention after the war, since Einem had good relations with the American occupiers. However, by pointing to the low attendance, Salmhofer did ensure that the work soon disappeared from the repertoire as swiftly as possible.

A better public reception was received by the scenic oratorio *Johanna auf dem Scheiterhaufen* (*Joan of Arc at the Stake*) by the French-Swiss composer Arthur Honegger (libretto: Paul Claudel) in 1950. The message of love and forgiveness was gladly received in Catholic Austria a few months after the National Assembly elections of 1949, the first in which former members of the NSDAP were allowed to vote again.

Works with a thematic connection to the present were well received by the public as long as they remained within the accustomed harmonic framework musically. For instance, *Der Konsul* (*The Consul*) by the Italo-American Giancarlo Menotti was a great success in Vienna in 1951. The work took up the fate of displaced persons, a topic that was of great contemporary relevance in Austria too. The totalitarian power it depicted could easily be decoded as an "Eastern" dictatorship, which corresponded to the anti-Soviet mood in the country and hence either went unmentioned or was scornfully panned in the Soviet-dominated media.[6] The opera *Penelope* by Rolf Liebermann, which premiered at the Salzburg Festival in 1954 and addressed the fate of soldiers returning from the war, thinly veiled as Greek myth, later arrived for a few performances in Vienna. Direct treatment would undoubtedly have led to Allied protests – that is, by the Soviets.

After *Dantons Tod*, Einem became a member of the managerial board of the Salzburg Festival, where he ensured that contemporary musical works continued to be heard. Thanks to Hilbert, some of these productions then went to Vienna: for instance, Alban Berg's *Wozzeck* in 1952, the performance of which conservatives tried to prevent and which was extremely poorly attended. Einem's second opera, *Der Prozess* (The Trial), based on the novel by Franz Kafka, was even dropped by Salmhofer following loud public protests. The composer had supported making Bertolt Brecht an Austrian citizen, which made him a "cryptocommunist" in the eyes of many and cost him his post on the Salzburg management board.

The reintegration of artists with a National Socialist past into Vienna's cultural life proved much more successful, enjoying the untiring assistance of Egon Hilbert. Especially the former State Opera managers Clemens Krauss and Karl Böhm were most welcome permanent guests at the State Opera from 1947 onwards, after serving the ban the Allies had imposed on them as conductors. Josef Krips, who was largely responsible for the quality of the post-war ensemble, was thus increasingly pushed into the background. Disappointed, he left the State Opera in 1950.

On the other hand, renowned émigrés seeking to regain a foothold in Europe after the war were greeted in Vienna with cool distance. Guest appearances by important conductors such as Otto Klemperer, Fritz Busch, and Erich Kleiber remained isolated events at the State Opera. The house's former artistic director (*Oberspielleiter*) Lothar Wallerstein, who had fled to New York after the "An-

---

6 Cf. Österreichische Volksstimme, 4 March 1951.

schluss", returned to Vienna for a few productions, but died soon afterwards in the USA. Erich Wolfgang Korngold, who had been a favourite of Viennese audiences before the war and had since become a film composer in Hollywood, had a particularly infelicitous comeback. His opera *Die Kathrin*, which was originally supposed to have premiered at the State Opera in 1938, was mercilessly rejected by the public and the press alike. Korngold returned, embittered, to Los Angeles, convinced that "[t]here are only Nazis left in the city".[7] He was right, insofar as the strong antisemitism prevalent in Wien long before 1938 remained palpable in post-war Austria.

What the post-war Vienna State Opera remains fabled for to this day was its Mozart ensemble comprising a number of outstanding young singers with lean, flexible voices, unmistakable timbre, and individual personality. The difficult situation forced the company to put on the most important Mozart operas with sparse set designs on the Theater an der Wien's relatively small stage, mostly with the same cast. This resulted in exemplary performances. On the musical level, Josef Krips (and later Karl Böhm) ensured the highest quality, as did the Oscar Fritz Schuh on the level of staging. Over the years, the quality of the ensemble became one of the trademarks of the State Opera as well as a showcase for the Republic of Austria's cultural policy.[8] Triumphant guest performances in Western European cities (including Paris, London, Brussels, Wiesbaden, and Nice), especially with Mozart operas but also with *Fidelio* and *Der Rosenkavalier*, would demonstrate that the new Austria was a great power on the level of culture.

At the same time, these guest performances also sent a clear political signal. Negotiations over the peace treaty were faltering and there was the constant fear of a "sovietisation" of Austria mirroring that of its eastern neighbours and East Germany. During the Cold War between the global powers, Austrian officialdom distanced itself from the Soviet Union as much as possible. On the musical level, there was little artistic exchange with the USSR: Russian singers had made a brief visit to Vienna in the summer of 1945, and Josef Krips gave a few concerts in the Soviet Union in early 1947.[9] In contrast, the State Opera's guest performances in Western Europe were not only a welcome source of currency but also an ex-

---

7 Cf. Marcel Prawy: Die Wiener Oper, Vienna/Munich/Zurich 1969, 180.
8 Rathkolb points out that the aesthetic foundations of the post-war Mozart style presented in the State Opera's guest performances abroad also served as a cultural-political demonstration of Austria's doctrine of victimhood. This style had already been forged by Böhm, Schuh, and the set designer Caspar Neher during the National Socialist era. (Cf. Ratkolb, Paradoxe Republik, 307.)
9 Due to this guest performance, Krips was refused entry to the USA for a planned concert tour in July 1950. He was interned on Ellis Island and forced to return to Austria. (Cf. Arbeiter-Zeitung and Österreichische Volksstimme, 20 July 1950). The US immigration authorities during the McCarthy era eyed an Austrian artist with a Soviet visa in his passport with political distrust.

pression of the Western orientation that remained the political reality despite the neutrality later established by the State Treaty.

For the 1946/47 season, the Theater an der Wien and the Volksoper were organized separately, and Hermann Juch, a former casting manager at the State Opera, was appointed head of the Volksoper, although the ensemble continued to play both houses. Works requiring a larger stage (such as Wagner's *Tannhäuser* or Puccini's *Turandot*) were performed there. Above all, however, the Volksoper specialized in lighter pieces. The house had its greatest successes with lavish performances of operettas, but modern music dramas such as Benjamin Britten's *Bettleroper (The Beggar's Opera)*, Giancarlo Menotti's *Medium*, or Carl Orff's *Bernauerin* were also well received. The Volksoper nevertheless remained somewhat in the shadow of the Theater an der Wien, which was the city's number one opera house, not least due to its central location.

The Allied occupiers reined themselves in when it came to directly intervening in the running of the State Opera, although they attempted to influence it on occasions. For instance, the Soviet occupying authorities blocked the Vienna performance of *Dantons Tod* because Einem had allegedly been a Nazi.[10] In the early post-war years, the Allies also banned individuals from performing, such as the singer Elisabeth Schwarzkopf, who was known to have been a member of the NSDAP.[11] Egon Hilbert repeatedly managed to repel such attacks on the State Opera.

The Allied occupation nevertheless had a certain influence on programming choices. For instance, the Russian repertoire had a strong presence in the early post-war years. Tchaikovsky's *Eugen Onegin* and *Pique Dame (The Queen of Spades)*, Mussorgsky's *Boris Godunov*, and Borodin's *Fürst Igor (Prince Igor)* were regularly staged at the Theater an der Wien. The Volksoper even tended to play less common works, such as Mussorgsky's *Jahrmarkt von Soroschintzi (The Fair at Sorochyntsi*, 1950) and Prokofiev's *Die Liebe zu den drei Orangen (Love of Three Oranges*, 1951). Under the patronage of French High Commissioner Béthouart, a visit was made by the Paris Opera with three performances of Debussy's *Pelléas et Mélisande*. And in 1952 a black ensemble caused a great sensation in Vienna with George Gershwin's *Porgy and Bess*. There were also guest performances by ballet companies from the countries of the Western occupying powers (Sadler's Wells Company [1946], Ballet de Théâtre de l'Opéra de Paris [1950], and Martha Graham Dance Company [1954]).

The death of Stalin in 1953 ushered in the global political Thaw to which Austria owes its State Treaty of 1955. A change was made at the top of the Federal

---

10 Cf. Michael Kraus: Die musikalische Moderne an den Staatsopern von Berlin und Wien. Paradigmen nationaler Kulturidentitäten im Kalten Krieg, Stuttgart 2017, 262.
11 Cf. Prawy, Wiener Oper, 173.

Theatre Administration in 1953: Egon Hilbert, who had already lost his political backing when Julius Raab replaced Figl as federal chancellor and Ernst Kolb replaced Hurdes as minister of education, was succeeded by Ernst Marboe, hitherto head of the Department of Culture at the ÖVP Press Service. Marboe's task was to prepare the opening of the rebuilt State Opera and the Burgtheater on the Ringstrasse. He also had to find new managers for the two houses. For the State Opera, the decision was ultimately between two former managers of the company, Clemens Krauss and Karl Böhm. Education Minister Kolb publicly backed Krauss, but was disavowed by Federal Chancellor Raab, who appointed Böhm as the new manager. The selection showed that the official Austria continued to back individuals who were compromised by their actions during the National Socialist era. At the time, however, this was not an issue of public debate. The ÖVP's cultural policy cleverly declared art a sphere free from politics; it should primarily be about "representative culturalism",[12] to cite Heinrich Drimmel, who succeeded the hapless Kolb as education minister in 1954. This approach concealed the rigorous rejection of anything that might have disturbed the recourse to the counter-reformatory image of Austria commissioned by the state. Celebrating the reopening of "Burg and Opera" as the crowning conclusion to Austria's regained freedom was the perfect fit for this image. In the new, free Austria, anything that was unpleasant – such as the communist Theater in der Scala – was increasingly marginalized until it was forced to give up.

Ernst Marboe – also a staunch advocate of Christian-conservative cultural policy – nevertheless had a nose for the currents of the day. For instance, despite strong internal resistance, he got Marcel Prawy to work as a dramaturg at the Volksoper, which from the 1955/56 season was run as an independent house as part of the federal theatres (with Franz Salmhofer as Juch's successor). Prawy, an émigré who had returned to Austria after the war as cultural officer of the US army, had previously organized very successful evenings at the Kosmos cinema, staging excerpts from American musicals, then completely unknown to Austrian audiences. He thereby laid the foundation for a Viennese tradition of musicals that has survived to this day.[13]

1955 has gone down in Austrian history as the year in which the country became free via the State Treaty and the withdrawal of the Allied troops. The reopening of the Burgtheater (14 October) and the State Opera (5 November) was celebrated as the crowning act of state marking liberation. As a symbol of freedom, Beethoven's *Fidelio* was chosen for the opening, an opera that all manner of political systems have used for their cultural self-legitimation. It is perhaps one of

---

12 Heinrich Drimmel: Österreichische Kulturpolitik seit dem Staatsvertrag, cit. Hans Heinz Fabris, Kurt Luger: Medienkultur in Österreich, Vienna 1988, 162.
13 Cf. Marcel Prawy erzählt aus seinem Leben, Vienna 2000, 119f.

the ironies of history that this premiere was largely considered not to have gone well. Nevertheless, in the long term it was the prelude to a development that enabled the Vienna State Opera to return to its status as one of the world's most renowned opera houses. Today, it is indisputably an integral component of the worldwide topos of Austria as a "nation of culture".

Fig. 2: The opening of Vienna State Opera, 1955 (Wien Museum, inv. no. 208970)

Christian Glanz

Out of Nowhere? Observations on the Characteristics and Locations of Jazz in Vienna in the Early Post-War Era

More or less eight months after the war, the great hall of Vienna's Konzerthaus was the venue for a matinee Sunday revue of Viennese jazz. On first impression, the date and content of this event might tempt one to place it in the popular "zero hour" category, not least in view of the organizer and the fact that revenues went to efforts to rebuild, specifically with the aim of protecting the interests of professional musicians. Likewise, this document could be interpreted as evidence of the "re-educational" effectiveness of Allied, particularly American cultural work expressed within it. Upon closer inspection, however, the document also reveals that jazz in Vienna had never disappeared and that the manifold aspects of continuity are thus most relevant.

Vienna's first experiences of jazz-like musician of various sorts go back to the turn of the century. In the 1920s, interest in jazz, not always articulated positively in public, was on the rise, and Vienna's Konzerthaus soon became one of its venues, especially in the context of the competitions for the Golden Ribbon.[1] Admittedly, here the term "jazz" was always subject to very generous interpretations, the spectrum ranging from playing that remained true to the style, oriented around international models, which could also be experienced as guest performances,[2] to *Schlager* and operetta, and indeed the *Wienerlied*, arranged for ensembles in which saxophones, muted trumpets and trombones, and combined percussion represented the "jazz-like" sound.[3] This interpretation of "jazz" was a fixture of the Viennese entertainment scene when the so-called "Anschluss" to

---

[1] Cf. Monika Kornberger: Der Wettbewerb der Wiener Jazzkapellen und Jazzsänger um das Goldene Band. Ein Beitrag zur Wiener Unterhaltungsmusik der 1930er-Jahre, in: Christian Glanz, Manfred Permoser (eds.): Anklaenge 2016. Studien zur österreichischen Popularmusik im 20. Jahrhundert, Vienna 2017, 93–129.

[2] Cf. Dietrich Heinz Kraner, Klaus Schulz: Jazz in Austria. Historische Entwicklung und Diskographie des Jazz in Österreich, Graz 1972 (Beiträge zur Jazzforschung, Vol. 2).

[3] "Die Jazz" was the usual term for such ensembles. Responses ranging from fascination to disdain are evident not least in Viennese literary texts, a notable example being Felix Dörmann's "Viennese novel" of 1925, *Jazz*.

Nazi Germany took place. Despite the universally known and heavily documented vehement rejection of "swing and hot music", persistently emphasized by propaganda – one need only think of the emblematic use of jazz symbols in the poster advertising the exhibition on "Entartete Musik" ("Degenerate Art") – in Vienna too it remained possible to play jazz-like music during the National Socialist era, in very differing conditions and with equally differing intensity, as extensively documented in the foundational and extremely detailed study by Klaus Schulz.[4] It would certainly be incorrect to say that jazz was entirely suppressed during these years, and hence it did not have to begin "from zero" after the war. The "Große Wiener Jazz-Revue" in the early January of 1945 provides a clear testament to that, while also showing the continuation of the local tradition with respect to a very generous interpretation of the term "jazz".

An initial look at those involved is in itself most revealing. In Karl ("Charly") Kaufmann and Hans Neroth, framing the programme with larger bands, we have two important exponents of Vienna's pre-war scene. Both had already headed large formations in the 1930s, had appeared on the radio regularly, and had been successful contestants for the abovementioned Golden Ribbon. Hans Neroth won the award in 1934 and 1937, in the category for smaller ensembles.[5] That the first entry in the revue's programme is termed a "Bühnenschau" (stage show; the title probably suggests a potpourri) also points to the pre-war era. In particular, the large orchestras – the model repeatedly mentioned was clearly Paul Whiteman's band – strove for a comprehensive stage concept in which show effects including costumes played a key role.[6] The other pieces on offer from Kaufmann and Neroth are part of the canon of traditional jazz ("Tiger Rag") and swing (Glenn Miller, Count Basie, Duke Ellington), and another important aspect is the indication of their own arrangements. Neroth's performance also ended with vocals by Marion Soremba and Horst Winter, who provided the *Schlager* style of the day with its swing influences. Here too, the traditions cannot be overlooked: Horst Winter's hit song "Ich liebe die Sonne (den Mond und die Sterne)" (I Love the Sun [the Moon and the Stars]) was from 1940.[7] Both Kaufmann and Neroth had continued to work as musicians under very different conditions during the

---

4 Cf. Klaus Schulz: Steffl Swing. Jazz in Wien zwischen 1938 und 1945, Vienna 2008.
5 Cf. ibid., 130.
6 This is consistently evident in interviews the author of this piece conducted with exponents of the post-war jazz scene many years ago, including Leo Jaritz (18 December 1985, Institut für Musikwissenschaft und Interpretationsforschung [Department of Musicology and Performance Studies], Archiv imi shelf mark I 18), Walter Heidrich (3 April 1986, Archiv imi shelf mark I 21), Josef Wimmer (14 April 1986, Archiv imi shelf mark I 23), Karl Grell (15 October 1985, Archiv imi shelf mark I 14), and Erwin Halletz (12 November 1985, Archiv imi shelf mark I 16).
7 Cf. Horst Winter: Dreh Dich noch einmal um. Erinnerungen des Kapellmeisters der Hoch- und Deutschmeister, Vienna 1989, 42.

National Socialist era too. In the case of Kaufmann, who was deemed a "half-Jew" by National Socialist law, this led to the multi-instrumentalist treading a careful line between emigration that never happened (he had an affidavit for the USA), continuing to perform at various establishments in Vienna, and brief membership of an SS orchestra in Berlin – the stuff of film.[8] The singer and clarinettist Horst Winter also had a successful pre-war career, in Berlin, although it was interrupted by his conscription. It was not until after the war that he had arrived and remained in Vienna.[9] Incidentally, Josef Menschik, who compèred the revue, had also continued an acting and film career launched during the National Socialist period.

The Original Swingtett, the second act on the revue's bill, featured personalities with pre-war experience of jazz (the trombonist Friedrich Meisinger) and others who had continued to play to the extent that they could under National Socialism (the singer and guitarist Viktor Duchini). The ensemble was heavily influenced by Erwin Halletz, who had released himself from military service at the end of the war.[10] As a clarinettist, paints, and arranger, he became a member of the entertainment orchestra put together by the saxophonist, clarinettist, and arranger Ludwig Babinski by order of the Russian military administration immediately after the war. Babinski, on the other hand, had succeeded Leo Jaritz (who had also been very successful with his jazz orchestra in the 1930s) as head of the Vienna dance band of the Deutscher Europa Sender (DES) radio station in 1944, an orchestra that had been selected to spread National Socialist propaganda via short wave with swing modelled on Charlie & Orchestra but with lyrics against the Allies.[11] With at least fourteen concerts entitled "Hallo! Swing – Swing!" between August and November 1945,[12] Babinski and his Neues Wiener Tanzorchester soon re-established jazz-like music at the large venues that could still be played in Vienna: the Großer Konzerthaussaal, the Bürgertheater, the Scala, and the Colosseum. Erwin Halletz wrote a foxtrot as the signature from which the successful series of concerts took its title, and the Swingtett with the singer and guitarist Viktor Duchini was a firm fixture. The Swingtett's appearance at our revue also serves as a direct link with another format that had become established. Unlike Kaufmann and Neroth, who focused on the US canon, the Swingtett presented its own new compositions. Erwin Halletz in particular would

---

8 Cf. Christian Glanz: Grautöne und blue notes. Zur Popularmusik in Wien zwischen 1938 und 1945, in: Carmen Ottner (ed.): Musik in Wien 1938–1945, Vienna 2006, 272–290 (Studien zu Franz Schmidt, Vol. 15).
9 Cf. Stefan Schmidl, Monika Kornberger: Winter, Horst, in: Barbara Boisits (ed.): Österreichisches Musiklexikon Online, https://dx.doi.org/10.11553/0x0001e714 (8 July 2024).
10 Schulz, Steffl Swing, 69f.; interview with Erwin Halletz, Archiv imi I 16.
11 Idid., 138–149.
12 Programmes and press cuttings in Archiv imi, SKS.

later become widely renowned for his own compositions, including for Horst Winter's Wiener Tanzorchester.[13]

As a "hot violinist" in the style of Stéphane Grappelli, Joe (Jozsi) Ribari had also made use of the limited opportunities to play jazz-like music during the National Socialist era. After the war, he was one of the first Viennese musicians to find employment at the US and British soldiers' clubs, in his case initially at Parkhotel Hietzing (British) and Hotel Bristol (American).[14] In his contributions to 1946 revue, we find both American jazz (for instance "Woodchopper's Ball", then the signature of the Woody Hermann Band) and Theo Mackeben *Schlager* "Bei Dir war es immer wieder so schön" (It Was Always So Nice with You), which had been very popular in the National Socialist era, further indication that Vienna's idea of jazz covered a very broad spectrum. Ribari's band also featured important exponents of the pre-war and wartime years, including the trumpet player Josef (Joschi) Wimmer. Successful both at home and abroad in the 1930s (with engagements in places such as Istanbul, Casablanca, and Beirut),[15] towards the end of the war Wimmer joined Babinski's abovementioned DES orchestra. Immediately after the war, the American and British clubs offered him interesting opportunities for work; happily, some related documents have survived. Like Erwin Halletz, Joschi Wimmer subsequently became widely renowned primarily as a member of Horst Winter's orchestra.

As outlined above, the Paul Whiteman Orchestra had been a firm model for the Vienna scene from an early stage; Walter Heidrich's Wiener Film-Tanz-Orchester, the next act on the bill, also followed in this tradition.[16] With his broad musical interests, Heidrich hardly had any intensive experience of playing jazz at the end of the war, but he was already looking to Whiteman. It was only after the war that he gained his first intensive encounter with the Blues, in American clubs like the Embassy or Grünes Tor. After being conscripted and wounded, Heidrich was in already in Vienna by the end of the war, and very soon he was making public appearances, playing entertainment music with orchestra-like bands: as early as May 1945, he put on a revue entitled "Schlager auf Schlager" (Hit after Hit) at the Apollo cinema. The renowned actor Fritz Imhoff and the writer, composer, and theatre critic Max Brod were involved. "Walter Heidrich, who is deserving of special recognition for organizing the event, indulged in modern rhythms with his soloists and the jazz soprano Hannerl Trenker; finally, one was

---

13 Cf. Monika Korberger: Artikel Halletz, Erwin, in: Barbara Boisits (ed.): Österreichisches Musiklexikon Online, https://dx.doi.org/10.11553/0x0001d04f (8 July 2024); interview with Erwin Halletz, Archiv imi I 16.
14 Schulz, Steffl Swing, 152.
15 Interview with Joschi Wimmer, Archiv imi I 23; cf. Schulz, Steffl Swing 143–145; cf. Jack Back: Triumph des Jazz, Vienna 1948, 232.
16 Interview with Walter Heidrich, Archiv im I 21.

Fig. 1: ID card for Joschi Wimmer as a civilian employee of the US Vienna Area Air Command (Department of Musicology and Performance Studies, Archiv imi/Klaus Schulz Collection, SKS)

hearing American and English dance music again!"[17] Like the abovementioned band leaders Charly Kaufmann and Ludwig Babinski, Heidrich was one of the first, then, to perform with large orchestras immediately after the war. For instance, on 27 May 1945, the third edition of the "Schlager auf Schlager" revue took place, this time in the Stadttheater in Skodagasse, and promotion was now already proclaiming, "W. Heidrich – production".[18] Heidrich's is the only contribution to the revue not to be listed in further detail; the author of the special arrangement mentioned was probably Gert Last, another exponent of the Vienna scene.[19] While the individuals examined hitherto continued their careers in the traditional framework, Walter Heidrich subsequently went his own way: in 1948, he founded the Institut für Jazzmusik, an authorized private educational institution providing training in the style.[20] Classrooms were found in various primary schools with the support of Vienna City School Council. According to Heidrich, the institute, which existed until 1954 and also ran several ensembles, some as big as orchestras, introduced a total of almost two thousand pupils to the practice of playing jazz music, at least on a part-time basis (including Franz

---

17 Neues Österreich, 10 May 1945, 4.
18 Neues Österreich, 25 May 1945, 4.
19 Interview with Gert Last, 3 February 1986, Archiv imi shelf mark I 19.
20 Interview with Walter Heidrich, Archiv imi I 21; cf. Elisabeth Th. Hilscher, Monika Kornberger: Heidrich, Walter, in: Barbara Boisits (ed.): Österreichisches Musiklexikon Online, https://dx.doi.org/10.11553/0x0001d0e9 (8 July 2024); Back, Triumph des Jazz, 168 f.; cf. Karin Schober: 1945 – "Stunde Null" der österreichischen Popularmusik? Diplomarbeit (unpublished), University of Music and Performing Arts Vienna 1994, 105–116.

Pressler, who would later become known as Fatty George).[21] Its teachers were renowned exponents of the Vienna scene, including Fred Krippner (clarinet), Rudi Kregcyk (saxophone), Joschi Wimmer (trumpet), Eugen Landwehr (trombone), Heinz Neubrand (piano), and Johannes Fehring (arrangement and theory). The institute had a number of educational works on instruments or style published by the Astoria – Musikverlag press, produced by the respective teachers, including "stylistic exercises" for the individual instruments and textbooks on modulation and arrangement. Thereafter, Heidrich, now also an academically-trained conductor as a pupil of Hans Swarowsky, moved on to pastures new, becoming the band leader for the Wiener Eisrevue.

That leaves us with the fifth act on the bill of our revue of 1946. In Herbert Mytteis and Jeff Palme, it included two people who had played jazz particularly intensively and sometimes at great personal risk during the National Socialist era. The violinist Herbert Mytteis (who had begun his musical career in the 1930s, in Charly Gaudriot's orchestra, a far cry from jazz) played during the war mainly with the pianist Ernst Landl (Mytteis, Landl & Co), often in the legendary Steffl-Diele bar, taking considerable risks under the National Socialists with his highly ironic and sometimes sarcastic self-representations.[22] The same holds for Jeff Palme (real name Joseph Grumbach-Palme), who, like Charly Kaufmann, was particularly endangered as a "half-Jew". The accordionist, pianist, and singer had already been banned from performing in 1941, but due to his "non-Aryan" descent he was not considered "worthy" of military service either. Not as active publicly as Mytteis, Palme also took enormous risks, mainly by regularly hosting private jam sessions, also attended by the young Hans Koller when he had leave from the front.[23] It was only fitting, then, that in Mytteis and Palme two further (also symbolically) very important exponents of Viennese jazz during the National Socialist participated in the post-war re-awakening represented by this revue.

Examination of an exemplary document shows, then, that the revival of jazz in Vienna in 1945 did not come out of nowhere; undoubtedly, in the first years after the war US and British efforts had a large impact on its development, but with respect to jazz (understood broadly, in line with the Viennese tradition), one cannot speak of a "zero hour" or a tabula rasa. In this context, we might consider a further, and for our purposes final, contribution from 1948: *Triumph des Jazz* is the title of a book published by Edition Alpha (that the paper was allocated by the USFA Information Branch Center is explicitly stated in the prelims), written by a certain "Jack Back"; the "German rendering" is by an equally mysterious "Dr.

---

21 Interview with Walter Heidrich, Archiv imi I 21.
22 Schulz, Steffl Swing, 97–104.
23 Cf. ibid., 75–81.

Hardo Nühring". Much about this book is remarkable. Firstly, there is the question as to its author's true identity. An author by this name is, of course, unknown; it seems likely that we are dealing with a not particularly original pseudonym. "Back" might be thus be an allusion to a remigrant, or a general reference to the triumphant return of jazz itself. The most notable feature of the book is the biographical section. After providing a historical overview of the history of jazz and making a passionate case for some specialist explanations, including on instrumentation and terminology, suggestive of the characteristics of a handbook, the book then goes on to introduce exponents of Vienna's jazz scene (but for two female singers, all men), virtually placing them on the same level as the famous, big names of US jazz. Walter Heidrich, for instance, enjoys the same size font and almost the same level of detail as Coleman Hawkins, Erwin Halletz is mentioned immediately before Lionel Hampton, and so on.[24] The intention seems clear, and quite telling, in the light of the above: Viennese jazz is presented as genuinely relevant; the "triumph of jazz" lies, then, not only in its return but also in its self-assertion. The selection of Viennese jazz players indicates good knowledge of the scene, but the question of the work's authorship must remain open – for now?

Fig. 2: Ernst Hausknost: jazz at the Artclub, from the series *Sterbende Musikstadt Wien* (Vienna, the Dying City of Music), 1952 (Wien Museum, inv. no. 208952)

---

24 Back, Triumph des Jazz, 168f., 164f.

Hans Petschar

Porgy and Bess: A Case Study of the Impact of US Cultural Policy in Vienna, 1945–1955

At 8:30 p.m. on 3 September 1952, a Boeing 337 Stratocruiser of the US army landed at the airfield in Tulln. On board was the Black artists' ensemble for George Gershwin's opera *Porgy and Bess.* The company of sixty-six people and one goat was welcomed by Ernst Haeusserman, who had returned to Austria from exile as an American occupation officer and who worked for the American Embassy in Vienna as head of the Department of Film, Theater, and Music from 1948 to 1953.

Fig. 1: The *Porgy and Bess* ensemble arriving at the Tulln-Langenlebarn airfield, 3 September 1952 (photo: Jeff Rainer, ANL/Vienna, US 10.377/12)

This was the start to the first European tour of a production that can be considered one of the most successful projects of 1950s American cultural policy and a prime example of cultural diplomacy during the Cold War in Austria. The tour also took in Berlin, London, and Paris in 1952 and 1953. In 1954, *Porgy and Bess* toured the USA before returning to Europe in the December with the support of the United States Information Agency (USIA). The USIA was an authority founded by President Dwight D. Eisenhower, who had become the thirty-fourth president of the United States on 20 January 1953. Cooperating closely with the State Department, it was responsible for the US government's public relations outside the USA.[1] The USIA's main remit was supporting American foreign policy by promoting radio stations such as Radio Free Europe and the export of films, exhibitions, and concerts.

The guest performance of *Porgy and Bess* in Vienna was a particularly successful start to the European tour and became an unexpected media triumph.

The *Porgy* ensemble was hosted in Vienna from 3 to 14 September and was accompanied throughout its stay by a film and photography crew from the United States Information Service (USIS). Running reports were also provided by the radio station Rot-Weiss-Rot and the flagship publication of American information policy in Austria, the *Wiener Kurier*. Extensive reports on the premiere and the total of eight performances appeared in the *Wiener Zeitung*, *Die Presse*, the *Salzburger Nachrichten*, the *Weltpresse*, *Neues Österreich*, the *Arbeiter-Zeitung*, *Der Abend*, and the *Neue Wiener Tageszeitung*.

The USIS film crew accompanied the ensemble on its journey to Vienna, on a trip up to the Leopoldsberg hill overlooking Vienna via the Höhenstrasse, on a visit to Schönbrunn Palace, at rehearsals in the Raimundtheater, at the premiere at the Volksoper, and finally at the farewell party in Vienna's Rathauskeller.

USIS's photographers provided equally extensive and media-savvy coverage. Over two hundred photos are listed in the archive of the Pictorial Section of the USIS; today the collection is housed by the Austrian National Library. The head of the USIS Pictorial Section himself, Yoichi Okamoto, provided some superb close-up shots of the ensemble's stars William Warfield (Porgy) and Leontyne Price (Bess), also photographing his USIS colleagues at work during the rehearsals. These pictures can be found in Okamoto's private photo archive, which has also been held at the Austrian National Library since 2019.[2]

The premiere on 7 September turned into a spectacular event: the new US ambassador and high commissioner to Vienna, Llewelyn Thompson, invited

---

[1] On USIA, cf.: Nicholas J. Cull: Cold War and the United States Information Agency. American Propaganda and Public Diplomacy, 1945–1989, New York 2008.
[2] For the biography and oeuvre of Okamoto, see: Marlies Dornig, Hans Petschar (eds.): Bild Macht Politik. Yoichi Okamoto. Ikone der Nachkriegsfotografie, Vienna 2023.

549 guests of honour to the premiere at the Volksoper and to a party afterwards at Hotel Bristol, where some of the illustrious guests from the USA were staying. The guest list included the Allied high commissioners, representatives of the diplomatic missions, and the highest office holders of the Republic, Federal President Theodor Körner, Federal Chancellor Leopold Figl, representatives of the federal government, and renowned figures from the spheres of art, culture, and business. Okamoto himself photographed the press conference in Hotel Bristol, where the Austrian press were informed about the production and the aims of the European tour.

Some three months earlier, the American State Department had issued a press release making it clear why *Porgy and Bess* should be sent to Europe: sending the ensemble was supposed to counter anti-American propaganda's assertions that the country was devoid of culture or home-grown artists with creative vitality and that Black Americans in the USA did not have any opportunities to develop their abilities beyond the status of slaves.[3]

Debunking this propaganda cost the American government a fair sum: almost 100,000 dollars were spent financing the productions in Vienna and Berlin alone. *Porgy*, according to a high-ranking State Department official, was a unique instrument for conveying a completely different message: *Porgy* as a manifestation of the American melting pot, with music and songs sung by Black people, written and composed by two New York Jews, based on the novel by a white Southerner, who had also co-authored the libretto. The ensemble was put together specifically for the European tour, the government would cover all the costs, and the Gershwin Estate would take all the royalties: in short, *Porgy* was "good art" but – repackaged by the State Department – "even better propaganda".[4]

The story of *Porgy and Bess* is set in the Black quarter of Charleston, South Carolina, and centres on the love and misery experienced by dockworkers in Catfish Row. One summer's evening, the residents dance to piano music. Clara sings the lullaby *Summertime* for her baby in her arms. The disabled Porgy appears on his cart pulled by the goat Jebob and asks about the beautiful drug addict Bess, who turns up with her giant, violent lover Crown. After a fight over a game of dice, Crown murders a man and flees. Porgy offers Bess his help and a place to live. Bess moves in with Porgy and begins a happy relationship with him, but she then bumps into Crown at a picnic and falls for him again. At night, Crown appears in Porgy's apartment to take Bess away. Porgy kills him with a knife in the back. A woman is accused of the murder and protests her innocence.

---

3 Cf. David Monod: "He is a Cripple an' Needs my Love": Porgy and Bess as Cold War Propaganda, in: Giles Scott-Smith, Hans Krabbendam (eds.): The Cultural Cold War in Western Europe 1945–1960, 300–312, 300.

4 Ibid.

Porgy is arrested for a week, since he refuses to identify the body. Bess relapses into drug addiction and moves to New York with the drug dealer Sportin' Life. Let out of jail, Porgy follows his love Bess to New York on his goat cart.

For David Monod, who analysed the reception of *Porgy and Bess* in Austria and Germany, it seems to have been only a partial success. Monod writes that this is due, firstly, to the opera's material itself, which the authors DuBose Heyward and George and Ira Gershwin adapted for the libretto in 1935. The second reason he sees in the new production and reworking of the original libretto in the early 1950s by Robert Breen, a New Deal liberal committed to equal rights for Black Americans.

According to Monod, Breen remained a prisoner of his own prejudices and the limitations of his New Deal thinking: for Breen, Black people represented the Other, exotic beings who undoubtedly deserved freedom but as a group were not yet ready for full democratic rights.[5] And this thoroughly ambivalent message, writes Monod, also had a crucial impact on the perception and reception of *Porgy and Bess* in Vienna and Berlin.

Monod went so far as to assert that the ambivalence of the piece and its staging was also reflected in the media reports and that particularly the media campaign and the premiere in Vienna with the many dignitaries in attendance were nothing more than an exercise in damage limitation driven by efforts to keep everything under control.[6] For Monod, the State Department's hopes of supporting the aims of American foreign policy, propagating American culture, and countering Soviet Cold War propaganda by sending over *Porgy and Bess* were only partly fulfilled; while the commentators in Vienna and Berlin celebrated the show, they expressed their enthusiasm in racist terms and only praised the performances because they reinforced their own negative prejudices.

In his criticism, Monod makes no distinction between the reception in Berlin and that in Vienna, nor does he give any consideration to the different political orientations of the individual newspapers or the American occupation authorities' influence over them. This is of crucial importance, however, particularly for Vienna – and the Western Zones in Austria beyond the capital.

After Austria's liberation, one of the Allies' most pressing aims was to create a democratic press. The first newspapers appeared as army group newspapers and propagated the aims of the respective occupation authorities. They were supported in their endeavours by their information services.[7]

---

5 Cf. David Monod, 303.
6 Cf. ibid. On the history of the reception of Porgy and Bess in general, cf.: Ellen Noonan: The Strange Career of Porgy and Bess. Race, Culture, and America's Most Famous Opera, Chapel Hill 2012, 143–257.
7 For further literature, see: Wolfgang Mueller: Informationsmedien in der "Besatzungszeit". Tagespresse, Rundfunk, Wochenschau 1945–1955, in: Matthias Karmasin, Christian Oggolder

The media resonance greeting the guest performance of *Porgy and Bess* in Austria was, of course, mostly due to the American information services: the USIS Film Section and Pictorial Section; the US-funded radio station Rot-Weiss-Rot; and the *Wiener Kurier*, the latter providing running reports.

Correspondingly, the report of the US high commissioner on Austria for 1952 reads euphorically with respect to *Porgy and Bess*.[8] Rot-Weiss-Rot aired the entire opera. The radio broadcaster had stations in Vienna, Linz, and Salzburg, and although it was formally restricted to eastern and western Austria, it broadcast to the entire country and deep into the neighbouring communist states. In 1953, almost four million people listened to the channel, which, along with Austrian programming, primarily propagated American culture, as well as parts of the Voice of American programme.

The thirty-minute documentary film *Porgy and Bess in Wien*,[9] produced locally by the USIS Film Section and including highlights from the opera, was screened in all Austrian newsreel cinemas and became an unexpectedly big hit.[10] Some venues demanded repeat screenings, and one newsreel cinema in Vienna played the *Porgy and Bess* film for the entire duration of the Soviet Congress of the Peoples for Peace in the mid-December of 1952 as a contrasting programme.

Let us now take a look at the reports in Vienna's daily newspapers themselves, starting with the communist press, which was predestined to be critical of America in its reporting: the *Österreichische Zeitung* and the *Volksstimme* ignored the guest performance, initially refusing to report on it entirely and limiting themselves to mentioning the performances at the Volksoper in their theatre programmes.

Der Abend,[11] which the *Report on Austria* mentions as a communist paper, actually published a review by Dezsö Hajas that was both positive and free from racist prejudices. "Life itself", he wrote, "permeated the music", and the subject matter of *Porgy and Bess* and everyday life in the American South played into the hands of the authors, who had created almost a reportage influenced by

---

(ed.): Österreichische Mediengeschichte, Vol. 2: Von Massenmedien zu sozialen Medien (1918 bis heute), Wiesbaden 2019, 75–98.
8 Cf. Report on Austria 1952. Office of the United States High Commissioner for Austria, Vienna 1952.
9 Porgy and Bess in Wien. Ein Film des U.S. Information Service, USIS Film, Vienna 1952.
10 The film was also intended for distribution in the USA. Cf. Ellen Noonan, 205.
11 *Der Abend* was founded by Bruno Frei (Benedikt Freistadt) in February 1948 as a paper without affiliation to a political party. It was printed by Globus-Verlag and followed the party line of the Communist Party of Austria. Cf. Deszö Hajas: Das Gastspiel in der Volksoper: "Porgy und Bess", in: Der Abend, 8 September 1952, 5.

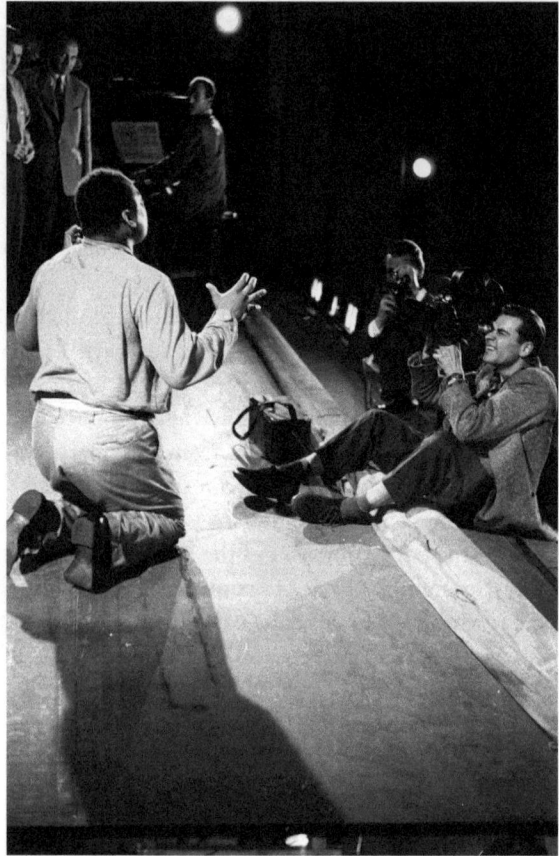

Fig. 2: Rehearsals for *Porgy and Bess*, September 1952 (photo: Yoichi Okamoto, ANL/Vienna, OKA03_087_06)

American Realism.[12] Gershwin's music, which drastically conveys the abrupt change of mood and emotional ambivalence, is emphasized with reference to Schönberg, and the review also notes the ensemble's consummate theatrical and vocal performance: "The opera's performance by the American Negro ensemble is theatrically and vocally so consummate that one could almost forget the propaganda aim that was probably the actual motivation for this guest performance." The report ends by quoting Brecht's *Dreigroschenoper* – "[Y]ou see those in the light. Those in the dark you do not see" (my trans.). That "individual extraordinarily talented Negroes can be successful in America was of course

---

12 Noonan cites this passage as an example of the piece's reception as "racially authentic and a depiction of daily life". Like Monod, however, she thereby overlooks the report's political dimension. Cf. Ellen Noonan, 207.

hardly in doubt". Hence if singers such as Lyontyne Price, Helen Colbert, William Warfield, John McCurry, Helen Thigpen, and Cab Calloway are placed in the light, one at least knows about those in the dark "and will not forget their suffering, even if the names of some of their brothers appear in lights intended to wash out that darkness".

The reviewer for the communist *Der Abend* thus addresses not only the propaganda mission behind the guest performance but also the racial conflicts and suffering of Black people in 1950s America. Nevertheless, the assessment of the guest performance of *Porgy and Bess* in *Der Abend* is ultimately a positive one, and, even if the author was certainly effusive in his praise, as the American high commissioner's report claimed, it can certainly be considered a remarkable success for American policy.

The culture editor of the *Arbeiter-Zeitung*,[13] Felix Hubalek, cites George Gershwin himself in describing *Porgy and Bess* as a "unified composition" and yet in essence and meaning a "popular opera". He writes that it has indeed become a popular opera, but it can only be an American popular opera "when the American people have identified fully with their black minority". The libretto remains "far from any allusions to the social or racial problem", the reviewer continues: it emphasizes humanity, embodied by Porgy's poignant love for Bess. In every scene, director Robert Breen has "conjured real, whirling life onto the stage", and the ensemble consummately bears the intellectual and artistic material. The review concludes: "This Negro ensemble is the best emissary of that section of the American people to whose spirit, intelligence, and human kindness it delivered an overwhelming testimony."

Like the editor of the *Arbeiter-Zeitung*, Max Graf, the culture editor at *Weltpresse*,[14] emphasized the "sound of humanity" and Gershwin's lover for "all forms of life". "In a mysterious way, Gershwin has made the big country (or at least part of it) resound: the houses of the poor, the stairwells, the corners of the docks of South Carolina, bustling crowds, childlike laughter and violent surging of the blood and sensuality, the cheerfulness and sadness of the blacks, and has transformed all this life into humanity that sings." After the *Wiener Kurier*, *Weltpresse* provided the most extensive coverage of *Porgy and Bess*, announcing it in advance and reporting on the premiere, with the main report on the front page and photos of scenes.

---

13 Cf. (Felix) Hubalek: "Porgy und Bess", in: Arbeiter-Zeitung, 9 September 1952, 5.
14 "Porgy and Bess": ein Gesellschaftsereignis. Glanzvolle Premiere des amerikanischen Negerensembles, in: Weltpresse, 9 September 1952, 1; Max Graf: Gershwins Meisterwerk. Erste Wiener Aufführung von "Porgy and Bess" in der Wiener Volksoper, in: Weltpresse, 10 September 1952, 6.

Before the premiere, the culture editor of the *Wiener Zeitung*,[15] Fritzi Beruth, also reported that Gershwin's music was "a resounding kaleidoscope", describing the performance as "splendid"; the "singer-actor" William Warfield painted a truly harrowing portrait of the lame beggar Porgy, and "Leontyne Price as Bessie is a dark-skinned Manon with a beautiful soprano revealing great skill and possessing a sweet piano. [...] A creature full of ravishing urges, high on cocaine in terrifyingly realistic fashion."

Somewhat less colourful reports featured in *Neues Österreich*[16] and the *Salzburger Nachrichten*, which were just as full of praise for the music, the staging, and the ensemble, however. *Neues Österreich* wrote that George Gershwin, who had already created a new type of classic standard in 1924 with *Rhapsody in Blue*, had succeeded in composing "the first genuine jazz opera" in *Porgy and Bess*. The premiere, launched with "all indications of a sensation and truly American publicity", had been a great success and the paper could only recommend that everyone take in the excellent performance.

A similar tone was taken by the culture editor at the *Salzburger Nachrichten*,[17] Hans Rutz, in his report on the start of the European tour of *Porgy and Bess*. The Volksoper had finally received a long-awaited experience, "a new popular opera hitherto unknown to this country". Perhaps one had already heard about it, but now one understood: "this is an opera that can only be played by Negroes." Now one also understood that Gershwin, whose love for Black people seemed to resonate in his early unhappy ending, only wanted his work to be sung and played by Blacks. What Gerschwin had created here was not an opera in the classical sense, but rather a "'production' depicting life as it is". The Vienna premiere had gathered all of Austrian officialdom, a picture of society that the theatre city of Vienna had not seen for a long time. "In the first performance following the premiere, the actual theatre audience then pronounced its judgement: a hurricane of enthusiasm roared through the house."

Heinrich Kralik in the *Presse*[18] and Fritz Skorzeny in the *Neuen Wiener Tageszeitung*[19] reported just as euphorically. And even if the bourgeois critics, like their colleague at the *Wiener Zeitung* and the left-wing editors of *Der Abend* and the *Arbeiter-Zeitung*, wrote about life in Catfish Row, the production, and the

---

15 Cf. Fritzi Beruth: Ein exotisches Lebensbild: George Gershwins Oper "Porgy and Bess", in: Wiener Zeitung, 9 September 1952, 3.
16 Cf. [Y.]: Gershwins "Porgy and Bess" in der Volksoper, in: Neues Österreich, 9 September, 5.
17 Cf. Hans Rutz: Die Ballade von der Catfish-Gasse, in: Salzburger Nachrichten, 11 September 1952, 4.
18 Cf. Hans Kralik: Begeisterung um "Porgy und Bess". Gastspiel des Gershwin-Ensembles in der Volksoper, in: Die Presse, 9 September 1952, 5.
19 Cf. Fritz Skorzeny: "Porgy and Bess". Sensationserfolg von Gershwins amerikanischer Volksoper am Währinger Gürtel, in: Neue Wiener Tageszeitung, 8.

ensemble in the language of their time, using terms like "Negro singers", "Negro ensemble", or "Negro artists", they are far removed from the latent racism and prejudice of which Monod accuses them almost across the board.

That is not to say, however, that racist prejudices and depictions were absent in post-war Austria. On the contrary, an examination of the report in the weekly paper *Berichte und Informationen*, founded in 1946 by the co-founder of the VdU, Herbert Alois Kraus, demonstrates this quite clearly. Editor Deutsch-Huslar titles his article on the performance of *Porgy and Bess* in Vienna "'Black' and 'white' music in America"[20] and makes clear from the outset that he is only able to write and think in racial and, it soon transpires, racist terms. He begins by distancing himself from the well-to-do premiere audience and the daily press, which "frothed" with enthusiasm, before getting to work: the word "Negro" is used no fewer than twelve times in various combinations ("Negro music", "Negro production", "Negro sound", etc.), along with "nigger songs" – concealed as a Gershwin quotation. The accumulation of these terms and the clearly articulated racial categorization – "the Negroes, a most musical race" – reveals the naked racism. Hence it is no surprise to read that Gershwin was "arguably a skilful and talented musician but hardly a first-rate composer" and that the Americans have yet to produce a "truly great" one or any great "white" musicians. For Bartók, Strawinsky, Schönberg, Krenek, or Hindemith, "who all went to America in recent years as a result of the European turmoil", could "certainly not be considered American composers".

The blatant anti-Americanism, the dismissive assessment of American music and, of course, jazz are not the result of successful Soviet Cold War propaganda. They are rooted in an attitude that has internalized all the prejudices and ideologemes of National Socialist propaganda – and which was still prevalent in Austria in the early 1950s, at least among members of the VdU and far beyond those circles. The Americans stationed in Austria were of course quite aware of this. They thus placed special emphasis on media work and promoted the "export" of American culture to Vienna and to the federal provinces beyond the occupation zones.[21]

Hence, when the *Wiener Kurier* reports in words and pictures[22] on the "storms of enthusiasm" for *Porgy and Bess*, celebrates the premiere of Gershwin's opera

---

20 Deutsch-Huslar: "Schwarze" und "weiße" Musik in Amerika. Zur Wiener Aufführung von "Porgy and Bess", in: Berichte und Informationen des österreichischen Forschungsinstituts für Wirtschaft und Politik 7 (1952) 322, 15.
21 On the establishment of American everyday culture in Austria, cf. Reinhold Wagnleitner: Coca-Colonisation und Kalter Krieg: Die Kulturmission der USA in Österreich nach dem Zweiten Weltkrieg, Vienna 1991.
22 The photo supplement of Saturday, 6 September 1952, a day before the premiere, then, featured an exclusive photo report with shots of the rehearsals. The report on the premiere

by "American Negro artists", and communicates this to a broad public, the attempt to dismantle prejudices and propagate a humane attitude via music and culture cannot be underestimated.

In 1952, the *Wiener Kurier* still had a midweek circulation of 160,000 copies and a weekend output of 230,000. A substantial number of those copies were distributed in the Soviet Occupation Zone – very much to the disgruntlement of the Soviets, who made several attempts to prevent delivery and confiscated issues.[23] A considerable factor behind the *Wiener Kurier*'s success was a lavish photo supplement; from February 1949 to mid-1954, it was edited and produced by Yoichi Okamoto, head of the Pictorial Section of the American Information Service.[24]

Okamoto was well aware of the propaganda effect of pictures and set completely new standards for reportage photography in Austria. However, he was not only a gifted head of the American photo service but also had an affinity for art, himself being an outstanding art photographer with very good connections in Vienna's art scene. The artists of the Art Club regularly met at the Strohkoffer nightclub, a favourite haunt of artists, writers, and jazz musicians, in a cellar beneath the famous Loos Bar in Vienna. Okamoto shot portraits of almost all of them, and even exhibited some of his artistic photos at Strohkoffer. A regular patron at Strohkoffer was the Austrian pianist Friedrich Gulda, who in the early 1950s had begun an intensive exploration of American jazz, thoroughly irritating aficionados of a strictly conservative musical high culture. This barely concerned Gulda, who played the piano and saxophone at Strohkoffer and gave talks on jazz at the Kosmos theatre and on the radio in order to counter the reactionary and racist criticism of "Negermusik". "Negermusik" ("Negro music") was a pejorative term used during the Third Reich to denigrate musical styles particularly influenced by Black Americans, such as Blues and jazz. Driven by racist resentment, the term continued to be used in conservative and right-wing discourses in Germany and Austria well into the 1960s.

The performance of *Porgy and Bess* in Vienna must also be seen in this context. It was just not just a Cold War propaganda tool of the American occupation authorities; for the parties and artists involved, it was also an opportunity to take a stance and combat prejudices and stereotypes.

---

appeared on Monday 8 September. The photo supplement of 13 September published one more report, on the party in Hotel Bristol. Wiener Kurier, 6 September 1952, Bildbeilage, 4.; 8 September 1952, 7; 13 September 1952 Bildbeilage, 1.
23 Cf. Report on Austria, 35.
24 Cf. Marion Krammer, Margarethe Szeless: "Let's hit the reorientation line every time we can!" Amerikanische Bildpolitik in Österreich am Beispiel der *Pictorial Section*, in: medien & zeit 1 (2017), 4–33; 28–31.

When the ensemble of *Porgy and Bess* celebrated in Hotel Bristol and in Strohkoffer after the premiere and in the Rathauskeller after the final performance, the USIS film crew, Okamoto, and the USIS photographers were in attendance: Cab Calloway gave his best rendition of "Lady Be Good" and "Minnie the Moocher" and introduced his accompaniment to the audience. "I am accompanied on the piano by Vienna's best: Friedrich Gulda."[25]

---

25 Porgy and Bess in Wien. Ein Film des U.S. Information Service, USIS Film, Vienna 1952.

Selected Bibliography

General surveys

Angerer, Thomas, Frankreich, die alliierte Besatzung Österreichs und die Staatsvertragsverhandlungen / Französische Staatsvertragsverhandler, in: Karner, Stefan/Stangler, Gottfried (eds.), Österreich ist frei – Der Österreichische Staatsvertrag 1955 (Beitragsband zur Ausstellung "Kriegsende – Besatzungszeit – Freiheit" auf Schloß Schallaburg), Horn/Vienna 2005, 82–87 / 388–393.

Angerer, Thomas, Towards a New Anschluss? France, the German and the Austrian Questions, 1945–55, in: Frédéric Bozo, Christian Wenkel (eds.), France and the German Question during the Cold War, 1945–1990, New York/Oxford 2019, 241–256.

Angerer, Thomas, Französische Freundschaftspolitik in Österreich nach 1945: Gründe, Grenzen und Gemeinsamkeiten mit Frankreichs Deutschlandpolitik, in: Rauchensteiner, Manfried/Kriechbaumer, Robert (eds.), Die Gunst des Augenblicks. Neuere Forschungen zu Staatsvertrag und Neutralität, Cologne/Vienna 2005, 113–138.

Angerer, Thomas, Kontinuitäten und Kontraste der französischen Österreichpolitik 1919–1955, in: Koch, Klaus/Rauscher, Walter/Suppan, Arnold/Vyslonzil, Eliasbeth (eds.), Von Saint-Germain zum Belvedere. Österreich und Europa 1919–1955 (Außenpolitische Dokumente der Republik Österreich 1918–1938/special edition), Vienna 2007, 129–157.

Bischof, Günter/Leidenfrost, Josef (eds.), Die bevormundete Nation. Österreich und die Alliierten 1945–1949, Innsbruck 1988.

Graf, Maximilian/Meisinger, Agnes (eds.), Österreich im Kalten Krieg. Neue Forschungen im internationalen Kontext, Göttingen 2016.

Karner, Stefan/Stangler, Gottfried (eds.), Österreich ist frei – Der Österreichische Staatsvertrag 1955 / Beitragsband zur Ausstellung auf Schloß Schallaburg / Kriegsende – Besatzungszeit – Freiheit, Horn/Vienna 2005.

Rathkolb, Oliver, Die paradoxe Republik. Österreich 1945–2015, new, expanded edition, Vienna 2015 (= The Paradoxical Republic. Austria 1945–2005, Berghahn Books: New York und Oxford 2010).

Rauchensteiner, Manfried, Der Sonderfall. Die Besatzungszeit in Österreich 1945 bis 1955, Graz 1995 (1979).

Rauchensteiner, Manfried (ed.), Österreich 1945. Ein Ende und viele Anfänge, Graz/Vienna 1997.

Rauchensteiner, Manfried/Kriechbaumer, Robert (eds.), Die Gunst des Augenblicks. Neuere Forschungen zu Staatsvertrag und Neutralität, Cologne/Vienna 2005.

Stourzh, Gerald/Mueller, Wolfgang, A Cold War over Austria: The Struggle for the State Treaty, Neutrality, and the End of East–West Occupation, 1945–1955 (The Harvard Cold War Studies Book Series), Lanham 2018.

Cultural and media policy

Blaschitz, Edith, Zwischen re-orientation und "Kampf gegen Schmutz und Schund". Österreichische Kinder- und Jugendmedien in der Nachkriegszeit (1945–1960), in: Moser, Heinz/Sesink, Werner/Meister, Dorothee M./Hipfl, Brigitte/Hug, Theo (eds.), Jahrbuch Medien-Pädagogik 7. Medien. Pädagogik. Politik, Wiesbaden 2008, 169–186.

Ebel, Ursula/Englerth, Holger/Kiefer, Nicole (eds.), Bühne, Brücken, Buchpakete. Die Österreichische Gesellschaft für Literatur als Akteurin der internationalen Literaturvermittlung 1961–1990, Vienna 2024.

Falböck, Gaby/Feldinger, Norbert P., Vier Zonen, vier Konzepte, Akteure mit Vergangenheit – ein besondere Geschichte vom Anfang: Die Medienregulierung der Alliierten in Österreich, in: Krone, Jan/Pellegrini, Tassilo (eds.), Handbuch Medienökonomie, Wiesbaden 2020, 1309–1333.

Krammer, Marion/Szeless, Margarethe/Hausjell, Fritz (eds.), Alliierte Bildpolitik in Österreich 1945–1955, in: medien & zeit 1/2017.

Krammer, Marion/Szeless, Margarethe, "Let's hit the reorientation line every time we can!" Amerikanische Bildpolitik in Österreich am Beispiel der Pictorial Section, in: medien & zeit 1/2017, 4–33.

Krammer, Marion, Sowjetunion im Bild. Die sowjetische Medien- und Bildpropaganda in Österreich von 1945–1955, in: medien & zeit 1/2017, 52–56.

Maurer, Stefan, Wolfgang Kraus und der österreichische Literaturbetrieb nach 1945, Vienna 2020.

Moser, Karin, Besetzte Bilder: Film, Kultur und Propaganda in Österreich 1945–1955, Vienna 2005.

Szeless, Margarethe, Im Schatten der amerikanischen Bildpolitik. Zur Rolle der Fotografe im britischen und französischen Informationsdienst, in: medien & zeit 1/2017, 34–51.

Wimmer, Michael, Kultur und Demokratie Eine systematische Darstellung von Kulturpolitik in Österreich, Innsbruck/Vienna/Bozen 2011.

Exhibitions

Architekturzentrum Wien, Kalter Krieg und Architektur. Beiträge zur Demokratisierung Österreichs nach 1945 (exhibition from 17 October 2019 to 24 February 2020).

Österreichische Nationalbibliothek, 1945. Zurück in die Zukunft. 70 Jahre Ende Zweiter Weltkrieg (28 April 2015–10 May 2015).

US cultural policy

König, Thomas, Die Frühgeschichte des Fulbright Program in Österreich. Transatlantische "Fühlungnahme auf dem Gebiete der Erziehung", Innsbruck 2012.
Rathkolb, Oliver, Politische Propaganda der amerikanischen Besatzungsmacht in Österreich 1945–1950. Ein Beitrag zur Geschichte des kalten Krieges in der Presse-, Kultur- und Rundfunkpolitik, doctoral thesis, University of Vienna 1981.
Rathkolb, Oliver, "Ein garstig Lied! Pfui! Ein politisch' Lied!" – U.S. Kulturpolitik und Entnazifizierung von MusikerInnen in Oberösterreich, in: Thumser, Regina/Petermayr, Klaus (eds.), Klänge der Macht. Nationalsozialistische Musikpolitik in Oberösterreich, Linz 2010, 105–130.
Schlegel, Natalie, Die Beurteilung der "US-Kulturmission in Österreich 1945–1955": der Bereich der Medien am Beispiel von "Wiener Kurier", "Salzburger Nachrichten" und "Radio Rot-Weiß-Rot", Diplomarbeit, University of Vienna 2008.
Stifter, Christian H., Zwischen geistiger Erneuerung und Restauration: US-amerikanische Planungen zur Entnazifizierung und demokratischen Neuorientierung österreichischer Wissenschaft, 1941–1955, Vienna 2013.
Wagnleitner, Reinhold, Coca-Colonization and the Cold War. The Cultural Mission of the United States in Austria after the Second World War, Chapel Hill, NC/London 1994.

Soviet cultural policy

Golovlev, Alexander, Tchaikovsky meets Debussy: French and Soviet musical diplomacy in occupied Austria, 1945–1955, doctoral dissertation, European University Institute Florence 2017.
Kraus, Michael "Kultura". Der Einfluss der sowjetischen Besatzung auf die österreichische Kultur 1945–1955, Diplomarbeit, University of Vienna 2008.
Mueller, Wolfgang, Kulturpolitik oder Propaganda? Zur Funktion von Kunst und Kommunikation in der sowjetischen Besatzungspolitik in Österreich 1945–1955, in: Bauer, Ingrid (ed.), Kunst-Kommunikation-Macht (6. Österreichischer Zeitgeschichtetag 2004), Innsbruck/Vienna 2004, 57–62.
Mueller, Wolfgang, Die Kulturpolitik und Propaganda der sowjetischen Besatzungsmacht in Österreich, in: Karner, Stefan/Stangler, Gottfried (eds.), Österreich ist frei – Der Österreichische Staatsvertrag 1955 / Beitragsband zur Ausstellung auf Schloß Schallaburg / Kriegsende – Besatzungszeit – Freiheit, Horn/Vienna 2005, 241–244.
Mugrauer, Manfred, Die Politik der KPÖ 1945–1955: Von der Regierungsbank in die innenpolitische Isolation, Göttingen 2020.

British cultural policy

Beer, Siegfried, Die 'britische' Steiermark 1945–1955, Graz 1995.
Feichtinger, Johannes: Die Kulturpolitik der Besatzungsmacht Großbritannien in Österreich, in: Ableitinger, Alfred/Beer, Siegfried/Staudinger, Eduard G. (eds.), Österreich unter alliierter Besatzung 1945–1955 (Studien zu Politik und Verwaltung 63). Vienna/Cologne/Graz 1998, 495–529.
Lehner, Isabella, Anglo-Austrian Cultural Relations between 1944 and 1955: Influences, Cooperation and Conflicts, Diplomarbeit, University of Vienna 2011.
Stieber, Gabriela (ed.), Consolidated intelligence reports. Psychological Warfare Branch. Military Government Kärnten. Mai 1945 bis April 1946. Eine Quellenedition zur Geschichte der britischen Besatzungszeit in Kärnten, Klagenfurt 2005.
Stieber, Gabriela (ed.), Die Briten als Besatzungsmacht in Kärnten 1945–1955, Klagenfurt 2005.
Treiber, Gerda, Großbritanniens Informationspolitik gegenüber Österreich 1945 bis 1955: Publicity und Propaganda sowie deren Instrumente in Printmedien und Rundfunk, dargestellt anhand britischer Dokumente, doctoral thesis, Vienna 1997.

French cultural policy

Angerer, Thomas/Le Rider, Jacques (eds.), "Ein Frühling, dem kein Sommer folgte"? Französisch-österreichische Kulturtransfers seit 1945, Vienna 1999.
Dussault, Éric, La dénazification de l'Autriche par la France. La politique culturelle de la France dans la zone d'occupation, 1945–1955, Sainte-Foy, QC 2005.
Eisterer, Klaus, Französische Besatzungspolitik. Tirol und Vorarlberg 1945/46 (Innsbrucker Forschungen zur Zeitgeschichte 9), Innsbruck 1992.
Eisterer, Klaus, La présence française en Autriche (1945–1946). Occupation – dénazification – action culturelle (Etudes Autrichiennes 5), Rouen 1998.
Eisterer, Klaus, La présence française en Autriche (1945–1946), Vol. 2: Relations humaines – Questions économiques – Prisonniers de guerre – Le problème du Tyrol du Sud (Etudes Autrichiennes 13), Rouen 2005.
Feurstein-Prasser, Michaela, Von der Besatzungspolitik zur Kulturmission französische Schul- und Bildungspolitik in Österreich 1945–1955, doctoral thesis, University of Vienna 2002.
Porpaczy, Barbara, Frankreich – Österreich 1945–1960. Kulturpolitik und Identität (Innsbrucker Forschungen zur Zeitgeschichte, Vol. 18), Innsbruck 2002.
Unterweger, Sandra/Zankl, Verena, "Der kleine Prinz" goes Tirol. Die französische Kulturpolitik 1945–1955 in Westösterreich, in: Forschungsinstitut Brenner-Archiv der Universität Innsbruck (ed.), Zeitmesser – 100 Jahre "Brenner", Innsbruck 2010.
Werner, Juliane, Existentialismus in Österreich. Kultureller Transfer und literarische Resonanz, Berlin 2021.
Werner, Juliane, Fenster nach Frankreich. Existentialismus-Vermittlung in österreichischen Periodika (1945–1955), in: Hehl, Michael Peter/Tommek, Heribert (eds.), Transnationale Akzente. Zur vermittelnden Funktion von Literatur- und Kulturzeitschriften im Europa des 20. Jahrhunderts, Berlin 2021, 133–146.

Authors

THOMAS ANGERER
An Assistant Professor at the Department of History, University of Vienna, and lecturer at the Vienna School of International Studies, he has also been a Visiting Professor at the Universités Paris I and Paris VIII. A recipient of the Ludwig Jedlicka Memorial Prize and the Karl von Vogelsang State Prize, he specializes in the history of French policy towards Austria and Austria's position in Europe since 1918.

WOLFGANG DUCHKOWITSCH
studied Mass Media Science and Art History at the University of Vienna, where he received his doctorate. In 1997, he qualified (*Venia Legendi*) to teach all areas of Mass Media and Communication Science. He teaches at the University of Vienna and the St. Pölten University of Applied Sciences. His research focuses on the history of mass media and communication, cultural studies, and contemporary history.

VERONIKA FLOCH
An art historian, she works at Galerie nächst St. Stephan Rosemarie Schwarzwälder. As part of her dissertation in the field of History at the University of Vienna, she is currently researching cultural transfer in Austria in the early Cold War context with respect to integration into the West and the formation of European identity.

CHRISTIAN GLANZ
Associate Professor of Historical Musicology at the Department of Musicology and Performance Studies at the University of Music and Performing Arts in Vienna (mdw) and head of the Wissenschaftszentrum Gustav Mahler und die Wiener Moderne at the mdw, he researches and publishes on music and politics, Gustav Mahler, and Hans Eisler.

RICHARD HUFSCHMIED
is a historian and Senior Research Fellow at the Department of Contemporary History at the University of Vienna and member of the Department of Military History Research at the Museum of Military History/Federal Ministry of Defence. There he organizes exhibitions, research, and publishing projects, as well as at the Institute of Culture Studies and Theatre History of the Austrian Academy of Sciences.

MONIKA KNOFLER
studied Art History, Archaeology, and Psychology at Innsbruck and Munich, with a doctoral thesis on *Clemens Holzmeister – Das architektonische Werk* (The Architectural Works of Clemens Holzmeister). She worked at the Albertina from 1978 to 1982 and was art director for UNICEF in Geneva and New York from 1982 to 1995. From 1995 to 2012, she served as the director of the Print Room at the Academy of Fine Arts Vienna, with a focus on contemporary drawing and printmaking. She is currently working on a publication about the Academy with an emphasis on the history of its graphic art collection.

MARION KRAMMER
co-manages (together with Margarethe Szeless) the historical agency wesearch. agentur für geschichte und kommunikation in Vienna. She has collaborated on several exhibitions and contemporary history projects and currently leads the Austrian Science Fund project "Shaping the Visual under National Socialism. Press Photography in Austria 1938–1945" at the Department of Contemporary History at the University of Vienna (with Margarethe Szeless). Her research focuses on visual communication, propaganda, and the history of photography and media in the twentieth century. Her most recent publication is *Rasender Stillstand oder Stunde Null? Eine Kollektivbiografie österreichischer PressefotografInnen 1945–1955* (2022).

MICHAEL KRAUS
studied History, Romance Languages, Drama, and Vocal Studies in Vienna and Munich. He gained his first experience of the stage as an actor in Vienna. For many years, he has been an international opera and concert singer, as well as a translator of opera librettos and opera director. He wrote his Master's (*Magister*) thesis on *Der Einfluss der sowjetischen Besatzung auf die österreichische Kultur 1945–1955* (The Soviet Occupation's Influence on Austrian Culture; 2008) and his doctoral thesis on *Die musikalische Moderne an den Opernhäusern von Berlin und Wien 1945–1989* (Musical Moderism at the Opera Houses in Berlin and Vienna; 2016, published as a monograph in 2017) at the Department of Con-

temporary History at the University of Vienna. Since 2020 he has served as director of the opera studio at the Vienna State Opera.

JOHANNA LERCHNER
Since completing her Bachelor's degree in European Ethnology, she has been working on an interdisciplinary Master's degree in Contemporary History and Media at the University of Vienna since 2020. Since March 2023, her research for her Master's dissertation has focused on the topography of the Allied occupation of Vienna from 1945 to 1955.

AGNES MEISINGER
studied History and Political Science at the University of Vienna. Her research foci include the history of sport, Viennese municipal history, and Cold War Studies. She works at the Department of Contemporary History at the University of Vienna and at the Jewish Museum Vienna and is a member of the editorial board of the journal *zeitgeschichte*.

KARIN MOSER
is Visiting Professor of Political History and Media and Social History (University of Vienna, Univerzita Hradec Králové). She has worked in the field of documentary filmmaking (as a scriptwriter, co-director, historical advisor, and researcher). Her research focuses on the history of film, radio, and media, twentieth-century political history, public history, the history of consumption, advertising, and social history.

WOLFGANG MUELLER
is Professor of Russian History at the University of Vienna and a member of the Austrian Academy of Sciences (OeAW). He has also been a visiting lecturer or visiting researcher at the Universities of Salzburg, Rostock, Toruń, Nice, and Bern, at Stanford University, and at the Russian Academy of Sciences. His works include *Die sowjetische Besatzung in Österreich 1945–1955* (2005); *A Good Example of Peaceful Coexistence? The Soviet Union, Austria, and Neutrality, 1955–1991* (2011); and *A Cold War over Austria* (with Gerald Stourzh 2018).

MANFRED MUGRAUER
studied Political Science and History in Vienna and Berlin and works at the Documentation Centre of Austrian Resistance and as an academic secretary at the Alfred Klahr Gesellschaft. Publications: *Die Politik der KPÖ in der Provisorischen Regierung Renner* (2006), *Die Politik der KPÖ 1945–1955. Von der Regierungsbank in die innenpolitische Isolation* (2020).

WOLFGANG PENSOLD
A media historian, he has researched and published on various aspects of Austrian media history, including the history of radio (2018) and cinema (2024). The curator of historical mass media at Vienna Museum of Science and Technology and the permanent exhibition "medien.welten" (opened in 2003), most recently the centenary exhibition "100 Years of Radio. As Austria Went on Air" (opened in October 2024).

HANS PETSCHAR
studied History and German at the University of Salzburg. From 2002 to 2024, he served as the director of the Picture Archive and Graphics Department at the Austrian National Library. He has been a Visiting Professor and Austrian Marshall Plan Chair at the University of New Orleans 2015/2016 and is the author of several publications on Austrian history, latest: *Ein Jahrhundert in Bildern. Österreich 1925–2025* (together with Michaela Pfundner).

MONIKA PLATZER
studied Art History at the University of Vienna. She is currently head of collections and curator at the Architekturzentrum Wien (Az W). Her research focuses on twentieth-century Austrian architectural and cultural history. She teaches at the University of Vienna and TU Wien. She has served as the editor of *icam-print* (2004–2020), the members' journal of the International Confederation of Architectural Museums. In 2014, she was a Visiting Fellow at the Center for European Studies, Harvard University, USA.

OLIVER RATHKOLB
was Professor of Contemporary History at the University of Vienna from 2006 to 2024. He is currently chair of the Vienna Institute for Cultural and Contemporary History and Arts (VICCA) and the international scientific advisory board of the House of European History in Brussels and a member of the boards of the Jewish Museum Vienna and the Salzburg Festival Archive. He has authored, edited, and co-edited several publications on European and Austrian contemporary, cultural, and media history and is the editor of the journal *zeitgeschichte* and the series *Zeitgeschichte im Kontext*.

PETER ROESSLER
is Professor of Dramaturgy at the University of Music and Performing Arts Vienna (Max Reinhardt Seminar), chair of the Theodor Kramer Gesellschaft, and a member of the board of the Austrian Society for Exile Research. His most recent publications are: Theodor Kramer: *Wir lagen in Wolhynien im Morast … und*

weitere Gedichte zum Ersten Weltkrieg (ed. with Karl Müller, 2023) and Achim Benning: *In den Spiegel greifen. Texte zum Theater 1976–2023* (ed., 2024).

GÜNTHER STOCKER
Professor of Modern German Literature at the Department of German Studies, University of Vienna, he studied German Studies and Communication Science at the Universities of Salzburg and Zurich. His many publications and research projects focus on Austrian literature, the literature and culture of the Cold War, reading research, and digital reading.

MARKUS STUMPF
is a librarian and teaches at the Department of Contemporary History at the University of Vienna, where he heads the Contemporary History library as well as the Nazi provenance research at Vienna University Library.

MARGARETHE SZELESS
With a doctorate in Art History, she founded the historical agency wesearch. agentur für geschichte und kommunikation in Vienna (together with Marion Krammer) and teaches at the Department of Art History. She currently leads the Austrian Science Fund project "Shaping the Visual under National Socialism. Press Photography in Austria 1938–1945" at the Department of Contemporary History at the University of Vienna (with Marion Krammer). Her research focuses on Austrian press photography in the twentieth century. She has written for many exhibition catalogues and journals, most recently *Das Wiener Zinshaus. Bauen für die Metropole* (with Marion Krammer and Andreas Nierhaus, 2023).